ISBN 0-8373-5819-1

119 ADMISSION TEST SERIES

New RUDMAN'S QUESTIONS AND ANSWERS ON THE...

LAST
Liberal Arts and Sciences Test

Intensive preparation for the examination including...
- Science and Mathematics
- Social Sciences - History
- Humanities
- Communication Skills
- Written English Expression

NLC

NATIONAL LEARNING CORPORATION

(516) 921-8888
(800) 645-6337
FAX: (516) 921-8743
www.passbooks.com
sales @ passbooks.com
info @ passbooks.com

PRINTED IN THE UNITED STATES OF AMERICA

3 1327 00578 0929

PASSBOOK®

NOTICE

PASSBOOK SERIES®

THE *PASSBOOK SERIES®* has been created to prepare applicants and candidates for the ultimate academic battlefield – the examination room.

At some time in our lives, each and every one of us may be required to take an examination – for validation, matriculation, admission, qualification, registration, certification, or licensure.

Based on the assumption that every applicant or candidate has met the basic formal educational standards, has taken the required number of courses, and read the necessary texts, the *PASSBOOK SERIES®* furnishes the one special preparation which may assure passing with confidence, instead of failing with insecurity. Examination questions – together with answers – are furnished as the basic vehicle for study so that the mysteries of the examination and its compounding difficulties may be eliminated or diminished by a sure method.

This book is meant to help you pass your examination provided that you qualify and are serious in your objective.

The entire field is reviewed through the huge store of content information which is succinctly presented through a provocative and challenging approach – the question-and-answer method.

A climate of success is established by furnishing the correct answers at the end of each test.

You soon learn to recognize types of questions, forms of questions, and patterns of questioning. You may even begin to anticipate expected outcomes.

You perceive that many questions are repeated or adapted so that you can gain acute insights, which may enable you to score many sure points.

You learn how to confront new questions, or types of questions, and to attack them confidently and work out the correct answers.

You note objectives and emphases, and recognize pitfalls and dangers, so that you may make positive educational adjustments.

Moreover, you are kept fully informed in relation to new concepts, methods, practices, and directions in the field.

You discover that you are actually taking the examination all the time: you are preparing for the examination by "taking" an examination, not by reading extraneous and/or supererogatory textbooks.

In short, this PASSBOOK®, used directedly, should be an important factor in helping you to pass your test.

NEW YORK STATE TEACHER CERTIFICATION EXAMINATIONS™

INTRODUCTION

GENERAL INFORMATION

About the Testing Program

Those seeking a New York State teaching certificate for the common branch subjects in prekindergarten through grade 6 or for academic subjects in the secondary grades 7 through 12, i.e., English, a language other than English, mathematics, a science (biology, chemistry, earth science, physics), or social studies, must pass the New York State Teacher Certification Examinations (NYSTCE®) as part of the requirements for certification.

Those seeking a New York State teaching certificate in other areas may need to achieve qualifying scores on the NYSTCE® as indicated in the table which follows.

The New York State Teacher Certification Examinations™ program consists of the
- Liberal Arts and Sciences Test (LAST)
- Elementary and Secondary Assessment of Teaching Skills - Written (ATS-W)
- Content Specialty Tests (CSTs)
- Language Proficiency Assessments (LPAs)
- Assessment of Teaching Skills - Performance (ATS-P) (Video)

These exams provide an objective basis of competency and skill for teaching in New York State.

For the requirements, check the summary table of testing requirements which follows.

Test Development

The New York State Teacher Certification Examinations™ are criterion referenced and objective based. A criterion-referenced test is designed to measure a candidate's knowledge and skills in relation to an established standard rather than in relation to the performance of other candidates. The purpose of these exams is to certify candidates who have demonstrated requisite knowledge and skills necessary for a public school teacher.

An individual's performance on a test is evaluated against an established standard. The passing score for each test is established by the New York State Commissioner of Education based on the professional judgments and recommendations of New York State educators. Examinees who do not pass a test may retake it at any of the subsequent scheduled test administrations.

Description of the Tests

The following is a description of the tests within the NYSTCE® program.

Liberal Arts and Sciences Test (LAST). The Liberal Arts and Sciences Test consists of multiple-choice test questions and a written assignment. Candidates are asked to demonstrate conceptual and analytical skills, critical-thinking and communication skills, and multicultural awareness. The test covers scientific and mathematical processes, historical and social scientific awareness, artistic expression and the humanities, communication skills, and written analysis and expression. The Liberal Arts and Sciences Test is required for a provisional certificate.

Elementary and Secondary Versions of the Assessment of Teaching Skills - Written (ATS-W). There are two versions of the Assessment of Teaching Skills - Written (ATS-W). The elementary ATS-W should be taken by individuals seeking a PreK-6, common branch subject teaching certificate. The secondary ATS-W should be taken by individuals seeking a certificate for a secondary academic subject. Individuals seeking a certificate in other titles may take either the elementary or the secondary ATS-W. The ATS-W is required for a provisional certificate.

The elementary and secondary versions of the Assessment of Teaching Skills - Written consist of multiple-choice test questions and a written assignment. These tests address knowledge of the learner, instructional planning and assessment, instructional delivery, and the professional environment.

Content Specialty Tests (CSTs). There are currently 21 Content Specialty Tests. For a complete list of test titles, see the list that follows.

The Content Specialty Tests (except Japanese, Russian, Mandarin, Cantonese, Hebrew, and Greek) contain multiple-choice test questions. The CSTs for languages other than English also include audiotaped listening and speaking components and writing components. The CSTs are required for a permanent certificate.

Language Proficiency Assessments (ELPA-C, ELPA-N, TLPAs). The Language Proficiency Assessments are required for ESOL certificates and for bilingual education extension certificates in New York State.

Assessment of Teaching Skills - Performance (ATS-P)(video). The Assessment of Teaching Skills - Performance (ATS-P)(video) is one requirement for individuals seeking a permanent New York State teaching certificate in specified areas. For this assessment, candidates are required to prepare a videotape of their instruction with students who are part of their regular teaching assignments in grades PreK through 12. The teaching skills assessed by the ATS-P (video) are defined by the five objectives in the Instructional Delivery subarea of the Assessment of Teaching Skills test framework.

TESTS

Test (Test Code)

Liberal Arts and Sciences Test (LAST)(01)
Elementary Assessment of Teaching Skills - Written (ATS-W)(90)
Secondary Assessment of Teaching Skills - Written (ATS-W)(91)
Elementary Education (02)
English (03)
Mathematics (04)
Social Studies (05)
Biology (06)
Chemistry (07)
Earth Science (08)
Physics (09)
Early Childhood (21)
Latin (10)
Cantonese (11)
French (12)
German (13)
Greek (14)
Hebrew (15)
Italian (16)
Japanese (17)
Mandarin (18)
Russian (19)
Spanish (20)
English to Speakers of Other Languages (ESOL)(22)
English Language Proficiency Assessment for Classroom
    Personnel (ELPA-C)(23)
English Language Proficiency Assessment for Nonclassroom
    Personnel (ELPA-N)(25)
Target Language Proficiency Assessment - Spanish (24)
Target Language Proficiency Assessment other than Spanish

NEW YORK STATE TEACHER CERTIFICATION TESTING REQUIREMENTS

(Commissioner's Regulation) Teaching Certificates	Current Requirements	Projected Requirements
(8 NYCRR 80.15) PreK-6, Common Branch Subjects	LAST Provisional ATS-W Provisional CST (Elementary Permanent Education) ATS-P Permanent	Same as current requirements
7-9 Extension	Same as base certificate, PLUS: CST in academic Permanent subject	
Early Childhood Annotation (PreK-3)	CST in annotation Permanent	
(8 NYCRR 80.16) 7-12 Academic Subjects, e.g., English, Language other than English, Mathematics, Science (Biology, Chemistry, Earth Science, Physics), Social Studies	LAST Provisional ATS-W Provisional CST (in academic Permanent subject) ATS-P Permanent	Same as current requirements
5-6 Extension	Same as base certificate	

(8 NYCRR 80.9)
Bilingual Education [Extension]
	Same as base certificate, PLUS:
	LPA in English Prov./Perm.
	  (oral)*
	LPA in Target Prov./Perm.
	  Language (oral
	  & written)*
		Same as current requirements

(8 NYCRR 80.10) English to speakers of other languages (ESOL)	LAST* Provisional ATS-W* Provisional LPA in English Provisional (oral)* CST* (ESOL) Permanent ATS-P* Permanent	Same as current requirements
(8 NYCRR 80.5) Occupational Subjects, e.g. Agricultural Subjects, Business/Distributive Education, Health Occupations, Trade Subjects, Technical Subjects, Home Economics Subjects	Baccalaureate-based certificates: LAST + ATS-W or Provisional NTE Core Battery Associate & non-degree-based certificate titles: ATS-W Permanent or NTE Core Battery	Baccalaureate-based certificates: LAST Provisional ATS-W Provisional CST Permanent ATS-P Permanent Associate & non-degree-based certificate titles: ATS-W Provisional ATS-P Permanent

NEW YORK STATE TEACHER CERTIFICATION TESTING REQUIREMENTS

(Commissioner's Regulation) Teaching Certificates	Current Requirements		Projected Requirements	
8 NYCRR 80.6) pecial Education, e.g. pecial Education, Blind/ artially Sighted, Deaf/ earing Impaired ———————————— peech/Hearing Handicapped	LAST & ATS-W or NTE Core Battery	Provisional	Same as for PreK-6 or 7-12 certificate, PLUS: Special Education Supplement to ATS-W Special Education supplement to ATS-P	Provisional Permanent
3 NYCRR 80.7) eading	LAST & ATS-W or NTE Core Battery	Provisional	Same as for PreK-6 or 7-12 certificate, PLUS: CST in Reading	Permanent
3 NYCRR 80.8) chool Media Specialist	LAST + ATS-W or NTE Core Battery	Provisional	LAST ATS-W CST ATS-P	Provisional Provisional Permanent Permanent
3 NYCRR 80.17) pecial Subjects, e.g. ·t, Business/Distributive lucation, Dance, Health, me Economics, Music, ysical Education, ecreation, Speech, echnology Education	LAST + ATS-W or NTE Core Battery	Provisional	LAST ATS-W CST ATS-P	Provisional Provisional Permanent Permanent

Effective 9/2/95

LAST = Liberal Arts & Sciences Test
ATS-W = Assessment of Teaching Skills - Written
CST   = Content Specialty Test
ATS-P = Assessment of Teaching Skills - Performance (video)
LPA   = Language Proficiency Assessment

FOR FURTHER INFORMATION

If you have questions regarding which test(s) you must take, contact the teacher certification contact person at your college or:

NEW YORK STATE EDUCATION DEPARTMENT
OFFICE OF TEACHING
CULTURAL EDUCATION CENTER
ALBANY, N.Y. 12230

TELEPHONE: (518) 474-3901
9:00-11:45 A.M., 12:45-4:30 P.M. Eastern Time

Relay center telephone number for the deaf within New York State: 1-800-622-1220

Nationwide AT&T Relay Operator for the Deaf: 1-800-855-2880 (TTY)

If you have questions regarding the Test Registration, Administration Procedures, Admission Ticket, or Score Report, contact:

NYSTCE
NATIONAL EVALUATION SYSTEMS, INC.
30 GATEHOUSE ROAD
P.O. BOX 660
AMHERST, MA   01004-9008

TELEPHONE: (413) 256-2882
9:00 A.M. - 5:00 P.M. Eastern Time

Telephone number for the deaf: (413) 256-8032 (TTY)

ABOUT THE LIBERAL ARTS AND SCIENCES TEST (LAST)

Scientific, Mathematical, and Technological Processes
Historical and Social Scientific Awareness
Artistic Expression and the Humanities
Communication and Research Skills
Written Analysis and Expression

> The educator has the knowledge and skills necessary to teach effectively in public schools. The teacher has a broad understanding of the fundamental concepts of mathematics, science, and technology and is familiar with the basic principles and procedures associated with scientific inquiry. The teacher recognizes the interrelatedness of geography and culture and can analyze varied interpretations of human history and society. The teacher has an understanding of the major traditions of art, literature, religion, and philosophy and how cultural contexts inform artistic and literary expression. The teacher can retrieve information from traditional and electronic sources, communicate effectively, reason clearly, and evaluate competing ideas and arguments. Most importantly, the teacher recognizes the fundamental connections among all realms of human thought and endeavor and the diverse perspectives that shape human societies.

SUBAREA I—SCIENTIFIC, MATHEMATICAL, AND TECHNOLOGICAL PROCESSES

0001   **Use mathematical reasoning in problem-solving situations to arrive at logical conclusions and to analyze the problem-solving process.**

For example:

- analyzing problem solutions for logical flaws

- examining problems to determine missing information needed to solve them

- analyzing a partial solution to a problem to determine an appropriate next step

- evaluating the validity or logic of an argument or advertising claim that is based on statistics or probability

0002   **Understand connections between mathematical representations and ideas; and use mathematical terms and representations to organize, interpret, and communicate information.**

For example:

- analyzing data and making inferences from two or more graphic sources (e.g., diagrams, graphs, equations)

- restating a problem related to a concrete situation in mathematical terms

- using mathematical modeling/multiple representations to present, interpret, communicate, and connect mathematical information and relationships

- selecting an appropriate graph or table summarizing information presented in another form (e.g., a newspaper excerpt)

0003 **Apply knowledge of numerical, geometric, and algebraic relationships in problem-solving and mathematical contexts.**

For example:

- representing and using numbers in a variety of equivalent forms (e.g., integer, fraction, decimal, percent)

- applying operational algorithms to add, subtract, multiply and divide fractions, decimals, and integers

- using scales and ratios to interpret maps and models

- using geometric concepts and formulas to solve problems (e.g., estimating the surface area of a floor to determine the approximate cost of floor covering)

- solving problems using algebraic concepts and formulas (e.g., calculating wages based on sales commission)

- applying appropriate algebraic equations to the solution of problems (e.g., determining the original price of a sale item given the rate of discount)

0004 **Understand major concepts, principles, and theories in science and technology; and use that understanding to analyze phenomena in the natural world and to interpret information presented in illustrated or written form.**

For example:

- using an appropriate illustration, graphic, or physical model to represent a scientific theory, concept, or relationship presented in an excerpt

- relating a major scientific principle, concept, or theory to a natural phenomenon

- using design processes and procedures to pose questions and select solutions to problems and situations

- applying technological knowledge and skills to evaluate the degree to which products and systems meet human and environmental needs

- analyzing excerpts describing recent scientific discoveries or technological advances in relation to underlying scientific principles, concepts, or themes

0005 **Understand the historical development and cultural contexts of mathematics, science, and technology; the relationships and common themes that connect mathematics, science, and technology; and the impact of mathematics, science, and technology on human societies.**

For example:

- analyzing the historical, societal, or environmental effects of given developments in science and technology (e.g., computerization)

- recognizing how mathematical models can be used to understand scientific, social, or environmental phenomena

- evaluating how historical and societal factors have promoted or hindered developments in science and technology

- analyzing how developments in scientific knowledge may affect other areas of life (e.g., recognizing types of scientific data likely to affect government policymaking regarding pollution control)

0006 Understand and apply skills, principles, and procedures associated with inquiry and problem solving in the sciences.

For example:

- applying scientific methods and principles (including nonquantitative methods such as case studies) to investigate a question or problem

- formulating questions to guide research and experimentation toward explanations for phenomena and observations

- inferring the scientific principles (e.g., reliance on experimental data, replication of results) or skills (e.g., observation, inductive reasoning, familiarity with statistics and probability) that contributed to a scientific development as described in an excerpt

- demonstrating familiarity with electronic means for collecting, organizing, and analyzing information (e.g., databases, spreadsheets)

- analyzing the components of a given experimental design (e.g., dependent and independent variables, experimental groups, control groups)

- demonstrating an understanding of the nature of scientific inquiry (including ethical dimensions) and the role of observation and experimentation in science

SUBAREA II—HISTORICAL AND SOCIAL SCIENTIFIC AWARENESS

0007 Understand the interrelatedness of historical, geographic, cultural, economic, political, and social issues and factors.

For example:

- assessing the likely effects of human activities or trends (described in written or graphic form) on the local, regional, or global environment

- assessing ways in which major transformations related to human work, thought, and belief (e.g., industrialization, the scientific revolution, the development of various religions and belief traditions) have affected human society

- inferring aspects of a society's social structure or group interactions based on information presented in an excerpt

- analyzing ways in which social, cultural, geographic, and economic factors influence intergroup relations and the formation of values, beliefs, and attitudes

- assessing the social or economic implications of political views presented in an excerpt

0008 Understand principles and assumptions underlying historical or contemporary arguments, interpretations, explanations, or developments.

For example:

- inferring the political principles (e.g., popular sovereignty, separation of powers, due process of the law) illustrated in given situations or arguments

- recognizing assumptions (e.g., regarding the nature of power relationships) that inform the positions taken by political parties

- analyzing assumptions on which given U.S. policies (e.g., national health insurance, foreign relations) are based

- recognizing concepts and ideas underlying alternative interpretations of past events

- inferring the economic principle (e.g., supply and demand, redistribution of wealth) upon which a given explanation is based

0009 **Understand different perspectives and priorities underlying historical or contemporary arguments, interpretations, explanations, or developments.**

For example:

- identifying the values (e.g., a commitment to democratic institutions) implicit in given political, economic, social, or religious points of view

- recognizing the motives, beliefs, and interests that inform differing political, economic, social, or religious points of view (e.g., arguments related to equity, equality, and comparisons between groups or nations)

- analyzing multiple perspectives within U.S. society regarding major historical and contemporary issues

- recognizing the values or priorities implicit in given public policy positions

- analyzing the perceptions or opinions of observers or participants from different cultures regarding a given world event or development

0010 **Understand and apply skills, principles, and procedures associated with inquiry, problem solving, and decision making in history and the social sciences.**

For example:

- analyzing a description of research results to identify additional unanswered questions or to determine potential problems in research methodology

- determining the relevance or sufficiency of given information for supporting or refuting a point of view

- assessing the reliability of sources of information cited in historical or contemporary accounts or arguments and determining whether specific conclusions or generalizations are supported by verifiable evidence

- evaluating the appropriateness of specific sources (e.g., atlas, periodical guide, economic database) to meet given information needs (e.g., the distribution of natural resources in a given region, the political philosophy of a presidential candidate)

- distinguishing between unsupported and informed expressions of opinion

0011 **Understand and interpret visual representations of historical and social scientific information.**

For example:

- translating written or graphic information from one form to the other (e.g., selecting an appropriate graphic representation of information from an article on historical changes in global population)

- relating information provided in graphic representations (e.g., regarding population or economic trends) to public policy decisions

- interpreting historical or social scientific information provided in one or more graphs, charts, tables, diagrams, or maps

- inferring significant information (e.g., geographic, economic, sociological) about a historical or contemporary society based on examination of a photograph, painting, drawing, cartoon, or other visual representation

SUBAREA III—ARTISTIC EXPRESSION AND THE HUMANITIES

0012 **Understand and analyze elements of form and content in works from the visual and performing arts from different periods and cultures.**

For example:

- recognizing important elements in a given work of the visual or performing arts (e.g., focal point, symmetry, repetition of shapes, perspective, motif, rhythm)
- determining how a sense of unity or balance is achieved in a given work from the visual or performing arts
- characterizing the theme, mood, or tone of a given work from the visual or performing arts
- determining how specific elements in a given work of the visual or performing arts (e.g., color, composition, scale, instrumentation, set design, choreography) affect audience perceptions of the content of the work

0013 **Analyze and interpret works from the visual and performing arts representing different periods and cultures and understand the relationship of works of art to their social and historical contexts.**

For example:

- identifying similarities and differences in forms and styles of art from different movements or periods of time
- comparing and contrasting two or more works from the visual or performing arts in terms of mood, theme, or technique
- demonstrating an understanding of art as a form of communication (e.g., conveying political or moral concepts, serving as a means of individual expression)
- analyzing ways in which the content of a given work from the visual or performing arts reflects a specific cultural or historical context

0014 **Understand forms and themes used in literature from different periods and cultures.**

For example:

- identifying characteristic features of various genres of fiction and nonfiction (e.g., novels, plays, essays, autobiographies)
- distinguishing the dominant theme in a literary passage
- recognizing common literary elements and techniques (e.g., imagery, metaphor, symbolism, allegory, foreshadowing, irony) and using those elements to interpret a literary passage
- determining the meaning of figurative language used in a literary passage

0015 **Analyze and interpret literature from different periods and cultures and understand the relationship of works of literature to their social and historical contexts.**

For example:

- analyzing how the parts of a literary passage contribute to the whole
- comparing and contrasting the tone or mood of two or more literary passages
- analyzing aspects of cultural or historical context implied in a literary passage
- distinguishing characteristic features of different literary genres, periods, and traditions reflected in one or more literary passages
- making inferences about character, setting, author's point of view, etc., based on the content of a literary passage
- recognizing how a text conveys multiple levels of meaning

0016 Analyze and interpret examples of religious or philosophical ideas from various periods of time and understand their significance in shaping societies and cultures.

For example:

- distinguishing the religious and philosophical traditions associated with given cultures and world regions

- recognizing assumptions and beliefs underlying ideas presented in religious or philosophical writing

- analyzing societal implications of philosophical or religious ideas

- comparing and contrasting key concepts presented in two excerpts reflecting different philosophical or religious traditions

SUBAREA IV—COMMUNICATION AND RESEARCH SKILLS

0017 Derive information from a variety of sources (e.g., magazine articles, essays, Web sites).

For example:

- identifying the stated or implied main idea of a paragraph or passage

- selecting an accurate summary or outline of a passage

- organizing information presented on a Web site or other electronic means of communication

- comprehending stated or implied relationships in an excerpt (e.g., cause-and-effect, sequence of events)

- recognizing information that supports, illustrates, or elaborates the main idea of a passage

0018 Analyze and interpret written materials from a variety of sources.

For example:

- recognizing a writer's purpose for writing (e.g., to persuade, to describe)

- drawing conclusions or making generalizations based on information presented in an excerpt

- interpreting figurative language in an excerpt

- comparing and contrasting views or arguments presented in two or more excerpts

0019 Use critical-reasoning skills to assess an author's treatment of content in written materials from a variety of sources.

For example:

- analyzing the logical structure of an argument in an excerpt and identifying possible instances of faulty reasoning

- distinguishing between fact and opinion in written material

- determining the relevance of specific facts, examples, or data to a writer's argument

- interpreting the content, word choice, and phrasing of a passage to determine a writer's opinions, point of view, or position on an issue

- evaluating the credibility, objectivity, or bias of an author's argument or sources

0020 **Analyze and evaluate the effectiveness of expression in a written paragraph or passage according to the conventions of edited American English.**

For example:

- revising text to correct problems relating to grammar (e.g., syntax, pronoun-antecedent agreement)

- revising text to correct problems relating to sentence construction (e.g., those involving parallel structure, misplaced modifiers, run-on sentences)

- revising text to improve unity and coherence (e.g., eliminating unnecessary sentences or paragraphs, adding a topic sentence or introductory paragraph, clarifying transitions between and relationships among ideas presented)

- analyzing problems related to the organization of a given text (e.g., logical flow of ideas, grouping of related ideas, development of main points)

0021 **Demonstrate the ability to locate, retrieve, organize, and interpret information from a variety of traditional and electronic sources.**

For example:

- demonstrating familiarity with basic reference tools (e.g., encyclopedias, almanacs, bibliographies, databases, atlases, periodical guides)

- recognizing the difference between primary and secondary sources

- formulating research questions and hypotheses

- applying procedures for retrieving information from traditional and technological sources (e.g., newspapers, CD-ROMs, the Internet)

- interpreting data presented in visual, graphic, tabular, and quantitative forms (e.g., recognizing level of statistical significance)

- organizing information into logical and coherent outlines

- evaluating the reliability of different sources of information

HOW TO TAKE A TEST

You have studied long, hard and conscientiously.

With your official admission card in hand, and your heart pounding, you have been admitted to the examination room.

You note that there are several hundred other applicants in the examination room waiting to take the same test.

They all appear to be equally well prepared.

You know that nothing but your best effort will suffice. The "moment of truth" is at hand: you now have to demonstrate objectively, in writing, your knowledge of content and your understanding of subject matter.

You are fighting the most important battle of your life—to pass and/or score high on an examination which will determine your career and provide the economic basis for your livelihood.

What extra, special things should you know and should you do in taking the examination?

BEFORE THE TEST

YOUR PHYSICAL CONDITION IS IMPORTANT
    If you are not well, you can't do your best work on tests. If you are half asleep, you can't do your best either. Here are some tips:

1) Get about the same amount of sleep you usually get. Don't stay up all night before the test, either partying or worrying—DON'T DO IT!
2) If you wear glasses, be sure to wear them when you go to take the test. This goes for hearing aids, too.
3) If you have any physical problems that may keep you from doing your best, be sure to tell the person giving the test. If you are sick or in poor health, you really cannot do your best on any test. You can always come back and take the test some other time.

AT THE TEST

EXAMINATION TECHNIQUES
1) Read the general instructions carefully. These are usually printed on the first page of the exam booklet. As a rule, these instructions refer to the timing of the examination; the fact that you should not start work until the signal and must stop work at a signal, etc. If there are any *special* instructions, such as a choice of questions to be answered, make sure that you note this instruction carefully.

2) When you are ready to start work on the examination, that is as soon as the signal has been given, read the instructions to each question booklet, underline any key words or phrases, such as *least, best, outline, describe* and the like. In this way you will tend to answer as requested rather than discover on reviewing your paper that you *listed without describing*, that you selected the *worst* choice rather than the *best* choice, etc.

3) If the examination is of the objective or multiple-choice type – that is, each question will also give a series of possible answers: A, B, C or D, and you are called upon to select the best answer and write the letter next to that answer on your answer paper – it is advisable to start answering each question in turn. There may be anywhere from 50 to 100 such questions in the three or four hours allotted and you can see how much time would be taken if you read through all the questions before beginning to answer any. Furthermore, if you come across a question or group of questions which you know would be difficult to answer, it would undoubtedly affect your handling of all the other questions.

4) If the examination is of the essay type and contains but a few questions, it is a moot point as to whether you should read all the questions before starting to answer any one. Of course, if you are given a choice – say five out of seven and the like – then it is essential to read all the questions so you can eliminate the two which are most difficult. If, however, you are asked to answer all the questions, there may be danger in trying to answer the easiest one first because you may find that you will spend too much time on it. The best technique is to answer the first question, then proceed to the second, etc.

5) Time your answers. Before the exam begins, write down the time it started, then add the time allowed for the examination and write down the time it must be completed, then divide the time available somewhat as follows:
   - If 3-1/2 hours are allowed, that would be 210 minutes. If you have 80 objective-type questions, that would be an average of 2-1/2 minutes per question. Allow yourself no more than 2 minutes per question, or a total of 160 minutes, which will permit about 50 minutes to review.
   - If for the time allotment of 210 minutes there are 7 essay questions to answer, that would average about 30 minutes a question. Give yourself only 25 minutes per question so that you have about 35 minutes to review.

6) The most important instruction is to *read each question* and make sure you know what is wanted. The second most important instruction is to *time yourself properly* so that you answer every question. The third most important instruction is to *answer every question*. Guess if you have to but include something for each question. Remember that you will receive no credit for a blank and will probably receive some credit if you write something in answer to an essay question. If you guess a letter – say "B" for a multiple-choice question – you may have guessed right. If you leave a blank as an answer to a multiple-choice question, the examiners may respect your

feelings but it will not add a point to your score. Some exams may penalize you for wrong answers, so in such cases *only*, you may not want to guess unless you have some basis for your answer.

7) Suggestions
   a. Objective-type questions
      1. Examine the question booklet for proper sequence of pages and questions
      2. Read all instructions carefully
      3. Skip any question which seems too difficult; return to it after all other questions have been answered
      4. Apportion your time properly; do not spend too much time on any single question or group of questions
      5. Note and underline key words – *all, most, fewest, least, best, worst, same, opposite,* etc.
      6. Pay particular attention to negatives
      7. Note unusual option, e.g., unduly long, short, complex, different or similar in content to the body of the question
      8. Observe the use of "hedging" words – *probably, may, most likely,* etc.
      9. Make sure that your answer is put next to the same number as the question
      10. Do not second-guess unless you have good reason to believe the second answer is definitely more correct
      11. Cross out original answer if you decide another answer is more accurate; do not erase until you are ready to hand your paper in
      12. Answer all questions; guess unless instructed otherwise
      13. Leave time for review

   b. Essay questions
      1. Read each question carefully
      2. Determine exactly what is wanted. Underline key words or phrases.
      3. Decide on outline or paragraph answer
      4. Include many different points and elements unless asked to develop any one or two points or elements
      5. Show impartiality by giving pros and cons unless directed to select one side only
      6. Make and write down any assumptions you find necessary to answer the questions
      7. Watch your English, grammar, punctuation and choice of words
      8. Time your answers; don't crowd material

8) Answering the essay question

Most essay questions can be answered by framing the specific response around several key words or ideas. Here are a few such key words or ideas:

M's: manpower, materials, methods, money, management
P's: purpose, program, policy, plan, procedure, practice, problems, pitfalls, personnel, public relations

a. Six basic steps in handling problems:
   1. Preliminary plan and background development
   2. Collect information, data and facts
   3. Analyze and interpret information, data and facts
   4. Analyze and develop solutions as well as make recommendations
   5. Prepare report and sell recommendations
   6. Install recommendations and follow up effectiveness

b. Pitfalls to avoid
   1. *Taking things for granted* – A statement of the situation does not necessarily imply that each of the elements is necessarily true; for example, a complaint may be invalid and biased so that all that can be taken for granted is that a complaint has been registered
   2. *Considering only one side of a situation* – Wherever possible, indicate several alternatives and then point out the reasons you selected the best one
   3. *Failing to indicate follow up* – Whenever your answer indicates action on your part, make certain that you will take proper follow-up action to see how successful your recommendations, procedures or actions turn out to be
   4. *Taking too long in answering any single question* – Remember to time your answers properly

EXAMINATION SECTION

EXAMINATION SECTION

TEST 1

DIRECTIONS: Each question or incomplete statement is followed by several suggested answers or completions. Select the one that BEST answers the question or completes the statement. *PRINT THE LETTER OF THE CORRECT ANSWER IN THE SPACE AT THE RIGHT.*

Use the passage below to answer Question #1:

The next time you see lightning and hear the accompanying thunder, you can easily estimate the distance between yourself and the lightning by using the following method.

When you see a lightning bolt, start counting the seconds until you hear the thunder. Divide the total number of seconds by five. The result is the approximate distance to the lightning. Thus, if you counted 10 seconds between the flash of the lightning and the sound of the thunder, the lightning struck about two miles away.

How does that method work? It's simple. The speed of sound in air is about 1,125 feet – approximately one-fifth of a mile – per second. The speed of light is approximately 186,000 miles per second. The light and sound created by the lightning bolt originate at the same time, but because the speed of light is much greater than the speed of sound, we see the flash of the lightning before we hear the rumble of the thunder.

When you count the seconds between the lightning and the thunder and divide the total by five, you are in fact estimating the distance in miles – one mile per five seconds – that the sound traveled since the lightning flash.

1. Which of the following is a fundamental assumption of this method of estimating the distance between an observer and a bolt of lightning?
   A. The wavelength of light is much shorter than the wavelength of sound
   B. The speed at which light travels is so great that the time required for the light waves to reach the observer is essentially zero
   C. Sound waves are more strongly affected by atmospheric conditions than are light waves
   D. The speed at which sound and light travel varies proportionately with the distance they travel

1._____

2. A small stream of water is poured at a constant rate into a flask (shown at the right), until the flask is full. Which of the following graphs best represents the way in which the height of the water in the flask changes in relation to the length of time the water is poured?

2._____

A.

B.

C.

D.

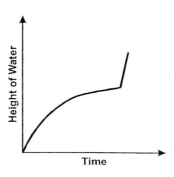

3. Which of the following situations best illustrates the mathematical concept of a *linear relationship* – a relationship between two variables such that a change in one is accompanied by a proportional change in the other?

3._____

   A. Joe's Pizza sells an 8-inch diameter pizza for $10, a 12-inch pizza for $14 and a 16-inch pizza for $16
   B. College Painters estimates that two people could paint a house in ten days, four people could paint the same house in four days, and eight people could paint the house in one day
   C. A recycling center offers $22 for 100 pounds of scrap aluminum, $33 for 150 pounds, and $44 for 200 pounds
   D. The world's population doubled in the 15 years from 1960 to 1975, doubled again in the 20 years from 1975 to 1995, and is expected to double once more in the 30 years from 1995 to 2025

4. Many systems in the living and physical worlds have mechanisms that use feedback to help maintain equilibrium – that is, help to keep the overall conditions of the system relatively constant over time. Which of the following processes is the best example of a mechanism that uses feedback to maintain equilibrium in the human body system?

    A. The increase in breathing rate while exercising
    B. The detection of temperature by a finger touching a cool surface
    C. The continual growth of hair and nails
    D. The loss of blood at the site of a cut

4._____

Use the following excerpt from *The Discoverers* by Daniel J. Boorstin to answer Question #5:

The Chinese had been making a rudimentary paper since about A.D. 105, when Ts'ai Lun, using mulberry, waste fish nets and rags, made the first known sheet of paper for the emperor. Chinese prisoners of war whom the Arabs had taken at Samarkand introduced the Arabs to the arts of papermaking. By 800 the brilliant caliph Harun al-Rashid (764?–809) was having paper made for him in Baghdad. Then through the Arabs paper was brought to Byzantium and across the Mediterranean to Spain, whence it spread over Europe. Even before the invention of printing, manuscripts written on paper were not uncommon, and there were paper mills in Spain, Italy, France and Germany.

5. This excerpt illustrates which of the following characteristics of the relationship between culture and technological discovery?

    A. Technological discovery may be hindered by political, cultural and religious restrictions on the sharing of ideas
    B. Technological discoveries may be spread by warfare and other interactions across cultures
    C. Technological discovery may be halted until seemingly unrelated scientific advances are made in widely diffuse cultural areas
    D. Technological discoveries initially designed for military purposes may soon be adapted for nonmilitary uses

5._____

6. Researchers are beginning to conduct clinical trials of a new medication
designed to reduce the itching associated with poison ivy. The
researchers randomly divide a group of trial participants in half. One
group of participants is treated with the actual medication, while the other
group is treated with a placebo, a substance that looks the same as the
medication but has none of the active ingredients. Only the researchers
know which participants receive the medication and which receive the
placebo. Which of the following best explains the purpose of having a
group of participants receive a placebo in a study such as this?

6._____

    A. It allows the researchers to test the medication's effectiveness
without exposing more people than necessary to potential side
effects

    B. It prevents the researchers from inadvertently allowing their own
preconceptions and expectations to influence the clinical trial or
the interpretation of results

    C. It helps the researchers distinguish between the actual effects of
the medication and effects participants might imagine they feel

    D. It keeps the overall research and development costs associated
with the medication to a minimum

Use the passage below, from the translated writings of Juan Batista Alberdi, a
19th-century Argentine political theorist, to answer Question #7:

What name will you give a land with 200,000 leagues of territory and a
population of 800,000? A desert…But what constitution best fits a desert?
One that will help to make it disappear: one that will enable it in the shortest
possible time to cease being a desert and become a populated country. This,
then, should and must be the political aim of the Argentine constitution and in
general of all South American constitutions. The constitutions of unpopulated
countries can have no other serious and rational end, at present and for
many years to come, than to give the solitary and abandoned countryside the
population it requires, as a fundamental condition for its development and
progress.

7. Based on the information contained in the passage, it is reasonable to
assume that its author would most strongly support which of the following
economic proposals?

7._____

    A. Limiting foreign investment in Argentine industries

    B. Using government land grants to promote highway and railroad
construction

    C. Taxing all goods produced for sale within Argentina

    D. Using monetary policy to tighten the supply of money and raise
interest rates

8. Which of the following excerpts from the U.S. Constitution best illustrates the principle of checks and balances?

    8._____

    A. "The judicial power shall extend to … controversies between two or more States;—between a State and citizens of another State;—between citizens of different States;—between citizens of the same State claiming land under grants of different States, and between a State, or the citizens thereof, and foreign states, citizens or subjects."

    B. "Each house may determine the rules of its proceedings, punish its members for disorderly behavior, and with the concurrence of two-thirds, expel a member."

    C. "Every bill which shall have passed the House of Representatives and the Senate, shall, before it become a law, be presented to the President of the United States; if he approve he shall sign it, but if not he shall return it with objections to that house in which it originated, who shall … proceed to reconsider it."

    D. "The times, places and manner of holding elections for Senators and Representatives shall be prescribed in each State by the legislature thereof; but the Congress may at any time by law make or alter such regulations, except as to the places of choosing Senators."

Use the passage below, adapted from a speech by Frances Harper at the 1893 Columbian Exposition in support of women's right to equal social status and political participation, to answer Question #9:

"[T]o-day we stand on the threshold of woman's era, and woman's work is grandly constructive. The social and political advancement which woman has already gained bears the promise of the rising of the full-orbed sun of emancipation. Yet I do not think the mere extension of the ballot a panacea for all the ills of our national life. What we need to-day is not simply more voters, but better voters. It is the women of a country who help to mold its character, and to influence if not determine its destiny. In coming into her political estate woman will find a mass of illiteracy to be dispelled. If knowledge is power, ignorance is also power."

9. Which of the following statements most closely expresses a central democratic value underlying the speaker's arguments in this selection?

9._____

    A. "I believe – indeed I know – that whatever is fine and beautiful in the human expresses and asserts itself in spite of government, and not because of it." –Emma Goldman

    B. "Every democratic system evolves its own conventions. It is not only the water but the banks which make the river." –Indira Gandhi

    C. "Democracy always makes for materialism, because the only kind of equality that you can guarantee to a whole people is, broadly speaking, physical." –Katherine Fullerton Gould

    D. "A democratic form of government, a democratic way of life, presupposes public education over a long period; it presupposes also an education for personal responsibility that too often is neglected." –Eleanor Roosevelt

10. Which of the following would be considered primary sources in researching the factors influencing U.S. involvement in Vietnam in the 1960s?

10._____

    I. the official correspondence of Lyndon Johnson from 1963 to 1968, the years of his presidency

    II. a journal article, published in 1975, about Robert S. McNamara, secretary of defense from 1961 to 1968

    III. a biography, published in 1969, of John F. Kennedy, president from 1961 to 1963

    IV. an interview, taped in 1976, with Dean Rusk, secretary of state from 1961 to 1969

    A. I and II only
    B. I and IV only
    C. II and III only
    D. III and IV only

Use the graphs below, charting statistics of a western farming state from 1926 to 1935, to answer Question #11:

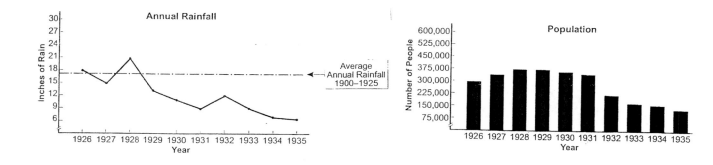

11. Which of the following conclusions about the relationship between rainfall
    and population from 1926 to 1935 is best supported by the information in
    the graphs?
    A. Increases and decreases in population directly paralleled
    increases and decreases in annual rainfall
    B. Despite a steady decline in annual rainfall during this period, the
    state's population remained stable, varying by no more than about
    10 percent
    C. There was no relationship between annual rainfall and fluctuations
    in the state's population during this period
    D. Population began to decline significantly only after several years
    of below-average rainfall

11._____

Use this reproduction of a woodcut by Suzuki Harunobu to answer Question #12:

12. The diagonal arrangement of the figures, faces and gestures in this
    woodcut serves to
    A. emphasize the difference in status between the woman and child
    B. draw the viewer's attention to the bird
    C. create a feeling of suspense and foreboding
    D. define the perspective from which the artist viewed the scene

12._____

Use the passage below, about Doris Humphrey's 1931 dance piece *The Shakers*, to answer Question #13:

> "Later [Humphrey] told her students that the Shakers attracted her because they believed in dancing; their religious ritual was, in fact, a dance and its original steps and formations served as the basis for her choreography ... The basic themes were few: hopping, swaying, falling forward and pulling back, shaking. The dancers moved in straight, symmetrical lines, often in unison but with individual "shaking" movements. Against the formal processions of the ritual, she pitted ecstatic falls; inspired speech; man and woman trembling as they approached one another, knowing they must not touch."

13. Which of the following views of Shaker society and culture is the choreography described in this passage most likely intended to suggest?   13._____
    A. Society centered on ambition and personal achievement
    B. Generally peaceful society, marked by occasional violence
    C. Society in which strong emotions are kept under control
    D. Belief system characterized by openness to new experiences

Use the excerpt, from Pablo Neruda's "The Pueblo," to answer Question #14:

> "That man I remember well, and at least two centuries
> have passed since I saw him;
> he traveled neither on horseback nor in a carriage–
> purely on foot
> he undid the distances,
> carrying neither sword nor weapon
> but nets on his shoulders,
> axe or hammer or spade;
> he never fought with another of his kind–
> his struggle was with water or with earth,
> with the wheat, for it to become bread,
> with the towering tree, for it to yield wood,
> with the walls, to open doors in them,
> with the sand, constructing walls,
> and with the sea, to make it bear fruit.
>
> I knew him and still he is there in me.
>
> The carriages splintered in pieces,
> war destroyed doorways and walls,
> the city was a fistful of ashes,
> all the dresses withered into dust,
> and he persists, for my sake,
> he survives in the sand,
> where everything previously
> seemed durable except him.

14. Which of the following statements best expresses an important theme of
    Neruda's poem?   14._____
     A. The human experience of previous centuries is lost and can never
        be regained
     B. The reality of modern existence must be cherished and preserved
        as energetically as the memory of the past
     C. Our picture of life in earlier times is distorted by our tendency to
        romanticize
     D. What is simple and constructive in humanity will endure despite
        the violent tendencies of modern society

Use the excerpts below from "A Vision Beyond Time and Place" by N. Scott
Momaday to answer Question #15:

When my father was a boy, an old man used to come to [my grandfather] Mammedaty's house
and pay his respects. He was a lean old man in braids and was impressive in his age and bearing.
His name was Cheney, and he was an arrowmaker. Every morning, my father tells me, Cheney
would paint his wrinkled face, go out, and pray aloud to the rising sun. . . .

I often think of old man Cheney, and of his daily devotion to the sun. . . . He was a man who
saw very deeply into the distance, I believe, one whose vision extended far beyond the physical
boundaries of his time and place. . . . In his mind's eye he could integrate all the realities and
illusions of the earth and sky; they became for him profoundly intelligible and whole. . . .

Most Indian people are able to see in these terms. . . . It is indeed the basis upon which they
identify themselves as individuals and as a race. . . . When old man Cheney looked into the
sunrise, he saw as far into himself, I suspect, as he saw into the distance. He knew certainly
of his existence and of his place in the scheme of things.

In contrast, most of us in this society are afflicted with a kind of cultural nearsightedness. . . .
[W]e do not see beyond the buildings and billboards that seem at times to be the monuments
of our civilization, and consequently we fail to see into the nature and meaning of our own
humanity. Now, more than ever, we might do well to enter upon a vision quest of our own,
that is, a quest after vision itself.

15. According to the excerpts, which of the following best describes a central   15._____
    aspect of the vision that Cheney achieved in his daily devotion?
     A. Faith in the reality of a spiritual life after death
     B. Belief in divine forgiveness and human redemption
     C. Perception of the interconnectedness of all things
     D. Rejection of the temptations and illusions of the material world

Use the poem below, translated from the works of Yang Kwang, to answer Question #16:

> In Spring when all the flowers are in bloom,
> The evening river appears smooth and motionless,
> Suddenly the tidewater comes with the reflection of glittering stars;
> The ebbing waves carry away the image of the moon.

16. This poem most closely reflects which of the following tenets of Asian belief systems?

    16._____

    A. Taoist emphasis on simplicity and contemplation of the effortless processes of nature
    B. Confucian emphasis on ethical precepts for the proper management of the social order
    C. Shintoist emphasis on the supernatural and the power of the divine forces of nature
    D. Buddhist emphasis on enlightenment and renunciation of worldly cravings and attachments

Use the selection below, from a letter written from the Birmingham jail in 1963 by Martin Luther King, Jr., to answer Questions #17 and #18:

> You express a great deal of anxiety over our willingness to break laws. This is certainly a legitimate concern. Since we so diligently urge people to obey the Supreme Court's decision of 1954 outlawing segregation in the public schools, at first glance it may seem rather paradoxical for us consciously to break laws. One may well ask: "How can you advocate breaking some laws and obeying others?" The answer lies in the fact that there are two types of laws: just and unjust. I would be the first to advocate obeying just laws. One has not only a legal but a moral responsibility to obey just laws. Conversely, one has a moral responsibility to disobey unjust laws. . . .
>
> A just law is a man-made code that squares with the moral law or the law of God. An unjust law is a code that is out of harmony with the moral law. . . . Any law that uplifts human personality is just. Any law that degrades human personality is unjust. All segregation statutes are unjust because segregation distorts the soul and damages the personality. It gives the segregator a false sense of superiority and the segregated a false sense of inferiority. . . .
>
> An unjust law is a code that a numerical or power majority group compels a minority group to obey but does not make binding on itself. This is *difference* made legal. By the same token, a just law is a code that a majority compels a minority to follow and that it is willing to follow itself. This is *sameness* made legal.

17. The views expressed in this selection are most consistent with which of   17._____
the following statements?
    A. In a democratic system, disobedience to the law can never be
justified
    B. Human law and moral law are inevitably in conflict
    C. Civil disobedience is an appropriate and necessary response to
immoral law
    D. A society that permits its citizens to disobey even unjust laws
cannot remain healthy

18. Which of the following assumptions is most fundamental to the   18._____
development of the argument presented in this selection?
    A. In a just society, the rights of the majority group outweigh the
rights of smaller and less powerful groups
    B. That government is best which governs least
    C. Law represents the collective historical wisdom of human society
    D. All human beings are created equal

Use the passage below to answer Question #19:

[1]Myths are traditional stories of unknown authorship that were originally
passed down by word of mouth. [2]Typically, myths evolved in preliterate
societies to explain natural events and forces, to come to terms with heroes
and gods, and to prescribe rituals to ward off evil. [3]In a society of this type,
an individual body of myths were developed to guide the community's
religious and social life. [4]Unlike fables and folk tales, which people told for
amusement but did not believe, myths were considered sacred and
completely true.

19. Which part of the passage should be revised to correct a grammatical   19._____
error?
    A. Part 1 – to correct an error in the placement of modifiers
    B. Part 2 – to correct an error in parallel structure
    C. Part 3 – to correct an error in subject-verb agreement
    D. Part 4 – to correct an error in prepositional phrasing

20. While researching a 19th-century presidential candidate, a researcher   20._____
locates four sources that provide conflicting information about a
controversial position that the candidate adopted during his campaign.
Which source is likely to be most reliable in explaining why the candidate
adopted the position?
   A. An autobiography that the candidate wrote later in life, covering
      the years during which the campaign was conducted
   B. A copy of the speech, written in the candidate's handwriting, in
      which the candidate announced the position
   C. A newspaper editorial opposing the candidate's position, written
      just after the candidate announced the position
   D. A series of notes on the issue between the candidate and a key
      advisor, written just before the candidate adopted the position

KEY (CORRECT ANSWERS)

1. B	11. D
2. C	12. B
3. C	13. C
4. A	14. D
5. B	15. C
6. C	16. A
7. B	17. C
8. C	18. D
9. D	19. C
10. B	20. D

READING COMPREHENSION
COMMENTARY

Questions on reading comprehension – the ability to understand and interpret written materials – are now universal, staple parts of almost all aptitude and achievement tests, as well as tests of general and mental ability.

By its very nature, the reading comprehension question is the most difficult of the question-types to cope with successfully, and, accordingly, it is usually weighted more heavily (assigned more credits) than other questions.

Generally, tests of aptitude and/or achievement derive their reading selections ("passages") from the several disciplines – art, biology, chemistry, economics, education, engineering, history, literature, mathematics, music, philosophy, physics, political science, psychology, and sociology. Thus, the student or applicant is not being tested for specific knowledge of, or proficiency in, these areas. Rather, he is being tested on his understanding and comprehension of the meaning of the materials contained in the specific passages presented, the theory being that his mental ability will be best tested by his reading power, not by his training or acquired knowledge in the different fields, since it may be reasonably expected that such training and/or knowledge will differ among the candidates for a variety of reasons. The great equalizing element is the reading comprehension test. Therefore, all the information and material needed for answering the questions are imbedded in the passages themselves. *The power or skill or ability of the testtaker, then, is to be shown in the extent and degree to which he succeeds in making the correct answers to the questions in the reading passages.*

Historically, many colleges and universities, leaning on the theory of transfer of training, regard the reading comprehension factor as, perhaps the most important of all criteria in measuring scholastic aptitude since, according to this view, the ability to read with understanding and to go on from this point, is basic to all academic professional, graduate, and research work.

Let us examine just what reading comprehension means in the context described above and analyze its basic components.

The factor of reading ability is a complex one which may be tested and measured at several discrete levels of ability.

Comparatively, the easiest type of reading question is that which tests understanding of the material to be read – to list facts or details as described in the passage, to explain the meanings of words or phrases used, to clarify references, etc.

The next level of difficulty is reached when the student is confronted with questions designed to show his ability to interpret and to analyze the material to be read, e.g., to discover the central thought of the passage, to ascertain the mood or point of view of the author, to note contradictions, etc.

The third stage consists of the ability to apply the principles and/or opinions expressed in the article, e.g., to surmise the recommendations that the writer may be expected to make later on or to formulate his stand on related issues.

The final and highest point is attained when the student is called upon to evaluate what he has read – agree with or to differ with the point of view of the writer, to accept or to refute the evidences or methods employed, to judge the efficacy or the inappropriateness of different proposals, etc.

All these levels will be broached and tested in this reading section.

SAMPLE PASSAGE - QUESTIONS AND ANSWERS

PASSAGE

(1) Our ignorance of the complex subject of social insurance was and remains colossal. (2) For years American business leaders delighted in maligning the British social insurance schemes. (3) Our industrialists condemned them without ever finding out what they were about. (4) Even our universities displayed no interest. (5) Contrary to the interest in this subject taken by organized labor abroad, our own labor movement bitterly opposed the entire program of social insurance up to a few years ago. (6) Since the success of any reform depends largely upon a correct public understanding of the principles involved, the adoption of social insurance measures presented peculiar difficulties for the United States under our Federal type of government of limited powers, our constitutional and judicial handicaps, our long conditioning to individualism, the traditional hostility to social reform by both capital and labor, the general inertia, and our complete lack of trained administrative personnel without which even the best law can be ineffective. (7) Has not bitter experience taught us that far more important than the passage of a law, which is at best only a declaration of intention, is a ready public opinion prepared to enforce it?

1. According to this writer, what attitude have we shown in this country toward social insurance?　　　1.__

   A. We have been extremely doubtful that it will work, but have been willing to give it a chance.
   B. We have opposed it on the grounds of a careful study of its defects.
   C. We have shown an unintelligent and rather blind antagonism toward it.
   D. We have been afraid that it would not work under our type of government.
   E. We have resented it because of the extensive propaganda in favor of it.

2. To what does the phrase, "our long conditioning to individualism," refer?　　　2.__

   A. Our habit of depending upon ourselves
   B. Our increasing dependence on the Federal Government
   C. Our long established distrust of "big business"
   D. Our policies of high protective tariff
   E. Our unwillingness to accept reforms

3. Which of these ideas is expressed in this passage?   3._____

   A. The surest way to cure a social evil is to get people to pass a law against it.
   B. Legislation alone cannot effect social reforms.
   C. The American people are seriously uninformed about all social problems.
   D. Our type of government makes social reform practically impossible.
   E. Capital and labor retard social progress.

ANALYSIS

These are the steps you must take to answer the questions:
First, scan the passage quickly, trying to gather at a glance the general import.
Then, read the passage carefully and critically, underlining with a pencil, what are apparently leading phrases and concepts.
Next, read each question carefully, and seek the answer in definite parts – sentences, clauses, phrases, figures of speech, adverbs, adjectives, etc. – in the text of the passage.
Finally, select the one answer which best answers the question, that is, it *best* matches what the paragraph says or is *best* supported by something in the passage.

The passage is concerned with the advent of social insurance to the United States. The author makes several points in this connection:

   1. Our gross ignorance of, and lack of interest in, the subject.
   2. The bitter opposition to social insurance in this country, particularly, of organized labor.
   3. Special and augmented difficulties in the United States in respect to this area; enumeration of these factors.
   4. The ultimate, certain method of achieving reform.

Having firmly encompassed the central meaning and basic contents of the passage, let us now proceed to examine each of the stated questions and proposed answers.

Question 1.   According to this writer, what attitude have we shown in this country toward social insurance?
   A. We have been extremely doubtful that it will work, but have been willing to give it a chance.
      Sentences 1, 2, 3, 4, 5 drastically negate the second clause of this statement ("but we have been willing to give it a chance").
   B. We have opposed it on the grounds of a careful study of its defects.
      This statement is completely refuted by sentences 2 and 3.
   C. We have shown an unintelligent and rather blind antagonism toward it.
      Just as A is fully denied by sentences 1-5, so these sentences fully Affirm the validity of this statement.
   D. We have been afraid that it would not work under our type of government.
      This is one – and only one – of the several difficulties facing the success of social insurance. Thus, this answer is only *partially* true.
   E. We have resented it because of the extensive propaganda in favor of it.
      Quite the contrary. Again, see sentences 1-5.

Looking back, you now see that the one suggested answer of the five (5) offered that BEST answers the question is item C, We have shown an unintelligent and rather blind antagonism toward it. The CORRECT answer, then, is C.

<u>Question 2</u>.   To what does the phrase, "our long conditioning to individualism," refer?
      A.   Our habit of depending upon ourselves.
          When a phrase is quoted from the text, as in this question, we should immediately locate it, review the context, and then consider it *in the light of the meaning of the passage as a whole.*
          We find the quoted phrase in long sentence 6, beginning "Since the success..."
          A is clearly the answer to question 2.
    Items B, C, D, E have little or no merit with reference to the meaning of the quoted phrase within the passage, and are, therefore, to be discarded as possible answers.

<u>Question 3</u>.   Which of these ideas is expressed in this passage?
      A.   The surest way to cure a social evil is to get people to pass a law against it.
          This is clearly refuted by the last sentence, "Has not bitter experience... it?"
      B.   Legislation alone cannot effect social reforms.
          This is just as clearly supported by this same last sentence.
      C.   The American people are seriously uninformed about all social problems.
        There is no evidence in the passage to support this statement.
      D.   Our type of government makes social reform practically impossible.
          Our democratic form of government does present serious handicaps to social reform, as stated in the next-to-last sentence, but does not make social reform "practically impossible."
      E.   Capital and labor retard social progress.
          American business leaders and the labor movement both opposed social *insurance*. They did not, however, retard social *progress*.

SUGGESTIONS FOR ANSWERING THE READING COMPREHENSION QUESTION

1. Be sure to answer the questions only on the basis of the passage, and not from any other source, unless specifically directed to do otherwise.

2. Note that the answers may not be found directly in the text. For the more difficult reading questions, answers are generally to be *inferred* or *derived* from the sense of one or more sentences, clauses, and even paragraphs.

3. Do not expect to find the bases for the answers in sequential parts of the textual material. The difficulty of questions is increased when the candidate is required to skip from one part of the passage to another without any order, i.e., Question 1 may have its root in the last sentence of the paragraph, let us say, and Question 5 may be based upon the second sentence, for example. This is a method of increasing the difficulty of the research and investigation required of the candidate.

4. When the question refers to a specific line, sentence, paragraph, or quotation, be sure to find this reference and to re-read it thoroughly. The answer to such a question is almost certain to be found in or near this reference in the passage.

5. Time for the reading question is limited, as it is for the examination as a whole. In other words, one must work speedily as well as effectively. The candidate, in seeking the answers to the reading questions, is not expected to go through all of the items in the thorough way presented in the sample questions above. That is, he has only to suit himself. It suffices, in order to attain to the right answer, to note mentally the basis for the answer in the text. There is no need to annotate your answer or to write out reasons for your answer. What we have attempted to do in the samples is to show that there is a definite and logical attack on this type of question, which, principally, consists of careful, critical reading, research and investigation, and evaluation of the material. One must learn to arrive at the correct answer through this process rather than through hit-or-miss tactics or guessing. There is no reading comprehension question, logically or fairly devised, which cannot be answered by the candidate provided he goes about this task in a systematic, sustained manner.

6. The candidate may be assisted by this advanced technique. Often, the general sense of the passage when fully captured, rather than specific parts in the passage, will lead to the correct answer. Therefore, it is most important that the candidate read the passage for total meaning first. This type of general understanding will be most helpful in answering those questions which have no specific background in the text but, rather, must be inferred from what has been read.

7. Beware of the following pitfalls:

   A. The categorical statement. – You can almost be sure that any answer which uses the words solely, wholly, always, never, at all times, forever, etc., is wrong.

   B. The too-easy answer. – When the question appears to be so simple that it can be answered almost word for word by reference to the text, be particularly on your guard. You will, probably, find that the language of the question may have been inverted or changed or that some important word has been added or omitted, so that you are being tested for alertness and attention to details. For example, if, in a passage, a comparison is made between Country A and Country B, and you are told that Country A has twice the area of Country B, and the question contains an item which states that "it is clear that the area of Country B is greater than Country A," note how easily you can be beguiled into accepting this statement as true.

C.   Questions requiring that the candidate show his understanding of the main point of a passage, e.g., to state the central theme, or to suggest a worthy title, must be answered on that basis alone. You may be sure that other worthy possibilities are available, but you should examine your choice from the points of view of both appropriateness and breadth. For the most part, answers that are ruled out will contain one, but not both of these characteristics.

D.   Make up your mind now that some, but not all, of the material in the various passages in the reading comprehension questions will be useful for finding the answer. Sometimes, passages are made purposely long to increase the difficulty and to further confuse the harried candidates. However, do not disregard any of the textual material without first having given it a thorough reading.

E.   If the question requires that you give the writer's opinion or feelings on possible future action, do just that, and do not substitute your own predilections or antidotes. Similarly, do not make inferences if there exists in the text a clear-cut statement of facts. Base your answer, preferably, on the facts; make inferences or assumptions when they are called for, or as necessary.

F.   Do not expect the passages to deal with your subject field(s) alone. The passages offered will illustrate all the academic areas. While interest is a major factor in attaining to success, resolve now that you are going to wade through all the passages, in a thorough way, be they science or mathematics or economics or art. Unfamiliarity with a subject is no excuse on this type of test since the answers are to be based upon the reading passage alone.

In corollary fashion, should you encounter a passage dealing with a field with which you are familiar, do not permit your special knowledge to play a part in your answer. Answer only on the basis of the passage, as directed.

G.   The hardest type of reading question is the one in which the fifth choice presented is "none of these." Should this phrase prove to be the correct answer, it would require a thorough, albeit rapid, examination of ALL the possibilities. This, of course, is time consuming and often frustrating.

H.   A final word of advice at this point. On the examination, leave the more difficult reading questions for the end. Try to answer those of lesser difficulty first. In this way, you will leave yourself maximum time for the really difficult part of the examination.

————

In accordance with the special challenge of the reading comprehension question, ten (10) selected passages, varying in subject matter, style, length, and form, are presented for solution by the candidate. However, the passages are all alike in one respect: they extend to the highest ranges of difficulty.

————

READING COMPREHENSION
UNDERSTANDING AND INTERPRETING WRITTEN MATERIAL
EXAMINATION SECTION
TEST 1

DIRECTIONS: Each question or incomplete statement is followed by several suggested
answers or completions. Select the one that *BEST* answers the question or
completes the statement. *PRINT THE LETTER OF THE CORRECT ANSWER
IN THE SPACE AT THE RIGHT.*

PASSAGE

It is a common belief that a thing is desirable because it is scarce and thereby has ostentation value. The notion that such a standard of value is an inescapable condition of settled social existence rests on one of two implicit assumptions. The first is that the attempt to educate the human race so that the desire to display one's possessions is not a significant feature of man's social behavior, is an infringement against personal freedom. The greatest obstacle to lucid discourse in these matters is the psychological anti-vaccinationist who uses the word freedom to signify the natural right of men and women to be unhappy and unhealthy through scientific ignorance instead of being healthy and happy through the knowledge which science confers. Haunted by a perpetual fear of the dark, the last lesson which man learns in the difficult process of growing up is "ye shall know the truth, and the truth shall make you free." The professional economist who is too sophisticated to retreat Into the obscurities of this curious conception of liberty may prefer to adopt the second assumption, that the truth does not and cannot make us free because the need for ostentation is a universal species characteristic, and all attempts to eradicate the unconscionable nuisance and discord which arise from overdeveloped craving for personal distinction artificially fostered by advertisement propaganda and so-called good breeding are therefore destined to failure. It may be earnestly, hoped that those who entertain this view have divine guidance. No rational basis for it will be found in textbooks of economics. Whatever can be said with any plausibility in the existing state of knowledge rests on the laboratory materials supplied by anthropology and social history.

1. According to the writer, the second assumption   1._____

   A. Is fostered by propaganda and so-called good breeding
   B. is basically opposite to the view of the psychological anti-vaccinationist
   C. is not so curious a conception of liberty as Is the first assumption
   D. is unsubstantiated
   E. is a religious explanation of an economic phenomenon

2. The author's purpose in writing this paragraph is MOST probably to   2._____

   A. denounce the psychological anti-vaccinationists
   B. demonstrate that the question under discussion is an economic rather than a psychological problem
   C. prove the maxim "ye shall know the truth, and the truth shall make you free"
   D. prove that ostentation is not an inescapable pheonomenon of settled social existence
   E. prove the inability of economics to account for ostentation

3. The writer implies that   3.__

    A. neither the psychological anti-vaccinationist nor the professional economist recognizes the undesirability of ostentation
    B. our cultural standards are at fault in enhancing ostentation value
    C. scarcity as a criterion of value Is an inexplicable concept
    D. his main objection Is to the inescapable standard of values
    E. the results of studies of ostentation in anthropology and social history are Irrational

4. The writer believes that both assumptions   4.__

    A. are invalid because they ignore the lesson "ye shall know the truth, and the truth shall make you free"
    B. are fallacious because they agree that a thing is desirable because it is scarce
    C. arise from overdeveloped craving for personal distinction
    D. are implicit in the conception of ostentation value
    E. dispute the efficacy of education in eliminating ostentation

5. In his reference to divine guidance, the writer is   5.__

    A. being ironic
    B. implying that only divine guidance can solve the problem
    C. showing how the professional economist is opposing divine laws
    D. referring to opposition which exists between religion and science
    E. indicating that the problem is not a matter for divine guidance

6. The writer believes that personal freedom is   6.__

    A. less important than is scientific knowledge
    B. a requisite for the attainment of truth
    C. attained by eradicating false beliefs
    D. no concern of the professional economist
    E. an unsophisticated concept

7. We may infer that this writer does NOT believe that   7.__

    A. education can solve the problem
    B. people have any "natural rights"
    C. science can solve the problem
    D. the psychological anti-vaccinationist is more than a lipservant of the cause of freedom
    E. people can be happy under the present value system

8. The writer would consider as MOST comparable to the effect of a vaccination on the body, the effect of   8.__

    A. fear upon personality
    B. science upon the supposed need for ostentation
    C. truth upon the mind
    D. knowledge upon ignorance
    E. knowledge upon happiness

KEY (CORRECT ANSWERS)

1.	D	5.	A
2.	D	6.	C
3.	B	7.	E
4.	D	8.	C

———

TEST 2

PASSAGE

In any country the wages commanded by laborers who have comparable skills but who work in various industries are determined by the productivity of the least productive unit of labor, i.e., that unit of labor which works in the industry which has the greatest economic disadvantage. We will represent the various opportunities of employment in a country like the United States by symbols: A, standing for a group of industries in which we have exceptional economic advantages over foreign countries; B, for a group in which our advantages are less; C, one in which they are still less; D, the group of industries in which they are least of all.

When our population is so small that all our labor can be engaged in the group represented by A, productivity of labor (and therefore wages) will be at their maximum. When our population increases so that some of the labor will have to be set to work in group B, the wages of all labor must decline to the level of the productivity in that group. But no employer, without government aid, will yet be able to afford to hire labor to exploit the opportunities represented by C and D, unless there is a further increase in population.

But suppose that the political party in power holds the belief that we should produce everything that we consume, that the opportunities represented by C and D should be exploited. The commodities that the industries composing C and D will produce have been hitherto obtained from abroad in exchange for commodities produced by A and B. The government now renders this difficult by placing high duties upon the former class of commodities. This means that workers in A and B must pay higher prices for what they buy, but do not receive higher prices for what they sell.

After the duty has gone into effect and the prices of commodities that can be produced by C and D have risen sufficiently, enterprisers will be able to hire labor at the wages prevailing in A and B, and establish industries in C and D. So far as the remaining laborers in A and B buy the products of C and D, the difference between the price which they pay for those products and the price that they would pay if they were permitted to import those products duty-free is a tax paid not to the government, but to the producers in C and D, to enable the latter to remain in business. It is an uncompensated deduction from the natural earnings of the laborers in A and B. Nor are the workers in C and D paid as much, estimated in purchasing power, as they would have received if they had been allowed to remain in A and B under the earlier conditions.

1. When C and D are established, workers in these industries   1.__

    A. receive higher wages than do the workers in A and B
    B. receive lower wages than do the workers in A and B
    C. must be paid by government funds collected from the duties on imports
    D. are not affected so adversely by the levying of duties as are workers in A and B
    E. receive wages equal to those workers in A and B

2. We cannot exploit C and D unless

    A.   the productivity of labor in all industries is increased
    B.   the prices of commodities produced by A and B are raised
    C.   we export large quantities of commodities produced by A and B
    D.   the producers in C and D are compensated for the disadvantages under which they operate
    E.   we allow duties to be paid to the producers in C and D rather than to the government

2.____

3. "No employer; without government aid, will yet be able to afford to hire labor to exploit the opportunities represented by C and D" because

    A.   productivity of labor is not at the maximum
    B.   we cannot produce everything we consume
    C.   the population has increased
    D.   enterprisers would have to pay wages equivalent to those obtained by workers in A and B, while producing under greater economic disadvantages
    E.   productivity would drop correspondingly with the wages of labor

3.____

4. The government, when it places high duties on imported commodities of classes C and D,

    A.   raises the price of commodities produced by A and B
    B.   is, in effect, taxing the workers in A and B
    C.   raises the wages of workers in C and D at the expense of the workers in A and B
    D.   does not affect the productivity of the workers in A and B, although the wages of these workers are reduced
    E.   is adopting a policy made necessary by the stability of the population

4.____

5. The author's MAIN point is that

    A.   it is impossible to attain national self-sufficiency
    B.   the varying productivity of the various industries leads to the inequalities in wages of workers in these industries
    C.   a policy that draws labor from the fields of greater natural productiveness to fields of lower natural productiveness tends to reduce purchasing power
    D.   wages ought to be independent of international trade
    E.   the government ought to subsidize C and D.

5.____

6. The author's arguments in this passage could BEST be used to

    A.   refute the belief that it is theoretically possible for us to produce everything that we consume
    B.   disprove the theory that national self-sufficiency can be obtained by means of protective tariffs
    C.   advocate the levying of duties on imported goods
    D.   advocate equal wages for workers who have comparable skills but who work in various industries
    E.   advocate free trade

6.____

7. When could C and D, as here defined, be exploited without the assistance of an artificially boosted price and without resultant lowering of wage levels?

7.___

   A. When a duty is placed on competing products from other countries
   B. When the products of C and D are exchanged in trade for other commodities
   C. When the country becomes economically self-sufficient
   D. When there is a favorable balance of trade
   E. At no time

8. In the last sentence in the selection, the statement is made: "Nor are the workers in C and D paid as much, estimated in purchasing power, as they would have received if they had been allowed to remain in A and B under the earlier conditions." This is because

8.___

   A. they must pay higher prices for commodities produced by C and D
   B. C and D cannot pay so high wages as can A and B
   C. products of C and D do not command sufficiently high prices
   D. there has not been an increase in population
   E. wages in all groups have declined

———

KEY (CORRECT ANSWERS)

1.	E	5.	C
2.	D	6.	E
3.	D	7.	B
4.	B	8.	E

———

TEST 3

DIRECTIONS: Each question or incomplete statement is followed by several suggested answers or completions. Select the one that *BEST* answers the question or completes the statement. *PRINT THE LETTER OF THE CORRECT ANSWER IN THE SPACE AT THE RIGHT.*

PASSAGE

In the Federal Convention of 1787, the members were fairly well agreed as to the desirability of some check on state laws; but there was sharp difference of opinion whether this check should be political in character as in the form of a congressional veto, or whether the principle of judicial review should be adopted.

Madison was one of the most persistent advocates of the congressional veto and in his discussion of the subject he referred several times to the former imperial prerogative of disallowing provincial statutes. In March, 1787, he wrote to Jefferson, urging the necessity of a federal negative upon state laws. He referred to previous colonial experience in the suggestion that there should be "some emanation" of the federal prerogative "within the several states, so far as to enable them to give a temporary sanction to laws of immediate necessity." This had been provided for in the imperial system through the action of the royal governor in giving immediate effect to statutes, which nevertheless remained subject to royal disallowance. In a letter to Randolph a few weeks later, Madison referred more explicitly to the British practice, urging that the national government be given "a negative, in all cases whatsoever, on the Legislative acts of the States, as the King of Great Britain heretofore had." Jefferson did not agree with Madison; on practical grounds rather than as a matter of principle, he expressed his preference for some form of judicial control.

On July 17, Madison came forward with a speech in support of the congressional veto, again supporting his contention by reference to the royal disallowance of colonial laws: "Its utility is sufficiently displayed in the British System. Nothing could maintain the harmony and subordination of the various parts of the empire, but the prerogative by which the Crown stifles in the birth every Act of every part tending to discord or encroachment. It is true the prerogative is sometimes misapplied thro' ignorance or a partiality to one particular part of the empire: but we have not the same reason to fear such misapplications in our System." This is almost precisely Jefferson's theory of the legitimate function of an imperial veto.

This whole issue shows that the leaders who wrestled with confederation problems during and after the war understood, in some measure at least, the attitude of British administrators when confronted with the stubborn localism of a provincial assembly.

1. Madison was advocating   1._____

    A.   royal disallowance of state legislation
    B.   a political check on state laws
    C.   the supremacy of the states over the federal government
    D.   the maintenance of a royal governor to give immediate effect to statutes
    E.   discord and encroachment among the states

2. From this passage there is no indication   2.___

    A. of what the British System entailed
    B. of Jefferson's stand on the question of a check on state laws
    C. that the royal negative had been misapplied in the past
    D. that Jefferson understood the attitude of British administrators
    E. of what judicial review would entail

3. According to this passage, Madison believed that the federal government   3.___

    A. ought to legislate for the states
    B. should recognize the sovereignty of the several states
    C. ought to exercise judicial control over state legislation
    D. should assume the king's veto power
    E. was equivalent to a provincial assembly

4. Madison's conception of a congressional veto   4.___

    A. was opposed to Jefferson's conception of a congressional veto
    B. developed from fear that the imperial negative might be misused
    C. was that the federal prerogative should be exercised in disallowing state laws
    D. was that its primary function was to give temporary sanction to laws of immediate
        necessity
    E. was that its primary function was to prevent such injustices as "taxation without
        representation"

5. Madison believed that   5.___

    A. the congressional veto would not be abused
    B. the royal prerogative ought to have some form of check to correct misapplications
    C. the review of state legislation by the federal government ought to remain subject to
        a higher veto
    D. the imperial veto had not been misused
    E. utility rather than freedom is the criterion for governmental institutions

6. Jefferson believed that   6.___

    A. the congressional veto would interfere with states' rights
    B. Madison's proposal smacked of imperialism
    C. the veto of state legislation was outside the limits of the federal prerogative
    D. the British System would be harmful if applied in the United States
    E. an imperial veto should include the disallowance of all legislation leading to discord

7. Madison's MAIN principle was that   7.___

    A. the national interest is more important than the interests of any one state
    B. the national government should have compulsive power over the states
    C. the king can do no wrong
    D. the United States should follow the English pattern of government
    E. the veto power of the royal governor should be included in the federal prerogative

8. Madison thought of the states as   8.____

    A. emanations of the federal government
    B. comparable to provinces of a colonial empire
    C. incapable of creating sound legislation
    D. having no rights specifically delegated to them
    E. incapable of applying judicial review of their legislation

9. Which of the following is the BEST argument which could be made against Madison's   9.____
   proposition?

    A. The United States has no king.
    B. The federal government is an entity outside the jurisdiction of the states.
    C. Each state has local problems concerning which representatives from other states
       are not equipped to pass judgment.
    D. The federal prerogative had been misused in the past.
    E. It provides no means of dealing with stubborn localism.

_____

KEY (CORRECT ANSWERS)

1.	B	5.	A
2.	E	6.	D
3.	D	7.	B
4.	C	8.	B
		9.	C

_____

TEST 4

PASSAGE

The nucleus of its population is the local businessmen, whose interests constitute the municipal policy and control its municipal administration. These local businessmen are such as the local bankers, merchants of many kinds and degrees, real estate promoters, local lawyers, local clergymen...The businessmen, who take up the local traffic in merchandising, litigation, church enterprise and the like, commonly begin with some share in the real estate speculation. This affords a common bond and a common ground of pecuniary interest, which commonly masquerades under the name of local patriotism, public spirit, civic pride, and the like. This pretense of public spirit is so consistently maintained that most of these men come presently to believe in their own professions on that head. Pecuniary interest in local land values involves an interest in the continued growth of the town. Hence any creditable misrepresentation of the town's volume of business traffic, population, tributary farming community, or natural resources, is rated as serviceable to the common good. And any member of this business-like community will be rated as a meritorious citizen in proportion as he is serviceable to this joint pecuniary interest of these "influential citizens."

1. The tone of the paragraph is   1.___

     A. bitter   B. didactic
     C. complaining   D. satirical
     E. informative

2. The foundation for the "influential citizens" interest in their community is   2.___

     A. their control of the municipal administration
     B. their interests in trade and merchandising
     C. their natural feeling of civic pride
     D. a pretense of public spirit
     E. ownership of land for speculation

3. The "influential citizens" type of civic pride may be compared with the patriotism of   3.___
believers in

     A. a balance of power in international diplomacy
     B. racial superiority
     C. laissez faire
     D. a high tariff
     E. dollar diplomacy

4. The IMPORTANT men in the town   4.___

     A. are consciously insincere in their local patriotism
     B. are drawn together for political reasons
     C. do not scruple to give their community a false boost
     D. regard strict economy as a necessary virtue
     E. are extremely jealous of their prestige

5. The writer considers that the influential men of the town   5.____

    A.   are entirely hypocritical in their conception of their motives
    B.   are blinded to facts by their patriotic spirit
    C.   have deceived themselves into thinking they are altruistic
    D.   look upon the welfare of their community as of paramount importance
    E.   form a closed corporation devoted to the interests of the town

6. PROBABLY the author's own view of patriotism is that it   6.____

    A.   should be a disinterested passion untinged by commercial motives
    B.   is found only among the poorer classes
    C.   is usually found in urban society
    D.   grows out of a combination of the motives of selfinterest and altruism
    E.   consists in the main of a feeling of local pride

––––––––––

KEY (CORRECT ANSWERS)

1.	B	4.	C
2.	E	5.	C
3.	E	6.	A

––––––––––

TEST 5

PASSAGE

Negative thinking and lack of confidence in oneself or in the pupils are probably the greatest hindrances to inspirational teaching. Confronted with a new idea, one teacher will exclaim: "Oh, my children couldn't do that! They're too young." Another will mutter, "If I tried that stunt, the whole class would be in an uproar." Such are the self-justifications for mediocrity.

Here and there it is good to see a teacher take a bold step away from the humdrum approach. For example, Natalie Robinson Cole was given a class of fourth-year pupils who could hardly speak English. Yet in her book, THE ARTS IN THE CLASSROOM, she describes how she tried clay work, creative writing, interpretive dancing and many other exciting activities with them. Did her control of the class suffer? Were the results poor? Was morale adversely affected? The answer is *NO* on all three counts.

But someone may point out that what Mrs. Cole could do on the fourth-grade could not be done in the primary grades. Wrong again! The young child is more malleable than his older brother. Furthermore, his radiant heritage of originality has not been enveloped in clouds of self-consciousness. Given the proper encouragement, he will paint an interesting design on the easel, contribute a sparkling expression to the "class poem" as it takes shape on the blackboard, make a puppet speak his innermost thoughts, and react with sensitivity in scores of other ways.

All teachers on all grade levels need to think positively and act confidently. Of course, any departure from the commonplace must be buttressed by careful preparation, firm handling of the situation, and consistent attention to routines. Since these assets are within the reach of all teachers there should be no excuse for not putting some imagination into their work.

1. The central idea of the above passage is BEST conveyed by the   1.__

    A. first sentence in the first paragraph
    B. last sentence in the first paragraph
    C. first sentence in the second paragraph
    D. last sentence in the passage
    E. third sentence in the third paragraph

2. If the concepts of this passage were to be expanded into a book, the one of the following   2.__
titles which would be MOST suitable is

    A. THE ARTS IN THE CLASSROOM
    B. THE POWER OF POSITIVE THINKING
    C. THE HIDDEN PERSUADERS
    D. KIDS SAY THE DARNDEST THINGS
    E. ARMS AND THE MAN

3. Of the following reasons for uninspired teaching, the one which is *NOT* given explicitly in the passage is

    3._____

    A. negative thinking
    B. teachers' underestimation of pupils' ability or stability
    C. teachers' failure to broaden themselves culturally
    D. teachers' lack of self-assurance
    E. teachers' rationalizations

4. From reading the passage one can gather that Natalie R. Cole

    4._____

    A. teaches in New York City
    B. has been married
    C. is an expert in art
    D. teaches in the primary grades
    E. is a specialist in child psychology

5. An activity for children in the primary grades which is NOT mentioned in the passage is

    5._____

    A. creative expression
    B. art work
    C. puppetry
    D. constructing with blocks
    E. work on the blackboard

6. A basic asset of the inspirational teacher NOT mentioned in the passage is

    6._____

    A. a pleasant, outgoing personality
    B. a firm hand
    C. a thorough, careful plan
    D. consistent attention to routines
    E. acting confidently

KEY (CORRECT ANSWERS)

1.	A	4.	B
2.	B	5.	D
3.	C	6.	A

TEST 6

PASSAGE

Of all the areas of learning the most important is the development of attitudes. Emotional reactions as well as logical thought processes affect the behavior of most people. "The burnt child fears the fire" is one instance; another is the rise of despots like Hitler. Both these examples also point up the fact that attitudes stem from experience. In the one case the experience was direct and impressive; in the other it was indirect and cumulative. The Nazis were indoctrinated largely by the speeches they heard and the books they read.

The classroom teacher in the elementary school is in a strategic position to influence attitudes. This is true partly because children acquire attitudes from these adults whose word they respect. Another reason it is true is that pupils often delve somewhat deeply into a subject in school that has only been touched upon at home or has possibly never occurred to them before. To a child who had previously acquired little knowledge of Mexico, his teacher's method of handling such a unit would greatly affect his attitude toward Mexicans.

The media through which the teacher can develop wholesome attitudes are innumerable. Social studies (with special reference to races, creeds and nationalities), science, matters of health and safety, the very atmosphere of the classroom... these are a few of the fertile fields for the inculcation of proper emotional reactions.

However, when children come to school with undesirable attitudes, it is unwise for the teacher to attempt to change their feelings by cajoling or scolding them. She can achieve the proper effect by helping them obtain constructive experiences. To illustrate, firstgrade pupils afraid of policemen will probably alter their attitudes after a classroom chat with the neighborhood officer in which he explains how he protects them. In the same way, a class of older children can develop attitudes through discussion, research, outside reading and all-day trips.

Finally, a teacher must constantly evaluate her own attitude because her influence can be deleterious if she has personal prejudices. This is especially true in respect to controversial issues and questions on which children should be encouraged to reach their own decisions as a result of objective analysis of all the facts.

1. The central idea conveyed in the above passage is that   1._

    A. attitudes affect our actions
    B. teachers play a significant role in developing or changing pupils' attitudes
    C. by their attitudes, teachers inadvertently affect pupils' attitudes
    D. attitudes can be changed by some classroom experiences
    E. attitudes are affected by experience

2. The author implies that   2.____

    A. children's attitudes often come from those of other children
    B. in some aspects of social studies a greater variety of methods can be used in the upper grades than in the lower grades
    C. the teacher should guide all discussions by revealing her own attitude
    D. people usually act on the basis of reasoning rather than on emotion
    E. parents' and teachers' attitudes are more often in harmony than in conflict

3. A statement NOT made or implied in the passage is that   3.____

    A. attitudes cannot easily be changed by rewards and lectures
    B. a child can develop in the classroom an attitude about the importance of brushing his teeth
    C. attitudes can be based on the learning of falsehoods
    D. the attitudes of children are influenced by all the adults in their environment
    E. the children should accept the teacher's judgment in controversial matters

4. The passage SPECIFICALLY states that   4.____

    A. teachers should always conceal their own attitudes
    B. whatever attitudes a child learns in school have already been introduced at home
    C. direct experiences are more valuable than indirect ones
    D. teachers can sometimes have an unwholesome influence on children
    E. it is unwise for the teacher to attempt to change children's attitudes

5. The first and fourth paragraphs have all the following points in common EXCEPT   5.____

    A. how reading affects attitudes
    B. the importance of experience in building attitudes
    C. how attitudes can be changed in the classroom
    D. how fear sometimes governs attitudes
    E. how differences in approach change attitudes

KEY (CORRECT ANSWERS)

    1. B
    2. B
    3. D
    4. D
    5. C

TEST 7

PASSAGE

The word geology refers to the study of the composition, structure, and history of the earth. The term is derived from the Latin, geologia. coined by Bishop Richard de Bury in 1473 to distinguish lawyers who study "earthy things" from theologians. It was first consistently used in its present sense in the latter part of the 17th century. The great mass of detail that constitutes geology is classified under a number of subdivisions which, in turn, depend upon the fundamental sciences, physics, chemistry and biology.

The principal subdivisions of geology are: mineralogy, petrology, structural geology, physiography (geomorphology), usually grouped under physical or dynamical geology; and paleontology, stratigraphy and paleogeography, grouped under historical geology. The term economic geology usually refers to the study of valuable mineral "ore" deposits, including coal and oil. The economic aspects of geology are, however, much more embracive, including many subjects associated with civil engineering, economic geography, and conservation. Some of the more important of these subjects are: meteorology, hydrology, agriculture, and seismology. Subjects which are also distinctly allied to geology are geophysics, geochemistry, and cosmogony.

1. The statement that geology treats of the history of the earth and its life, especially as recorded in the rocks, is   1.__

    A. contrary to the paragraph
    B. made in the paragraph
    C. neither made nor implied in the paragraph
    D. not made, but implied in the paragraph
    E. unclear from the passage

2. The statement that the principal branches or phases of geology are dynamical geology and historical geology are   2.__

    A. contrary to the paragraph
    B. made in the paragraph
    C. neither made nor implied in the paragraph
    D. not made, but implied in the paragraph
    E. unclear from the passage

3. The statement that mining geology is a subdivision of geophysics is   3.__

    A. contrary to the paragraph
    B. made in the paragraph
    C. neither made nor implied in the paragraph
    D. not made, but implied in the paragraph
    E. unclear from the passage

4. The statement that the study of both the exterior of the earth and its inner constitution constitutes the fundamental subject matter of geology is

    4.____

    A. contrary to the paragraph
    B. made in the paragraph
    C. neither made nor implied in the paragraph
    D. not made, but implied in the paragraph
    E. unclear from the passage

5. The statement that geology utilizes the principles of astronomy, zoology, and botany is

    5.____

    A. contrary to the paragraph
    B. made in the paragraph
    C. neither made nor implied in the paragraph
    D. not made, but implied in the paragraph
    E. unclear from the passage

6. The statement that geology is synonymous with the study of the attributes of rocks, rock formation, or rock attributes is

    6.____

    A. contrary to the paragraph
    B. made in the paragraph
    C. neither made nor implied in the paragraph
    D. not made, but implied in the paragraph
    E. unclear from the passage

_____

KEY (CORRECT ANSWERS)

1.	D	4.	D
2.	B	5.	D
3.	C	6.	A

_____

TEST 8

DIRECTIONS: Each question or incomplete statement is followed by several suggested answers or completions. Select the one that *BEST* answers the question or completes the statement. *PRINT THE LETTER OF THE CORRECT ANSWER IN THE SPACE AT THE RIGHT.*

PASSAGE

1   Schiller was the first to ring a change on this state of things
2   by addressing himself courageously to the entire population of his
3   country in all its social strata at one time. He was the great popularizer of our
4   theatre, and remained for almost a century the guiding
5   spirit of the German drama of which Schiller's matchless tragedies
6   are still by many people regarded as the surpassing manifestoes.
7   Schiller's position, while it demonstrates a whole people's gratitude
8   to those who respond to its desires, does not however furnish a
9   weapon of self-defense to the "popularizers" of drama, or rather its
10 diluters. Schiller's case rather proves that the power of popular
11 influence wrought upon a poet may be vastly inferior to the strength
12 that radiates from his own personality. Indeed, whereas the secret
13 of ephemeral power is only too often found in paltriness or mediocrity,
14 an influence of enduring force such as Schiller exerts on the Germans
15 can only emanate from a strong and self-assertive character. No poet
16 lives beyond his day who does not exceed the average in mental stature
17 or who, through a selfish sense of fear of the general, allows
18 himself to be ground down to the conventional size and shape.
19 Schiller, no less than Ibsen, forced his moral demands tyrannically
20 upon his contemporaries. And in the long run your moral despot, pro-
21 vided he be high-minded, vigorous, and able, has a better chance of
22 fame than the pliant time-server. However, there is a great difference
23 between the two cases. For quite apart from the striking dissimilarities
24 between the poets themselves, the public, through the
25 gradual growth of social organization, has become greatly altered.

1. Schiller's lasting popularity may be attributed to

    A. his meeting the desires of a whole people, not just a segment of the people
    B. his abiding by his inmost convictions
    C. his mediocrity and paltriness
    D. his courageous facing up to the problems of his day
    E. his ability to popularize the unknown

1.___

2. In the first line, "on this state of things" refers to

    A. romantic drama
    B. the French play of contrived construction
    C. drama directed to the rich and well-born
    D. the popularizers of the theatre of today
    E. the ruling class

2.___

3. In the second sentence from the last, "the two cases" refer to 3.____

    A. pliant time-server and moral despot
    B. the one who exceeds the average In mental stature and the one who allows him-self to be ground down to conventional size
    C. the popularizer and the poet of enduring fame
    D. Ibsen and Schiller
    E. the man of character and the man of wealth

4. We may assume that the author 4.____

    A. is no believer in the democratic processes
    B. has no high opinions of the "compact majority"
    C. regards popularity with the people as a measure of enduring success
    D. is opposed to the aristocracy
    E. has no fixed opinions

5. A word used in an ambiguous sense (having two or more possible meanings) in this passage is 5.____

    A. "poet" (lines 11,15, 24)
    B. "power" (lines 10, 13)
    C. "people" (lines 6, 7)
    D. "popularizer" (lines 3, 9)
    E. "moral" (lines 19, 20)

KEY (CORRECT ANSWERS)

    1. B
    2. C
    3. D
    4. B
    5. D

TEST 9

PASSAGE

In one sense, of course, this is not a new insight: all our great social and philosophical thinkers have been keenly aware of the fact of individual differences. It has remained, however, for psychologists to give the insight scientific precision.

What all this adds up to is more than just a working body of information about this and that skill. It adds up to a basic recognition of one important factor in the maturing of the individual. If each individual has a certain uniqueness of power, his maturing will best be accomplished along the line of that power. To try to develop him along lines that go in directions contrary to that of his major strength is to condition him to defeat. Thus, the non-mechanical person who is arbitrarily thrust into a mechanical occupation cannot help but do his work poorly and reluctantly, with some deep part of himself in conscious or unconscious rebellion.

He may blame himself for the low level of his accomplishment or for his persistent discontent; but not all his self-berating, nor even all his efforts to become more competent by further training, can make up for the original aptitude-lack. Unless he discovers his aptitude-lack, he may be doomed to a lifetime of self-blame, with a consequent loss of self-confidence and a halting of his psychological growth.

Or he may take refuge in self-pity — finding reason to believe that his failure is due to one or another bad break, to the jealousy of a superior, to lack of sympathy and help at home, to an initial bad start, to a lack of appreciation of what he does. If he thus goes the way of self-pity, he is doomed to a lifetime of self-commiseration that makes sound growth impossible.

The characteristic of the mature person is that he affirms life. To affirm life he must be involved, heart and soul, in the process of living. Neither the person who feels himself a failure nor the person who consciously or unconsciously resents what life has done to him can feel his heart and soul engaged in the process of living. That experience is reserved for the person whose full powers are enlisted. This, then, is what this fourth insight signifies: to mature, the individual must know what his powers are and must make them competent for life.

1. It is the author's view that   1.__

    A. "all men are created equal"
    B. "each man in his life plays many parts"
    C. "all comes to him who waits"
    D. "no kernel of nourishing corn can come to one but through his toil bestowed on that plot of ground given to him to till...."
    E. "that is what it is not to be alive. To move about in a cloud of ignorance... to live with envy... in quiet despair... to feel oneself sunk into a common grey mass..."

2. Ignorance of this fourth insight   2.____

    A. may very likely cause one to take refuge in self pity or conscious or unconscious rebellion

    B. constitutes a failure to understand that each individual is different and must cultivate his special powers in socially rewarding ways

    C. is a major deterrent to a growth to maturity

    D. means unawareness of the fact that each must use all his energy and powers to the best of his ability to make him competent for life

    E. may becloud the use of scientific precision

3. Two possible maladjustments of a man thrust into a position he is unfitted for may be summed up in the phrase,   3.____

    A. conscious and unconscious rebellion

    B. guilt-feelings and scapegoating

    C. halting of psychological growth and blaming the "breaks"

    D. "Peccavi – I have sinned" and "all the world is made except thee and me and I am not so sure of thee"

    E. light and darkness

4. We will expect a person placed in a job he is unequal to, to   4.____

    A. strike out for himself as an extrepreneur

    B. display quick angers and fixed prejudices

    C. show a great love of life outside of his work

    D. engage in labor union activities

    E. join political and social movements

KEY (CORRECT ANSWERS)

1.	D	3.	B
2.	B	4.	B

TEST 10

PASSAGE

1   "For the ease and pleasure of treading the old road, accepting
2   the fashions, the education, the religion of society, he takes the
3   cross of making his own, and, of course, the self-accusation, the
4   faint heart, the frequent uncertainty and loss of time, which are the
5   nettles and tangling vines in the way of the self-relying and self-
6   directed; and the state of virtual hositility in which he seems to
7   stand to society, and especially to educated society. For all this
8   loss and scorn, what offset? He is to find consolation in exercising
9   the highest functions of human nature. He is one who raises himself
10   from private consideration and breathes and lives on public and
11   illustrious thoughts. He is the world's eye. He is the world's
12   heart. He is to resist the vulgar prosperity that retrogrades ever
13   to barbarism, by preserving and communicating heroic sentiments,
14   noble biographies, melodious verse, and the conclusions of history.
15   Whatsoever oracles the human heart, in all emergencies, in all solemn
16   hours, has uttered as its commentary on the world of actions – these
17   he shall receive and impart. And whatsoever new verdict Reason from
18   her inviolable seat pronounces on the passing men and events of
19   today – this he shall hear and promulgate.
20   "These being his functions, it becomes him to feel all confidence
21   in himself, and to defer never to the popular cry. He and he only
22   knows the world. The world of any moment is the merest appearance.
23   Some great decorum, some fetish of a government, some ephemeral
24   trade, or war, or man, is cried up by half mankind and cried down by
25   the other half, as if all depended on this particular up or down.
26   The odds are that the whole question is not worth the poorest thought
27   which the scholar has lost in listening to the controversy. Let him
28   not quit his belief that a popgun is a popgun, though the ancient and
29   honorable of the earth affirm it to be the crack of doom. In silence,
30   in steadiness, in severe abstraction, let him hold by himself; add
31   observation to observation, patient of neglect, patient of reproach,
32   and bide his own time – happy enough if he can satisfy himself alone
33   that this day he has seen something truly. Success treads on every
34   right step. For the instinct is sure, that prompts him to tell his
35   brother what he thinks. He then learns that in going down into the
36   secrets of his own mind he has descended into the secrets of all
37   minds. He learns that he who has mastered any law in his private
38   thoughts, is master to the extent of all translated. The poet, in
39   utter solitude remembering his spontaneous thoughts and recording
40   them, is found to have recorded that which men in crowded cities
41   find true for them also. The orator distrusts at first the fitness

42 of his frank confessions, his want of knowledge of the persons he
43 addresses, until he finds that he is the complement of his hearers–
44 that they drink his words because he fulfills for them their own
45 nature; the deeper he delves into his privatest, secretest presentiment,
46 to his wonder he finds this is the most acceptable, most public, and
47 universally true. The people delight in it; the better part of every
48 man feels. This is my music; this is myself."

1. It is a frequent criticism of the scholar that he lives by himself, in an "ivory tower," remote from the problems and business of the world. Which of these below constitutes the *BEST* refutation by the writer of the passage to the criticism here noted?   1._____

  A. The world's concern being ephemeral, the scholar does well to renounce them and the world.
  B. The scholar lives in the past to interpret the present.
  C. The scholar at his truest is the spokesman of the people.
  D. The scholar is not concerned with the world's doing because he is not selfish and therefore not engrossed in matters of importance to himself and neighbors.
  E. The scholar's academic researches of today are the businessman's practical products of tomorrow.

2. The scholar's road is rough, according to the passage. Which of these is his GREATEST difficulty?   2._____

  A. He must renounce religion.
  B. He must pioneer new approaches.
  C. He must express scorn for, and hostility to, society.
  D. He is uncertain of his course.
  E. There is a pleasure in the main-traveled roads in education, religion, and all social fashions.

3. When the writer speaks of the "world's eye" and the "world's heart" he means   3._____

  A. the same thing
  B. culture and conscience
  C. culture and wisdom
  D. a scanning of all the world's geography and a deep sympathy for every living thing
  E. mind and love

4. By the phrase, "nettles and tangling vines," the author PROBABLY refers to   4._____

  A. "self-accusation" and "loss of time"
  B. "faint heart" and "self accusation"
  C. "the slings and arrows of outrageous fortune"
  D. a general term for the difficulties of a scholar's life
  E. "self-accusation" and "uncertainty"

5. The various ideas in the passage are BEST summarized in which of these groups?   5._

    1. (a) truth versus society
        (b) the scholar and books
        (c) the world and the scholar
    2. (a) the ease of living traditionally
        (b) the glory of a scholar's life
        (c) true knowledge versus trivia
    3. (a) the hardships of the scholar
        (b) the scholar's function
        (c) the scholar's justifications for disregarding the world's business

    A. 1 and 3 together
    B. 3 only
    C. 1 and 2 together
    D. 1 only
    E. 1, 2, and 3 together

6. "seems to stand" (lines 6 and 7) means   6._

    A. is
    B. gives the false impression of being
    C. ends probably in becoming
    D. is seen to be
    E. the quicksands of time

7. "public and illustrious thoughts" (lines 10 and 11) means   7._

    A. what the people think
    B. thoughts for the good of mankind
    C. thoughts in the open
    D. thoughts transmitted by the people
    E. the conclusions of history

_____

KEY (CORRECT ANSWERS)

1.	C	5.	B
2.	B	6.	B
3.	C	7.	B
4.	E		

_____

READING COMPREHENSION
EXAMINATION SECTION

DIRECTIONS FOR THIS SECTION:
Each question or incomplete statement is followed by several suggested answers or completions. Select the one that *BEST* answers the question or completes the statement. *PRINT THE LETTER OF THE CORRECT ANSWER IN THE SPACE AT THE RIGHT.*

TEST 1

In its current application to art, the term "primitive" is as vague and unspecific as the term "heathen" is in its application to religion. A heathen sect is simply one which is not affiliated with one or another of three or four organized systems of theology. Similarly, a primitive art is one which flourishes outside the small number of cultures which we have chosen to designate as civilizations. Such arts differ vastly and it is correspondingly difficult to generalize about them. Any statements which will hold true for such diverse aesthetic experiences as the pictographs of the Australians, the woven designs of the Peruvians, and the abstract sculptures of the African tribes must be of the broadest and simplest sort. Moveover, the problem is complicated by the meaning attached to the term "primitive" in its other uses. It stands for something simple, undeveloped, and, by implication, ancestral to more evolved forms. Its application to arts and cultures other than our own is an unfortunate heritage from the nineteenth-century scientists who laid the foundations of anthropology. Elated by the newly enunciated doctrines of evolution, these students saw all cultures as stages in a single line of development and assigned them to places in this series on the simple basis of the degree to which they differed from European culture, which was blandly assumed to be the final and perfect flower of the evolutionary process. This idea has long since been abandoned by anthropologists, but before its demise it diffused to other social sciences and became a part of the general body of popular misinformation. It still tinges a great deal of the thought and writing about the arts of non-European peoples and has been responsible for many misunderstandings.

1. The *MAIN* purpose of the passage is to   1. ...
   A. explain the various definitions of the term "primitive"
   B. show that the term "primitive" can be applied validly to art
   C. compare the use of the term "primitive" to the use of the term "heathen"
   D. deprecate the use of the term "primitive" as applied to art
   E. show that "primitive" arts vary greatly among themselves
2. The nineteenth-century scientists believed that the theory   2. ...
   of evolution
   A. could be applied to the development of culture
   B. was demonstrated in all social sciences
   C. was substantiated by the diversity of "primitive" art
   D. could be applied only to European culture
   E. disproved the idea that some arts are more "primitive" than others
3. With which of the following would the author agree?   3. ...
   A. The term "primitive" is used only by the misinformed.

    B. "Primitive" arts may be as highly developed as "civilized" arts.
    C. The arts of a culture often indicated how advanced that culture was.
    D. Australian, Peruvian, and African tribal arts are much like the ancestral forms from which European art evolved.
    E. A simple culture is likely to have a simple art.
4. According to the author, many misunderstandings have been   4. ...
   caused by the belief that
    A. most cultures are fundamentally different
    B. inferior works of art in any culture are "primitive" art
    C. "primitive" arts are diverse
    D. non-European arts are diverse
    E. European civilization is the final product of the evolutionary process

TEST 2

One of the ways the intellectual *avant-garde* affects the technical intelligentsia is through the medium of art, and art is, if only implicitly, a critique of experience. The turning upon itself of modern culture in the forms of the new visual art, the utilization of the detritus of daily experience to mock that experience, constitutes a mode of social criticism. Pop art, it is true, does not go beyond the surface of the visual and tactile experience of an industrial (and a commercialized) culture. Dwelling on the surface, it allows its consumers to mock the elements of their daily life, without abandoning it. Indeed, the consumption of art in the organized market for leisure serves at times to encapsulate the social criticism of the *avant-garde*. However, the recent engagement of writers, artists and theater people in contemporary issues suggests that this sort of containment may have begun to reach its limits.

In an atmosphere in which the intellectually dominant group insists on the contradictions inherent in daily experience, the technical intelligentsia will find it difficult to remain unconscious of those contradictions. The technical intelligentsia have until now avoided contradictions by accepting large rewards for their expertise. As expertise becomes increasingly difficult to distinguish from ordinary service on the one hand, and merges on the other with the change of the social environment, the technical intelligentsia's psychic security may be jeopardized. Rendering of labor services casts it back into spiritual proletarianization; a challenge to the social control exercised by elites, who use the technical intelligentsia's labor power, pushes it forward to social criticism and revolutionary politics. That these are matters, for the moment, of primarily spiritual import does not diminish their ultimate political significance. A psychological precondition for radical action is usually far more important than an "objectively" revolutionary situation -- whatever that may be.

The chances for a radicalization of the technical intelligentsia, thus extending the student revolt, cannot be even approximated. I believe I have shown there is a chance.

2

1. It may be *inferred* that the technical intelligentsia are: 1. ...
    I. The executives and employers in society
   II. Critics of *avant-garde* art
  III. Highly skilled technical workers
The *CORRECT* answer is:
    A. I *only*   B. I and III C. I, II, and III
    D. III *only*   E. I and II

2. The engagement of the intellectual *avant-garde* in con-   2. ...
temporary issues
    A. indicates that people tire of questioning the contra-
       dictions inherent in day-to-day living
    B. indicates that the technical intelligentsia are close
       to the point where they will rebel against the *avant-
       garde*
    C. could cause a challenge to the social control of the
       elites
    D. could cause the public to become more leisure-oriented
    E. could cause an increase in the consumption of art in
       the organized market for leisure services

3. The *possible* effect of the intellectual *avant-garde* on   3. ...
the technical intelligentsia is that
    A. the intellectual *avant-garde* makes the technical
       intelligentsia conscious of society's contradictions
    B. rapid curtailment of large rewards for expertise will
       result
    C. it may cause a strong likelihood of a radicalization
       of the technical intelligentsia
    D. the *avant-garde* will replace the employment of the
       technical intelligentsia in contemporary issues
    E. the rendering of labor services will be eliminated

4. If it is assumed that the technical intelligentsia become   4. ...
fully aware of the contradictions of modern life, it is
the author's position that
    A. revolution will result
    B. the technical intelligentsia may refuse to perform
       manual labor
    C. the technical intelligentsia will be pushed forward
       to social criticism and revolutionary politics
    D. the technical intelligentsia will experience some
       psychic dislocation
    E. ordinary service will replace technical expertise

5. According to the author,   5. ...
    A. the state of mind of a particular group may have more
       influence on its action than the effect of environmental
       factors
    B. the influence of art will often cause social upheaval
    C. matters of primarily spiritual import necessarily lack
       political significance
    D. the detritus of day-to-day living should be mocked by
       the intellectual *avant-garde*
    E. the technical intelligentsia can only protect their
       psychic security by self-expression through art

6. *With which* of the following would the author *agree*?   6. ...
    I. As contradictions are less contained, the psychic
       security of all members of the working class would
       be jeopardized.
   II. The expertise of the technical intelligentsia evolved
       from the ownership and management of property.
  III. The technical intelligentsia are not accustomed to
       rendering labor services.
   The *CORRECT* answer is:
     A. I only   B. III only   C. I and III
     D. II only   E. None of the above
7. The *MAIN* purpose of the passage is to   7. ...
     A. discuss the influence of the *avant-garde* art form on
        the expertise of the technical intelligentsia
     B. discuss the effect of the intellectual *avant-garde* on
        the working classes
     C. discuss the social significance of the technical
        intelligentsia
     D. discuss the possible effects of the deencapsulation
        of *avant-garde* social criticism
     E. point out that before a change psychological precon-
        ditions are first established

TEST 3

Turbulent flow over a boundary is a complex phenomenon for which
there is no really complete theory even in simple laboratory cases.
Nevertheless, a great deal of experimental data has been collected
on flows over solid surfaces, both in the laboratory and in nature,
so that, from an engineering point of view at least, the situation
is fairly well understood. The force exerted on a surface varies
with the roughness of that surface and approximately with the square
of the wind speed at some fixed height above it. A wind of 10 meters
per second (about 20 knots, or 22 miles per hour) measured at a height
of 10 meters will produce a force of some 30 tons per square kilometer
on a field of mown grass or of about 70 tons per square kilometer on
ripe wheat field. On a really smooth surface, such as glass, the force
is only about 10 tons per square kilometer.

When the wind blows over water, the whole thing is much more complicated. The roughness of the water is not a given characteristic
of the surface but depends on the wind itself. Not only that, the
elements that constitute the roughness - the waves - themselves move
more or less in the direction of the wind. Recent evidence indicates
that a large portion of the momentum transferred from the air into
the water goes into waves rather than directly into making currents
in the water; only as the waves break, or otherwise lose energy, does
their momentum become available to generate currents, or produce
Ekman layers. Waves carry a substantial amount of both energy and
momentum (typically about as much as is carried by the wind in a layer
about one wavelength thick), and so the wave-generation process is far
from negligible.

A violently wavy surface belies its appearance by acting, as far
as the wind is concerned, as though it were very smooth. At 10 meter

per second, recent measurements seem to agree, the force on the surface is quite a lot less than the force over mown grass and scarcely more than it is over glass; some observations in light winds of two or three meters per second indicate that the force on the wavy surface is less than it is on a surface as smooth as glass. In some way the motion of the waves seems to modify the airflow so that air slips over the surface even more freely than it would without the waves. This seems not to be the case at higher wind speeds, above about five meters per second, but the force remains strikingly low compared with that over other natural surfaces.

One serious deficiency is the fact that there are no direct observations at all in those important cases in which the wind speed is greater than about 12 meters per second and has had time and fetch (the distance over water) enough to raise substantial waves. The few indirect studies indicate that the apparent roughness of the surface increases somewhat under high-wind conditions, so that the force on the surface increases rather more rapidly than as the square of the wind speed.

Assuming that the force increases at least as the square of the wind speed, it is evident that high-wind conditions produce effects far more important than their frequency of occurrence would suggest. Five hours of 60-knot storm winds will put more momentum into the water than a week of 10-knot breezes. If it should be shown that, for high winds, the force on the surface increases appreciably more rapidly than as the square of the wind speed, then the transfer of momentum to the ocean will turn out to be dominated by what happens during the occasional storm rather than by the long-term average winds.

1. According to the passage, several hours of storm winds   1. ...
   (60 miles per hour) over the ocean would
   A. be similar to the force exerted by light winds for
      several hours over glass
   B. create an ocean roughness which reduces the force
      exerted by the high winds
   C. have proved to be more significant in creating ocean
      momentum than light winds
   D. create a force not greater than 6 times the force of
      a 10-mile-per-hour wind
   E. eventually affect ocean current
2. According to the passage, a rough-like ocean surface   2. ...
   A. is independent of the force of the wind
   B. has the same force exerted against it by high and
      light winds
   C. is more likely to have been caused by a storm than
      by continuous light winds
   D. nearly always allows airflow to be modified so as to
      cause the force of the wind to be less than on glass
   E. is a condition under which the approximate square of
      wind speed can never be an accurate figure in measur-
      ing the wind force

3. The author indicates that, where a hurricane is followed   3. ...
   by light winds of 10 meters per second or less,
     I. ocean current will be unaffected by the light winds
    II. ocean current will be more affected by the hurricane
         winds than the following light winds
   III. the force of the light winds on the ocean would be
         less than that exerted on a wheat field
   The *CORRECT* combination is:
     A. I only   B. III only   C. II and III
     D. I and III   E. II only
4. The *MAIN* purpose of the passage is to discuss   4. ...
     A. oceanic momentum and current
     B. turbulent flow of wind over water
     C. wind blowing over water as related to causing tidal
         flow
     D. the significance of high wind conditions on ocean
         momentum
     E. experiments in wind force
5. The author would be *incorrect* in concluding that the   5. ...
   transfer of momentum to the ocean is dominated by the
   occasional storm if
     A. air momentum went directly into making ocean current
     B. high speed winds slipped over waves as easily as low
         speed winds
     C. waves did not move in the direction of wind
     D. the force exerted on a wheat field was the same as
         on mown grass
     E. the force of wind under normal conditions increased
         as the square of wind speed
6. A wind of 10 meters per second measured at a height of   6. ...
   10 meters will produce a force close to 30 tons per square
   mile on *which* of the following?
     A. Unmown grass   B. Mown grass   C. Glass
     D. Water   E. A football field

TEST 4

Political scientists, as practitioners of a negligibley formalized
discipline, tend to be accommodating to formulations and suggested
techniques developed in related behavioral sciences. They even tend,
on occasion, to speak of psychology, sociology and anthropology as
"hard core sciences." Such a characterization seems hardly justified.
The disposition to uncritically adopt into political science non-
indigenous sociological and general systems concepts tends, at times,
to involve little more than the adoption of a specific, and sometimes
barbarous, academic vocabulary which is used to redescribe reasonably
well-confirmed or intuitively-grasped low-order empirical generalizations.

At its worst, what results in such instances is a runic explanation, a redescription in a singular language style, i.e., no explanation at all. At their best, functional accounts as they are
found in the contemporary literature provide explanation sketches,
the type of elliptical explanation characteristic of historical and

psychoanalytic accounts. For each such account there is an in-determinate number of equally plausible ones, the consequence of either the complexity of the subject matter, differing perspectives, conceptual vagueness, the variety of sometimes mutually exclusive empirical or quasi-empirical generalizations employed, or syntactical obscurity, or all of them together.

Functional explanations have been most reliable in biology and physiology (where they originated) and in the analysis of servo-mechanical and cybernetic systems (to which they have been effec-tively extended). In these areas we possess a well-standardized body of lawlike generalizations. Neither sociology nor political science has as yet the same resource of well-confirmed lawlike statements. Certainly sociology has few more than political science. What passes for functional explanation in sociology is all too frequently para-sitic upon suggestive analogy and metaphor, trafficking on our familiarity with goal directed-systems.

What is advanced as "theory" in sociology is frequently a non-theoretic effort at classification or "codification," the search for an analytic conceptual schema which provides a typology or a classificatory system serviceable for convenient storage and ready retrieval of independently established empirical regularities. That such a schema takes on a hierarchic and deductive character, impart-ing to the collection of propositions a *prima facie* theoretical appearance, may mean no more than that the terms employed in the high-order propositions are so vague that they can accommodate al-most any inference and consequently can be made to any conceivable state of affairs.

1. The author *implies* that, when the political scientist is   1. ...
   at his best, his explanations
      A. are essentially a retelling of events
      B. only then form the basis of an organized discipline
      C. plausibly account for past occurrences
      D. are prophetic of future events
      E. are confirmed principles forming part of the
         political scientist's theory
2. With *which* of the following would the author probably   2. ...
   agree?
      I. Because of an abundance of reasonable explanations
         for past conduct, there is the possibility of contend-
         ing schools within the field of political science
         developing.
     II. Political science is largely devoid of predictive power.
    III. Political science has very few verified axioms.
   The *CORRECT* answer is:
      A. III only   B. I and III   C. I and II
      D. I, II, and III E. I only
3. The passage *implies* that many sociological theories   3. ...
      A. are capable of being widely applied to various situations
      B. do not even appear to be superficially theoretical in
         appearance
      C. contrast with those of political science in that there
         are many more confirmed lawlike statements
      D. are derived from deep analysis and exhaustive research
      E. appear theoretical but are really very well proved

4. The author's thesis would be *UNSUPPORTABLE if*   4. ...
    A. the theories of the political scientist possessed
       predictive power
    B. political science did not consist of redescription
    C. political scientists were not restricted to "hard
       core sciences"
    D. political science consisted of a body of theories
       capable of application to any situation
    E. None of the above
5. The author believes that sociology   5. ...
    A. as a "hard core science," contains reliable and func-
       tional explanations
    B. is never more than a compilation of conceptual schema
    C. is in nearly every respect unlike political science
    D. is a discipline which allows for varied inferences to be
       drawn from its general propositions
    E. is a science indigenous to *prima facie* theoretical ap-
       pearance, containing very little codification posing
       as theory

TEST 5

James's own prefaces to his works were devoted to structural composition and analytics and his approach in those prefaces has only
recently begun to be understood. One of his contemporary critics,
with the purest intention to blame, wrote what might be recognized
today as sophisticated praise when he spoke of the later James as
"an impassioned geometer" and remarked that "what interested him was
not the figures but their relations, the relations which alone make
pawns significant." James's explanations of his works often are so
bereft of interpretation as to make some of our own austere defenses
against interpretation seem almost embarrassingly rich with psychological meanings. They offer, with a kind of brazen unselfconsciousness,
an astonishingly artificial, even mechanical view of novelistic invention. It's not merely that James asserts the importance of technique; more radically, he tends to discuss character and situation
almost entirely as functions of technical ingenuities. The very
elements in a Jamesian story which may strike us as requiring the
most explanation are presented by James either as a *solution* to a
problem of compositional harmony or else as the *donnee* about which
it would be irrelevant to ask any questions at all.

James should constantly be referred to as a model of structuralist
criticism. He consistently redirects our attention from the referen-
tial aspect of a work of art (its extensions into "reality") to its
own structural coherence as the principal source of inspiration.

What is most interesting about James's structurally functional
view of character is that a certain devaluation of what we ordinarily
think of as psychological interest is perfectly consistent with an
attempt to portray reality. It's as if he came to feel that a kind
of autonomous geometric pattern, in which the parts appeal for their
value to nothing but their contributive place in the essentially abstract pattern, is the artist's most successful representation of
life. Thus he could perhaps even think that verisimilitude - a word
he liked - has less to do with the probability of the events the

novelist describes than with those processes, deeply characteristic of life, by which he creates sense and coherence from *any* event. The only faithful picture of life in art is not in the choice of a significant subject (James always argues against the pseudorealistic prejudice), but rather in the illustration of sense-, of design-making processes. James proves the novel's connection with life by deprecating its derivation from life; and it's when he is most abstractly articulating the growth of a structure that James is almost most successfully defending the mimetic function of art (and of criticism). His deceptively banal position that only execution matters means most profoundly that verisimilitude, properly considered, is the grace and the truth of a formal unity.

1. The author suggests that James, in explanations of his own art,   1. ...
    A. was not bound by formalistic strictures but concentrated on verisimilitude
    B. was deeply psychological and concentrated on personal insight
    C. felt that his art had a one-to-one connection with reality
    D. was basically mechanical and concentrated on geometrical form
    E. was event-and-character-oriented rather than technique-oriented

2. The passage indicates that James's method of approaching reality was   2. ...
    A. that objective reality did not exist and was patterned only by the mind
    B. that formalism and pattern were excellent means of approaching reality
    C. not to concentrate on specific events but rather on character development
    D. that the only objective reality is the psychological processes of the mind
    E. that in reality events occur which are not structured but rather as random occurrences

3. The *MAIN* purpose of the paragraph is to   3. ...
    A. indicate that James's own approach to his work is only now beginning to be understood
    B. deprecate the geometrical approach towards the novel
    C. question whether James's novels were related to reality
    D. indicate that James felt that society itself could be seen as a geometric structure
    E. discuss James's explanation of his works

4. In discussing his own works, James   4. ...
    I. talks of people and events as a function of technique to the exclusion of all else
    II. is quick to emphasize the referential aspect of the work
    III. felt that verisimilitude could be derived not from character but rather from the ordering of events
    The *CORRECT* answer is:
    A. I *only*   B. II *only*   C. III *only*
    D. I and III   E. I and II

9

5. The author   5. ...
   - A. *approves* of James's explanations of his own work but *disapproves* his lack of discussion into the psychological makings of his characters
   - B. *disapproves* of James's explanation of his own work and his lack of discussion into the psychological makings of his characters
   - C. *approves* of James's explanations of his works in terms of structure as being well related to life
   - D. *disapproves* of James's explanation of his works in terms of structure as lacking verisimilitude
   - E. *approves* of James's explanation of his works because of the significance of the subjects chosen
6. The *following* is *NOT* true of James's explanation of his   6. ...
   own works: He
   - A. did not explain intriguing elements of a story except as part of a geometric whole
   - B. felt the artist could represent life by its patterns rather than its events
   - C. defended the imitative function of art by detailing the growth of a structure
   - D. attempted to give the reader insight into the psychology of his characters by insuring that his explanation followed a strict geometrical pattern
   - E. was able to devalue psychological interest and yet be consistent with an attempt to truly represent life
7. James believed it to be *essential* to   7. ...
   - A. carefully choose a subject which would lend itself to processes by which sense and cohesion is achieved
   - B. defend the mimetic function of art by emphasizing verisimilitude
   - C. emphasize the manner in which different facets of a story could fit together
   - D. explain character in order to achieve literary harmony
   - E. be artificial and unconcerned with representing life

TEST 6

The popular image of the city as it is now is a place of decay, crime, of fouled streets, and of people who are poor or foreign or odd. But what is the image of the city of the future? In the plans for the huge redevelopment projects to come, we are being shown a new image of the city. Gone are the dirt and the noise - and the variety and the excitement and the spirit. That it is an ideal makes it all the worse; these bleak new utopias are not bleak because they have to be; they are the concrete manifestation - and how literally - of a deep, and at times arrogant, misunderstanding of the function of the city.

Being made up of human beings, the city is, of course, a wonderfully resilient institution. Already it has reasserted itself as an industrial and business center. Not so many years ago, there was much talk of decentralizing to campus-like offices, and a wholesale exodus of business to the countryside seemed imminent. But a business pastoral is something of a contradiction in terms, and for the simple reason that the city is the center of things because it is a center, the suburban heresy never came off. Many industrial campuses have been built, but the overwhelming proportion of new office building has been taking place in the big cities.

But the rebuilding of downtown is not enough; a city deserted at night by its leading citizens is only half a city. If it is to continue as the dominant cultural force in American life, the city must have a core of people to support its theatres and museums, its shops and its restaurants - even a Bohemia of sorts can be of help. For it is the people who like living in the city who make it an attraction to the visitors who don't. It is the city dwellers who support its style; without them there is nothing to come downtown to.

The cities have a magnificent opportunity. There are definite signs of a small but significant move back from suburbia. There is also evidence that many people who will be moving to suburbia would prefer to stay in the city - and it would not take too much more in amenities to make them stay.

But the cities seem on the verge of muffing their opportunity - and muffing it for generations to come. In a striking failure to apply marketing principles and an even more striking failure of aesthetics, the cities are freezing on a design for living ideally calculated to keep everybody in suburbia. These vast, barracks-like superblocks are not designed for people who *like* cities, but for people who have no other choice. A few imaginative architects and planners have shown that redeveloped blocks don't have to be repellent to make money, but so far their ideas have had little effect. The institutional approach is dominant, and,unless the assumptions embalmed in it are re-examined,the city is going to be turned into a gigantic bore.

1. The author would *NOT* be pleased with   1. ...
    A. a crowded, varied, stimulating city
    B. the dedication of new funds to the reconstruction of the cities
    C. a more detailed understanding of the poor
    D. the elimination of assumptions which do not reflect the function of the city
    E. the adoption of a laissez faire attitude by those in charge of redevelopment.
2. "The rebuilding of downtown" (1st sentence, 3d paragraph)   2. ...
    refers to
    A. huge redevelopment projects to come
    B. the application of marketing and aesthetic principles to rejuvenating the city
    C. keeping the city as the center of business
    D. attracting a core of people to support the city's functions
    E. the doing away with barracks-like structures
3. According to the author, the city, in order to better it-   3. ...
    self, *must*
    A. increase its downtown population
    B. attract an interested core of people to support its cultural institutions

  C. adhere to an institutional approach rather than be
     satisfied with the status quo
  D. erect campus-like business complexes
  E. establish an ideal for orderly future growth
4. The *MAIN* purpose of the passage is to   4. ...
  A. show that the present people inhabiting the city do
     not make the city viable
  B. discuss the types of construction which should and
     should not take place in the city's future
  C. indicate that imaginative architects and planners have
     shown that redeveloped areas don't have to be ugly to
     make money
  D. discuss the human element in the city
  E. point out the lack of understanding by many city plan-
     ners of the city's functions
5. The author's thesis would be *LESS* supportable *if*   5. ...
    I. city planners presently understood that stereotyped
       reconstruction is doomed to ultimate failure
   II. the institutional approach referred to in the passage
       was based upon assumptions which took into account
       the function of the city
  III. there were signs that a shift back to the city from
       suburbia were occurring
The *CORRECT* answer is:
  A. II *only*   B. II and III   C. I and II
  D. I *only*   E. III *only*

TEST 7

In estimating the child's conceptions of the world,the first
question is to decide whether external reality is as external and
objective for the child as it is for adults. In other words, can
the child distinguish the self from the external world? So long as
the child supposes that everyone necessarily thinks like himself,
he will not spontaneously seek to convince others, nor to accept
common truths, nor,above all, to prove or test his opinions. If
his logic lacks exactitude and objectivity it is because the social
impulses of maturer years are counteracted by an innate egocentricity.
In studying the child's thought, not in this case in relation to
others but to things, one is faced at the outset with the analogous
problem of the child's capacity to dissociate thought from self in
order to form an objective conception of reality.

The child, like the uncultured adult, appears exclusively concerned with things. He is indifferent to the life of thought and
the originality of individual points of view escapes him. His
earliest interests, his first games, his drawings are all concerned
solely with the imitation of what is. In short, the child's thought
has every appearance of being exclusively realistic.

But realism is of two types, or,rather, objectivity must be dis-
tinguished from realism. Objectivity consists in so fully realizing
the countless intrusions of the self in everyday thought and the
countless illusions which result - illusions of sense, language,
point of view, value, etc. - that the preliminary step to every
judgment is the effort to exclude the intrusive self. Realism, on

the contrary, consists in ignoring the existence of self and thence regarding one's own perspective as immediately objective and absolute. Realism is thus anthropocentric illusion, finality - in short, all those illusions which teem in the history of science. So long as thought has not become conscious of self, it is a prey to perpetual confusions between objective and subjective, between the real and the ostensible; it values the entire content of consciousness on a single plane in which ostensible realities and the unconscious interventions of the self are inextricably mixed. It is thus not futile, but, on the contrary, indispensable to establish clearly and before all else the boundary the child draws between the self and the external world.

1. The result of a child's not learning that others think   1. ...
   differently than he does is that
   - A. the child will not be able to function as an adult
   - B. when the child has matured, he will be innately egocentric
   - C. when the child has matured, his reasoning will be poor
   - D. upon maturity, the child will not be able to distinguish thought from objects
   - E. upon maturity, the child will not be able to make non-ego-influenced value judgments
2. Objectivity is the ability to   2. ...
   - A. distinguish ego from the external world
   - B. dissociate oneself from others
   - C. realize that others have a different point of view
   - D. distinguish illusion from realism
   - E. dissociate ego from thought
3. When thought is *not* conscious of self,   3. ...
   - A. one is able to draw the correct conclusions from his perceptions
   - B. the apparent may not be distinguishable from the actual
   - C. conscious thought may not be distinguishable from the unconscious
   - D. the ego may influence the actual
   - E. ontogony recapitulates phylogony
4. The *MAIN* purpose of the passage is to   4. ...
   - A. argue that the child should be made to realize that others may not think like he does
   - B. estimate the child's conception of the world
   - C. explain the importance of distinguishing the mind from external objects
   - D. emphasize the importance of non-ego-influenced perspective
   - E. show how the child establishes the boundary between himself and the external world
5. The author *implies* that, if an adult is to think logically, 5. ...
   - A. his reasoning, as he matures, must be tempered by other viewpoints
   - B. he must be able to distinguish one physical object from another
   - C. he must be exclusively concerned with thought instead of things

13

D. he must be able to perceive reality without the
   intrusions of the self
E. he must not value the content of consciousness
   on a single plain
6. Realism, according to the passage, is   6. ...
   A. the realization of the countless intrusions of the self
   B. final and complete objectivity
   C. a desire to be truly objective and absolute
   D. the ability to be perceptive and discerning
   E. none of the above
7. The child who is exclusively concerned with things   7. ...
   A. thinks only objectively
   B. is concerned with imitating the things he sees
   C. must learn to distinguish between realism and
      anthropomorphism
   D. has no innate ability
   E. will,through interaction with others,often prove his
      opinions

TEST 8

Democracy is not logically antipathetic to most doctrines of
natural rights, fundamental or higher law, individual rights, or any
similar ideals - but merely asks citizens to take note of the fact
that the preservation of these rights rests with the majority, in
political processes, and does not depend upon a legal or constitutional Maginot line. Democracy may, then, be supported by believers
in individual rights providing they believe that rights - or any
transcendental ends - are likely to be better safeguarded under
such a system. Support for democracy on such instrumental grounds
may, of course, lead to the dilemma of loyalty to the system vs.
loyality to a natural right - but the same kind of dilemma may
arise for anyone, over any prized value, and in any political system,
and is insoluble in advance.

There is unanimous agreement that - as a matter of fact and law,
not of conjecture - no single right can be realized, except at the
expense of other rights and claims. For that reason their absolute
status, in some philosophic sense, is of little political relevance.
Political policies involve much more than very general principles
or rights. The main error of the older natural rights school was
not that it had an absolute right, but that it had too many absolute
rights. There must be compromise, and,as any compromise destroys
the claim to absoluteness, the natural outcome of experience was the
repudiation of all of them. And now the name of "natural right" can
only creep into sight with the reassuring placard, "changing content
gurranteed." Nor is it at all easy to see how any doctrine of inalienable, natural, individual rights can be reconciled with a
political doctrine of common consent - except in an anarchist society,
or one of saints. Every natural right ever put forward, and the lists
are elusive and capricious, is every day invaded by governments, in
the public interest and with widespread public approval.

To talk of relatively attainable justice or rights in politics
is not to plump for a moral relativism - in the sense that all

14

values are equally good. But while values may be objective, the specific value judgments and policies are inevitably relative to a context, and it is only when a judgment divorces context from general principle that it looks like moral relativism. Neither, of course, does the fact of moral diversity invalidate all moral rules.

Any political system, then, deals only with relatively attainable rights, as with relative justice and freedoms. Hence we may differ in given instances on specific policies, despite agreement on broad basic principles such as a right or a moral "ought"; and, per contra, we may agree on specific policies while differing on fundamental principles or long-range objectives or natural rights. Politics and through politics, law and policies, give these rights – and moral principles – their substance and limits. There is no getting away from the political nature of this or any other prescriptive ideal in a free society.

1. With *which* of the following would the author *agree*?   1. ...
   A. Natural and individual rights can exist at all only under a democracy.
   B. While natural rights may exist, they are only relatively attainable.
   C. Civil disobedience has no place in a democracy where natural rights have no philosophic relevance.
   D. Utilitarianism, which draws its criteria from the happiness and welfare of individuals, cannot logically be a goal of a democratic state.
   E. Some natural rights should never be compromised for the sake of political policy.

2. It can be *inferred* that a democratic form of government   2. ...
   A. can be supported by natural rightists as the best pragmatic method of achieving their aims
   B. is a form of government wherein fundamental or higher law is irrelevant
   C. will in time repudiate all inalienable rights
   D. forces a rejection of moral absolutism
   E. will soon exist in undeveloped areas of the world

3. The *MAIN* purpose of the passage is to   3. ...
   A. discuss natural rights doctrine
   B. compare and contrast democracy to individual rights
   C. discuss the reconciliation of a doctrine of inalienable natural rights with a political system
   D. discuss the safegurrding of natural rights in a democratic society
   E. indicate that moral relativism is antipathetic to democracy

4. The author indicates that natural rights   4. ...
   I. are sometimes difficult to define
   II. are easily definable but at times unreconcilable with a system of government predicated upon majority rule
  III. form a basis for moral relativism
  The *CORRECT* answer is:
   A. I *only*   B. I *only*   C. I and II
   D. III *only*   E. II and III

5. The fact that any political system deals with relatively   5. ...
   attainable rights
   - A. shows that all values are equally good or bad
   - B. is cause for divorcing political reality from moral rules
   - C. shows·that the list of natural rights is elusive and capricious
   - D. is inconsistent with the author's thesis
   - E. does not necessarily mean that natural rights do not exist

6. The passage indicates that an important conflict which   6. ...
   can exist in a democracy is the
   - A. rights of competing groups, i.e., labor versus management
   - B. adherence to the democratic process versus non-democratic actions by government
   - C. difficulty in choosing between two effective compromises
   - D. adherence to the democratic process versus the desire to support a specific right
   - E. difficulty in reconciling conflict by natural rights

KEYS (CORRECT ANSWERS)

TEST 1	TEST 2	TEST 3	TEST 4
1. D	1. D	1. E	1. C
2. A	2. C	2. C	2. D
3. B	3. A	3. C	3. A
4. E	4. D	4. B	4. A
	5. A	5. B	5. D
	6. B	6. A	
	7. D		

TEST 5	TEST 6	TEST 7	TEST 8
1. D	1. D	1. C	1. B
2. B	2. C	2. E	2. A
3. E	3. B	3. B	3. C
4. C	4. E	4. D	4. A
5. C	5. C	5. A	5. E
6. D		6. E	6. D
7. C		7. B	

READING COMPREHENSION
UNDERSTANDING AND INTERPRETING WRITTEN MATERIAL
EXAMINATION SECTION
TEST 1

DIRECTIONS: Each question or incomplete statement is followed by several suggested answers or completions. Select the one that BEST answers the question or completes the statement. *PRINT THE LETTER OF THE CORRECT ANSWER IN THE SPACE AT THE RIGHT.*

1. Most managers make the mistake of using absolutes as signals of trouble or its absence.   1.____
   A quality problem emerges — that means trouble; a test is passed — we have no problems. Outside of routine organizations, there are always going to be such signals of trouble or success, but they are not very meaningful. Many times everything looks good, but
   the roof is about to cave in because something no one thought about and for which there
   is no rule, procedure, or test has been neglected. The specifics of such problems cannot
   be predicted, but they are often signaled in advance by changes in the organizational
   system: Managers spend less time on the project; minor problems proliferate; friction in
   the relationships between adjacent work groups or departments increases; verbal
   progress reports become overly glib, or overly reticent; changes occur in the rate at
   which certain events happen, not in whether or not they happen. And they are monitored
   by random probes into the organization — seeing how things are going. According to the
   above paragraph,

   A.   managers do not spend enough time managing
   B.   managers have a tendency to become overly glib when writing reports
   C.   managers should be aware that problems that exist in the organization may not
        exhibit predictable signals of trouble
   D.   managers should attempt to alleviate friction in the relationship between adjacent
        work groups by monitoring random probes into the organization's problems

2. *Lack of challenge* and *excessive zeal* are opposite villains. You cannot do your best on a   2.____
   problem unless you are motivated. Professional problem solvers learn to be motivated
   somewhat by money and future work that may come their way if they succeed. However,
   challenge must be present for at least some of the time, or the process ceases to be
   rewarding. On the other hand, an excessive motivation to succeed, especially to succeed
   quickly, can inhibit the creative process. The tortoise-and-the-hare phenomenon is often
   apparent in problem solving. The person who thinks up the simple elegant solution,
   although he or she may take longer in doing so, often wins. As in the race, the tortoise
   depends upon an inconsistent performance from the rabbit. And if the rabbit spends so
   little time on conceptualization that the rabbit merely chooses the first answers that
   occur, such inconsistency is almost guaranteed. According to the above paragraph,

   A.   excessive motivation to succeed can be harmful in problem solving
   B.   it is best to spend a long time on solving problems
   C.   motivation is the most important component in problem solving
   D.   choosing the first solution that occurs is a valid method of problem solving

3. Virginia Woolf's approach to the question of women and fiction, about which She wrote extensively, polemically, and in a profoundly feminist way, was grounded in a general theory of literature. She argued that the writer was the product of her or his historical circumstances and that material conditions were of crucial importance. Secondly, she claimed that these material circumstances had a profound effect on the psychological aspects of writing, and that they could be seen to influence the nature of the creative work itself. According to this paragraph,

   3.___

   A. the material conditions and historical circumstances in which male and female writers find themselves greatly influence their work
   B. a woman must have an independent income to succeed as a writer
   C. Virginia Woolf preferred the writings of female authors, as their experiences more clearly reflected hers
   D. male writers are less likely than women writers to be influenced by material circumstances

4. A young person's first manager is likely to be the most influential person in his or her career. If this manager is unable or unwilling to develop the skills the young employee needs to perform effectively, the latter will set lower personal standards than he or she is capable of achieving, that person's self-image will be impaired, and he or she will develop negative attitudes toward the job, the employer, and—in all probability—his or her career. Since the chances of building a successful career with the employer will decline rapidly, he or she will leave, if that person has high aspirations, in hope of finding a better opportunity. If, on the other hand, the manager helps the employee to achieve maximum potential, he or she will build a foundation for a successful career. According to the above paragraph,

   4.___

   A. if an employee has negative attitudes towards his or her job, the manager is to blame
   B. managers of young people often have a great influence upon their careers
   C. good employees will leave a job they like if they are not given a chance to develop their skills
   D. managers should develop the full potential of their young employees

5. The reason for these differences is not that the Greeks had a superior sense of form or an inferior imagination or joy in life, but that they thought differently. Perhaps an illustration will make this clear. With the historical plays of Shakespeare in mind, let the reader contemplate the only extant Greek play on a historical subject, the Persians of Aeschylus, a play written less than ten years after the event which it deals with, and performed before the Athenian people who had played so notable a part in the struggle—incidentally, immediately below the Acropolis which the Persians had sacked and defiled. Any Elizabethan dramatist would have given us a panorama of the whole war, its moments of despair, hope, and triumph; we should see on the stage the leaders who planned and some of the soldiers who won the victory. In the persians we see nothing of the sort. The scene is laid in the Persian capital, one action is seen only through Persian eyes, the course of the war is simplified so much that the naval battle of Artemisium is not mentioned, nor even the heroic defense of Thermopylae, and not a single Greek is mentioned by name. The contrast could hardly be more complete. Which sentence is BEST supported by the above paragraph?

   5.___

   A. Greek plays are more interesting than Elizabethan plays.
   B. Elizabethan dramatists were more talented than Greek dramatists.

C. If early Greek dramatists had the same historical material as Shakespeare had, the final form the Greek work would take would be very different from the Elizabethan work.

D. Greeks were historically more inaccurate than Elizabethans.

6. The problem with present planning systems, public or private, is that accountability is weak. Private planning systems in the global corporations operate on a set of narrow incentives that frustrate sensible public policies such as full employment, environmental protection, and price stability. Public planning is Olympian and confused because there is neither a clear consensus on social values nor political priorities. To accomplish anything, explicit choices must be made, but these choices can be made effectively only with the active participation of the people most directly involved. This, not nostalgia for small-town times gone forever, is the reason that devolution of political power to local communities is a political necessity. The power to plan locally is a precondition for sensible integration of cities, regions, and countries into the world economy. According to the author,

6.____

A. people most directly affected by issues should participate in deciding those issues
B. private planning systems are preferable to public planning systems
C. there is no good system of government
D. county governments are more effective than state governments

Questions 7-11.

DIRECTIONS: Questions 7 through 11 are to be answered SOLELY on the basis of the following passage.

The ideal relationship for the interview is one of mutual confidence. To try to pretend, to put on a front of cordiality and friendship is extremely unwise for the interviewer because he will certainly convey, by subtle means, his real feelings. It is the interviewer's responsibility to take the lead in establishing a relationship of mutual confidence.

As the interviewer, you should help the interviewee to feel at ease and ready to talk. One of the best ways to do this is to be at ease yourself. If you are, it will probably be evident; if you are not, it will almost certainly be apparent to the interviewee. Begin the interview with topics for discussion which are easy to talk about and non-menacing. This interchange can be like the conversation of people when they are waiting for a bus, at the ballgame, or discussing the weather. However, do not prolong this warm-up too long since the interviewee knows as well as you do that these are not the things he came to discuss. Delaying too long in getting down to business may suggest to him that you are reluctant to deal with the topic.

Once you get onto the main topics, do all that you can to get the interviewee to talk freely with as little prodding from you as possible. This will probably require that you give him some idea of the area and of ways of looking at it. Avoid, however, prejudicing or coloring his remarks by what you say; especially, do not in any way indicate that there are certain things you want to hear, others which you do not want to hear. It is essential that he feel free to express his own ideas unhampered by your ideas, your values and preconceptions.

Do not appear to dominate the interview, nor have even the suggestion of a patronizing attitude. Ask some questions which will enable the interviewee to take pride in his knowledge. Take the attitude that the interviewee sincerely wants the interview to achieve its purpose. This creates a warm, permissive atmosphere that is most important in all interviews.

7. Of the following, the BEST title for the above passage is 7.___

    A. PERMISSIVENESS IN INTERVIEWING
    B. INTERVIEWING TECHNIQUES
    C. THE FACTOR OF PRETENSE IN THE INTERVIEW
    D. THE CORDIAL INTERVIEW

8. Which of the following recommendations on the conduct of an interview is made by the above passage? 8.___

    A. Conduct the interview as if it were an interchange between people discussing the weather.
    B. The interview should be conducted in a highly impersonal manner.
    C. Allow enough time for the interview so that the interviewee does not feel rushed.
    D. Start the interview with topics which are not threatening to the interviewee.

9. The above passage indicates that the interviewer should 9.___

    A. feel free to express his opinions
    B. patronize the interviewee and display a permissive attitude
    C. permit the interviewee to give the needed information in his own fashion
    D. provide for privacy when conducting the interview

10. The meaning of the word *unhampered*, as it is used in the last sentence of the fourth paragraph of the above passage, is MOST NEARLY 10.___

    A. unheeded   B. unobstructed
    C. hindered   D. aided

11. It can be INFERRED from the above passage that 11.___

    A. interviewers, while generally mature, lack confidence
    B. certain methods in interviewing are more successful than others in obtaining information
    C. there is usually a reluctance on the part of interviewers to deal with unpleasant topics
    D. it is best for the interviewer not to waiver from the use of hard and fast rules when dealing with clients

Questions 12-19.

DIRECTIONS: Questions 12 through 19 are to be answered SOLELY on the basis of the following passage.

Disabled cars pose a great danger to bridge traffic at any time, but during rush hours it is especially important that such vehicles be promptly detected and removed. The term *disabled car* is an all inclusive label referring to cars stalled due to a flat tire, mechanical failure, an accident, or locked bumpers. Flat tires are the most common reason why cars become disabled. The presence of disabled vehicles caused 68% of all traffic accidents last year. Of these, 75% were serious enough to require hospitalization of at least one of the vehicle's occupants.

The basic problem in the removal of disabled vehicles is detection of the car. Several methods have been proposed to aid detection. At a 1980 meeting of traffic experts and engineers, the idea of sinking electronic eyes into roadways was first suggested. Such *eyes* let officers know when traffic falls below normal speed and becomes congested. The basic argument against this approach is the high cost of installation of these *eyes*. One midwestern state has, since 1978, employed closed circuit television to detect the existence and locations of stalled vehicles. When stalled vehicles are seen on the closed circuit television screen, the information is immediately communicated by radio to units stationed along the roadway, thus enabling the prompt removal of these obstructions to traffic. However, many cities lack the necessary manpower and equipment to use this approach. For the past five years, several east-coast cities have used the method known as *safety chains*, consisting of mobile units which represent the links at the *safety chain*. Thses mobile units are stationed as posts one or two miles apart along roadways to detect disabled cars. Standard procedure is for the units in the *safety chain* to have roof blinker lights turned on to full rotation. The officer, upon spotting a disabled car, at once assumes a post that gives him the most control in directing traffic around the obstruction. Only after gaining such control does he investigate and decide what action should be taken.

12. From the above passage, the PERCENTAGE of accidents caused by disabled cars in which hospitalization was required by at least one of the occupants of a vehicle last year was   12.____

    A. 17%   B. 51%   C. 68%   D. 75%

13. According to the above passage, vehicles are MOST frequently disabled because of   13.____

    A. flat tires   B. locked bumpers
    C. brake failure   D. overheated motors

14. According to the above passage, in the electronic eye method of detection, the *eyes* are placed   14.____

    A. on lights along the roadway
    B. on patrol cars stationed along the roadway
    C. in booths spaced two miles apart
    D. into the roadway

15. According to the above passage, the factor COMMON to both the *safety chain* method and the *closed circuit television* method of detecting disabled vehicles is that both   15.____

    A. require the use of *electronic eyes*
    B. may be used where there is a shortage of officers
    C. employ units that are stationed along the highway
    D. require the use of trucks to move the heavy equipment used

16. The one of the following which is NOT discussed in the above passage as a method that may be used to detect disabled vehicles is   16.____

    A. closed circuit television   B. radar
    C. electronic *eyes*   D. safety chains

17. One DRAWBACK mentioned by the above passage to the use of the closed circuit television method for detection of disabled cars is that this technique   17.___

    A. cannot be used during bad weather
    B. does not provide for actual removal of the cars
    C. must be operated by a highly skilled staff of traffic engineers
    D. requires a large amount of manpower and equipment

18. The NEWEST of the methods discussed in the above passage for detection of disabled vehicles is   18.___

    A. electronic *eyes*
    C. the safety chain
    B. the mobile unit
    D. closed circuit television

19. When the *safety chain* method is being used, an officer who spots a disabled vehicle should FIRST   19.___

    A. turn off his roof blinker lights
    B. direct traffic around the disabled vehicle
    C. send a radio message to the nearest mobile unit
    D. conduct an investigation

20. The universe is 15 billion years old, and the geological underpinnings of the earth were formed long before the first sea creature slithered out of the slime. But it is only in the last 6,000 years or so that men have descended into mines to chop and scratch at the earth's crust. Human history is, as Carl Sagan has put it, the equivalent of a few seconds in the 15 billion year life of the earth. What alarms those who keep track of the earth's crust is that since 1950 human beings have managed to consume more minerals than were mined in all previous history, a splurge of a millisecond in geologic time that cannot be long repeated without using up the finite riches of the earth. Of the following, the MAIN idea of this paragraph is: 20.___

    A. There is true cause for concern at the escalating consumption of the earth's minerals in recent years
    B. Human history is the equivalent of a few seconds in the 15 billion year life of the earth
    C. The earth will soon run out of vital mineral resources
    D. The extraction of minerals from the earth's crust only began 6,000 years ago

21. The authors of the Economic Report of the President are collectively aware, despite their vision of the asset-rich household, of the real economy in which millions of Americans live. There are glimpses, throughout the Report, of the underworld in which about *23 million people* do not have public or private health insurance; in which *the number of people receiving unemployment compensation was 41 percent of the total unemployed*, in which the average dole for the compensated unemployed *is about one-half of take-home pay.* The authors understand, for example, that *a worker may become physically disabled and that individuals generally do not like the risk of losing their ability to earn income.* But such realities justify no more than the most limited interference in the (imperfect) market for disability insurance. There is only, as far as I can tell, one moment of genuine emotion in the entire Report when the authors' passions are stirred beyond market principles. They are discussing the leasing provisions of the 1981 Tax Act (conditions which so reduce tax revenues that they are apparently opposed in their present form by the Business Roundtable, the American Business Conference, and the National Association of Manufacturers).   21.___

In the dark days before the 1981 Act, according to the Report, *firms with temporary tax losses (a condition especially characteristic of new enterprises) were often unable to take advantage of investment tax incentives. The reason was that temporarily unprofitable companies had no taxable income against which to apply the investment tax deduction.* It was a piteous contingency for the truly needy entrepreneur. But all was made right with the Tax Act. Social security for the disabled incompetent corporation: the compassionate soul of Reagan's new economy. According to the above passage,

   A.   the National Association of Manufacturers and those companies that are temporarily unprofitable oppose the leasing provisions of the 1981 Tax Act

   B.   the authors of the Report are willing to ignore market principles in order to assist corporations unable to take advantage of tax incentives

   C.   the authors of the Report feel the National Association of Manufacturers and the Business Roundtable are wrong in opposing the leasing provisions of the 1981 Tax Act

   D.   the authors of the Report have more compassion for incompetent corporations than for disabled workers

22.   Much of the lore of management in the West regards ambiguity as a symptom of a variety of organizational ills whose cure is larger doses of rationality, specificity, and decisiveness. But is ambiguity sometimes desirable? Ambiguity may be thought of as a shroud of the unknown surrounding certain events. The Japanese have a word for it, ma, for which there is no English translation. The word is valuable because it gives an explicit place to the unknowable aspect of things. In English, we may refer to an empty space between the chair and the table; the Japanese don't say the space is empty but *full of nothing.* However amusing the illustration, it goes to the core of the issue. Westerners speak of what is unknown primarily in reference to what is known (like the space between the chair and the table), while most Eastern languages give honor to the unknown in its own right.

Of course, there are many situations that a manager finds himself in where being explicit and decisive is not only helpful but necessary. There is considerable advantage, however, in having a dual frame of reference—recognizing the value of both the clear and the ambiguous. The point to bear in mind is that in certain situations, ambiguity may serve better than absolute clarity. Which sentence is BEST supported by the above passage?
      22.____

   A.   We should cultivate the art of being ambiguous.

   B.   Ambiguity may sometimes be an effective managerial tool.

   C.   Westerners do not have a dual frame of reference.

   D.   It is important to recognize the ambiguous aspects of all situations.

23.   Everyone ought to accustom himself to grasp in his thought at the same time facts that are at once so few and so simple, that he shall never believe that he has knowledge of anything which he does not mentally behold with a distinctiveness equal to that of the objects which he knows most distinctly of all. It is true that some people are born with a much greater aptitude for such discernment than others, but the mind can be made much more expert at such work by art and exercise. But there is one fact which I should here emphasize above all others; and that is everyone should firmly persuade himself that none of the sciences, however abstruse, is to be deduced from lofty and
      23.____

obscure matters, but that they all proceed only from what is easy and more readily understood. According to the author,

    A.   people should concentrate primarily on simple facts
    B.   intellectually gifted people have a great advantage over others
    C.   even difficult material and theories proceed from what is readily understood
    D.   if a scientist cannot grasp a simple theory, he or she is destined to fail

24.   Goethe's casual, observations about language contain a profound truth. Every word in every language is a part of a system of thinking unlike any other. Speakers of different languages live in different worlds; or rather, they live in the same world but can't help looking at it in different ways. Words stand for patterns of experience. As one generation hands its language down to the next, it also hands down a fixed pattern of thinking, seeing, and feeling. When we go from one language to another, nothing stays put; different peoples carry different nerve patterns in their brains, and there's no point where they fully match. According to the above passage,   24.___

    A.   language differences and their ramifications are a major cause of tensions between nations
    B.   it is not a good use of one's time to read novels that have been translated from another language because of the tremendous differences in interpretation
    C.   differences in languages reflect the different experiences of people the world over
    D.   language students should be especially careful to retain awareness of the subtleties of their native language

Questions 25-27.

DIRECTIONS: Questions 25 through 27 are to be answered SOLELY on the basis of the following passage.

The context of all education is twofold — individual and social. Its business is to make us more and more ourselves, to cultivate in each of us our own distinctive genius, however modest it may be, while showing us how this genius may be reconciled with the needs and claims of the society of which we are a part. Thought it is not education's aim to cultivate eccentrics, that society is richest, most flexible, and most humane that best uses and most tolerates eccentricity. Conformity beyond a point breeds sterile minds and, therefore, a sterile society.

The function of secondary — and still more of higher education is to affect the environment. Teachers are not, and should not be, social reformers. But they should be the catalytic agents by means of which young minds are influenced to desire and execute reform. To aspire to better things is a logical and desirable part of mental and spiritual growth.

25.   Of the following, the MOST suitable title for the above passage is   25.___

    A.   EDUCATION'S FUNCTION IN CREATING INDIVIDUAL DIFFERENCES
    B.   THE NEED FOR EDUCATION TO ACQUAINT US WITH OUR SOCIAL ENVIRONMENT
    C.   THE RESPONSIBILITY OF EDUCATION TOWARD THE INDIVIDUAL AND SOCIETY
    D.   THE ROLE OF EDUCATION IN EXPLAINING THE NEEDS OF SOCIETY

26. On the basis of the above passage, it may be inferred that

    A. conformity is one of the forerunners of totalitarianism
    B. education should be designed to create at least a modest amount of genius in everyone
    C. tolerance of individual differences tends to give society opportunities for improvement
    D. reforms are usually initiated by people who are somewhat eccentric

26._____

27. On the basis of the above passage, it may be inferred that

    A. genius is likely to be accompanied by a desire for social reform
    B. nonconformity is an indication of the inquiring mind
    C. people who are not high school or college graduates are not able to affect the environment
    D. teachers may or may not be social reformers

27._____

Questions 28-30.

DIRECTIONS: Questions 28 through 30 are to be answered SOLELY on the basis of the following passage.

Disregard for odds and complete confidence in one's self have produced many of our great successes. But every young man who wants to go into business for himself should appraise himself as a candidate for the one percent to survive. What has he to offer that is new or better? Has he special talents, special know-how, a new invention or service, or more capital than the average competitor? Has he the most important qualification of all, a willingness to work harder than anyone else? A man who is working for himself without limitation of hours or personal sacrifice can run circles around any operation that relies on paid help. But he must forget the eight-hour day, the forty-hour week, and the annual vacation. When he stops work, his income stops unless he hires a substitute. Most small operations have their busiest day on Saturday, and the owner uses Sunday to catch up on his correspondence, bookkeeping, inventorying, and maintenance chores. The successful self-employed man invariably works harder and worries more than the man on a salary. His wife and children make corresponding sacrifices of family unity and continuity; they never know whether their man will be home or in a mood to enjoy family activities.

28. The title that BEST expresses the ideas of the above passage is

    A. OVERCOMING OBSTACLES
    B. RUNNING ONE'S OWN BUSINESS
    C. HOW TO BECOME A SUCCESS
    D. WHY SMALL BUSINESSES FAIL

28._____

29. The above passage suggests that

    A. small businesses are the ones that last
    B. salaried workers are untrustworthy
    C. a willingness to work will overcome loss of income
    D. working for one's self may lead to success

29._____

30. The author of the above passage would MOST likely believe in

    A. individual initiative
    B. socialism
    C. corporations
    D. government aid to small business

30.____

KEY (CORRECT ANSWERS)

1.	C		16.	B
2.	A		17.	D
3.	A		18.	A
4.	B		19.	B
5.	C		20.	A
6.	A		21.	D
7.	B		22.	B
8.	D		23.	C
9.	C		24.	C
10.	B		25.	C
11.	B		26.	C
12.	B		27.	D
13.	A		28.	B
14.	D		29.	D
15.	C		30.	A

READING COMPREHENSION
UNDERSTANDING AND INTERPRETING WRITTEN MATERIAL

EXAMINATION SECTION

DIRECTIONS: Each question or incomplete statement is followed by several suggested answers or completions. Select the one that BEST answers the question or completes the statement. *PRINT THE LETTER OF THE CORRECT ANSWER IN THE SPACE AT THE RIGHT.*

TEST 1

1. The question *Who shall now teach Hegel?* is shorthand for the question *Who is going to teach this genre - all the so-called Continental philosophers?* The obvious answer to this question is *Whoever cares to study them.* This is also the right answer, but we can only accept it whole-heartedly if we clear away a set of factitious questions. One such question is *Are these Continental philosophers really philosophers?* Analytic philosophers, because they identify philosophical ability with argumentative skill and notice that there is nothing they would consider an argument in the bulk of Heidegger or Foucault, suggest that these must be people who tried to be philosophers and failed--incompetent philosophers. This is as silly as saying that Plato was an incompetent sophist, or that a hedgehog is an incompetent fox. Hegel knew what he thought about philosophers who imitated the method and style of mathematics. He thought they were incompetent. These reciprocal charges of incompetence do nobody any good. We should just drop the questions of what philosophy really is or who really counts as a philosopher.
Which sentence is BEST supported by the above paragraph?
   A. The study of Hegel's philosophy is less popular now than in the past.
   B. Philosophers must stop questioning the competence of other philosophers.
   C. Philosophers should try to be as tolerant as Foucault and Heidegger.
   D. Analytic philosophers tend to be more argumentative than other philosophers.

1.____

2. It is an interesting question: the ease with which organizations of different kinds at different stages in their history can continue to function with ineffectual leadership at the top, or even function without a clear system of authority. Certainly, the success of some experiments in worker self-management shows that *bosses* are not always necessary, as some contemporary Marxists argue. Indeed, sometimes the function of those at the top is merely to symbolize organizational accountability, especially in dealing with outside authorities, but not to guide the actions of those within the organization. A vice president of a large insurance company remarked to us that *Presidents are powerless; no one needs them. They should all be sent*

2.____

off to do public relations for the company. While this is clearly a self-serving statement from someone next in line to command, it does give meaning to the expression *being. kicked upstairs.*
According to the author,
- A. organizations function very smoothly without bosses
- B. the function of those at the top is sometimes only to symbolize organizational accountability
- C. company presidents are often inept at guiding the actions of those within the organization
- D. presidents of companies have less power than one might assume they have

3. The goal of a problem is a terminal expression one wishes to cause to exist in the world of the problem. There are two types of goals: specified goal expressions in proof problems and incompletely specified goal expressions in find problems. For example, consider the problem of finding the value of X, given the expression 4X + 5 = 17. In this problem, one can regard the goal expression as being of the form X = ____, the goal expression. The goal expression in a find problem of this type is incompletely specified. If the goal expression were specified completely - for example, X = 3 - then the problem would be a proof problem, with only the sequence of operations to be determined in order to solve the problem. Of course, if one were not guaranteed that the goal expression X = 3 was true, then the terminal goal expression should really be considered to be incompletely specified - something like the statement *X = 3 is (true or false).*
According to the preceding paragraph,
- A. the goal of the equation 4X + 5 = 17 is true, not false
- B. if the goal expression was specified as being equal to 3, the problem 4X + 5 = 17 would be a proof problem
- C. if the sequence of operations of the problem given in the paragraph is predetermined, the goal of the problem becomes one of terminal expression, or the number 17
- D. X cannot be found unless X is converted into a proof problem

3.____

4. We have human psychology and animal psychology, but no plant psychology. Why? Because we believe that plants have no perceptions or intentions. Some plants exhibit *behavior* and have been credited with *habits*. If you stroke the midrib of the compound leaf of a sensitive plant, the leaflets close. The sunflower changes with the diurnal changes in the source of light. The lowest animals have not much more complicated forms of behavior. The sea anemone traps and digests the small creatures that the water brings to it; the pitcher plant does the same thing and even more, for it presents a cup of liquid that attracts insects, instead of letting the surrounding medium drift them into its trap. Here as everywhere in nature where the great, general classes of living things diverge, the lines between them are not perfectly clear. A sponge is an animal; the pitcher plant is a flowering plant, but it comes nearer to

4.____

feeding itself than the animal. Yet the fact is that we credit all animals, and only the animals, with some degree of feeling.

Of the following, the MAIN idea expressed in the above paragraph is:
  A. The classification of plants has been based on beliefs about their capacity to perceive and feel
  B. Many plants are more evolved than species considered animals
  C. The lines that divide the classes of living things are never clear
  D. The abilities and qualities of plants are undervalued

5. Quantitative indexes are not necessarily adequate measures of true economic significance or influence. But even the raw quantitative data speak loudly of the importance of the new transnationalized economy. The United Nations estimates value added in this new sector of the world economy at $500 billion in 1971, amounting to one-fifth of total GNP of the non-socialist world and exceeding the GNP of any one other country except the United States. Furthermore, all observers agree that the share of this sector in the world economy is growing rapidly. At least since 1950, its annual rate of growth has been high and remarkably steady at 10 percent compared to 4 percent for noninternationalized output in the Western developed countries. One spokesman for the new system frankly envisages that within a generation some 400 to 500 multinational corporations will own close to two-thirds of the world's fixed assets.

According to the author, all of the following are true EXCEPT:
  A. Quantitative indexes are not necessarily adequate measures of actual economic influence
  B. The transnational sector of the world economy is growing rapidly
  C. Since 1950, the rate of growth of transnationals has been 10% compared to 4% for internationalized output in the Western developed countries
  D. Continued growth for multinational corporations is likely

5.___

6. A bill may be sent to the Governor when it has passed both houses. During the session, he is given ten days to act on bills that reach his desk. Bills sent to him within ten days of the end of the session must be acted on within 30 days after the last day of the session. If the Governor takes no action on a ten day bill, it automatically becomes a law. If he disapproves or vetoes a ten day bill, it can become law only if it is re-passed by two-thirds vote in each house. If he fails to act on a 30 day bill, the bill is said to have received a *pocket veto*. It is customary for the Governor to act, however, on all bills submitted to him, and give his reason in writing for approving or disapproving important legislation.

6.___

3

According to the above paragraph, all of the following are true EXCEPT:
- A. Bills sent to the Governor in the last ten days of the session must be acted on within thirty days after the last day of the session
- B. If the Governor takes no action on a 10 day bill, it is said to have received a *pocket veto*
- C. It is customary for the Governor to act on all bills submitted to him
- D. If the Governor vetoes a ten day bill, it can become law only if passed by a two-thirds vote of the Legislature

7. It is particularly when I see a child going through the mechanical process of manipulating numbers without any intuitive sense of what it is all about that I recall the lines of Lewis Carroll: *Reeling and Writhing, of course, to begin with...and then the different branches of Arithmetic- Ambition, Distraction, Uglification, and Derision.* Or, as Max Beberman has put it, much more gently: *Somewhat related to the notion of discovery in teaching is our insistence that the student become aware of a concept before a name has been assigned to the concept.* I am quite aware that the issue of intuitive understanding is a very live one among teachers of mathematics, and even a casual reading of the YEARBOOK of the National Council of Teachers of Mathematics makes it clear that they are also very mindful of the gap that exists between proclaiming the importance of such understanding and actually producing it in the classroom.
The MAIN idea expressed in the above paragraph is:
- A. Math teachers are concerned about the difficulties inherent in producing an understanding of mathematics in their students
- B. It is important that an intuitive sense in approaching math problems be developed, rather than relying on rote, mechanical learning
- C. Mathematics, by its very nature, encourages rote, mechanical learning
- D. Lewis Carroll was absolutely correct in his assessment of the true nature of mathematics

7.___

8. Heisenberg's Principle of Uncertainty, which states that events at the atomic level cannot be observed with certainty, can be compared to this: in the world of everyday experience, we can observe any phenomenon and measure its properties without influencing the phenomenon in question to any significant extent. To be sure, if we try to measure the temperature of a demitasse with a bathtub thermometer, the instrument will absorb so much heat from the coffee that it will change the coffee's temperature substantially. But with a small chemical thermometer, we may get a sufficiently accurate reading. We can measure the temperature of a living cell with a miniature thermo- meter, which has almost negligible heat capacity.
But in the atomic world, we can never overlook the dis- turbance caused by the introduction of the measuring apparatus.

8.___

Which sentence is BEST supported by the above paragraph?
  A. There is little we do not alter by the mere act of observation.
  B. It is always a good idea to use the smallest measuring device possible.
  C. Chemical thermometers are more accurate than bathtub thermometers.
  D. It is not possible to observe events at the atomic level and be sure that the same events would occur if we were not observing them.

9. It is a myth that American workers are pricing themselves out of the market, relative to workers in other industrialized countries of the world. The wages of American manufacturing workers increased at a slower rate in the 1970's than those of workers in other major western countries. In terms of American dollars, between 1970 and 1980, hourly compensation increased 489 percent in Japan and 464 percent in Germany, compared to 128 percent in the United States. Even though these countries experienced faster productivity growth, their unit labor costs still rose faster than in the United States, according to the Bureau of Labor Statistics. During the 1970's, unit labor costs rose 192 percent in Japan, 252 percent in Germany, and only 78 percent in the United States.
According to the above passage,
  A. unit labor costs in the 1970's were higher in Japan than they were in Germany or the United States
  B. the wages of American workers need to be increased to be consistent with other countries
  C. American workers are more productive than Japanese or German workers
  D. the wages of American workers in manufacturing increased at a slower rate in the 1970's than the wages of workers in Japan or Germany

9._____

10. No people have invented more ways to enjoy life than the Chinese, perhaps to balance floods, famines, warlords, and other ills of fate. The clang of gongs, clashing cymbals, and beating of drums sound through their long history. No month is without fairs and theatricals when streets are hung with fantasies of painted lanterns and crowded with *carriages that flow like water, horses like roaming dragons.* Night skies are illumined by firecrackers - a Chinese invention - bursting in the form of flowerpots, peonies, fiery devils. The ways of pleasure are myriad. Music plays in the air through bamboo whistles of different pitch tied to the wings of circling pigeons. To skim a frozen lake in an ice sleigh with a group of friends on a day when the sun is warm is rapture, like *moving in a cup of jade.* What more delightful than the ancient festival called *Half an Immortal,* when everyone from palace officials to the common man took a ride on a swing? When high in the air, one felt like an Immortal, when back to earth once again human - no more than to be for an instant a god.

10._____

According to the above passage,
   A. if the Chinese hadn't had so many misfortunes, they wouldn't have created so many pleasurable pasttimes·
   B. the Chinese invented flowerpots
   C. every month the Chinese have fairs and theatricals
   D. pigeons are required to play the game *Half an Immortal*

11. In our century, instead, poor Diphilus is lost in the crowd of his peers. We flood one another. No one recognizes him as he loads his basket in the supermarket. What grevious fits of melancholy have I not suffered in one of our larger urban bookstores, gazing at the hundreds, thousands, tens of thousands of books on shelves and tables? And what are they to the hundreds of thousands, the millions that stand in our research libraries? More books than Noah saw raindrops. How many readers will read a given one of them - mine, yours - in their lifetimes? And how will it be in the distant future? Incomprehensible masses of books, Pelion upon Ossa, hordes of books, each piteously calling for attention, respect, love, in competition with the vast disgorgements of the past and with one another in the present. Neither is it at all helpful that books can even now be reduced to the size of a postage stamp. Avanti! Place the Bible on a pinhead! Crowding more books into small spaces does not cram more books into our heads. Here I come to the sticking point that unnerves the modern Diphilus. The number of books a person can read in a given time is, roughly speaking, a historical constant. It does not change significantly even when the number of books available for reading does. Constants are pitted against variables to confound both writer and reader.

   11.___

Of the following, the MAIN idea in this passage is:
   A. It is difficult to attain immortality because so many books are being published
   B. Too many books are being published, so fewer people are reading them
   C. Because so many books are being published, the quality of the writing is poorer
   D. Because so many books are available, but only a fixed amount of time to read them, frustration results for both the reader and the writer

12. Until recently, consciousness of sexual harassment has been low. But workers have become aware of it as more women have arrived at levels of authority in the workplace, feminist groups have focused attention on rape and other violence against women, and students have felt freer to report perceived abuse by professors. In the last 5 years, studies have shown that sexual misconduct at the workplace is a big problem. For example, in a recently published survey of federal employees, 42% of 694,000 women and 15% of 1,168,000 men said they had experienced some form of harassment.

   12.___

According to the author,
   A. the awareness of sexual harassment at the workplace is increasing

   B. the incidence of harassment is higher in universities
       than workplaces
   C. sexual harassment is much more commonly experienced
       by women than men
   D. it is rare for men to experience sexual harassment

Questions 13-17.

DIRECTIONS: Questions 13 through 17 are to be answered SOLELY on
              the basis of the following paragraph.

     Since discounts are in common use in the commercial world and
apply to purchases made by government agencies as well as business
firms, it is essential that individuals in both public and private
employment who prepare bills, check invoices, prepare payment
vouchers, or write checks to pay bills have an understanding of
the terms used. These include cash or time discount, trade discount, and discount series. A cash or time discount offers a reduc-
tion in price to the buyer for the prompt payment of the bill and
is usually expressed as a percentage with a time requirement, stated
in days, within which the bill must be paid in order to earn the
discount. An example would be 3/10, meaning a 3% discount may be
applied to the bill if the payment is forwarded to the vendor within
ten days. On an invoice, the cash discount terms are usually
followed by the net terms, which is the time in days allowed for
ordinary payment of the bill. Thus, 3/10, Net 30 means that full
payment is expected in thirty days if the cash discount of 3% is
not taken for having paid the bill within ten days. When the expression Terms Net Cash is listed on a bill, it means that no deduction for early payment is allowed. A trade discount is normally
applied to list prices by a manufacturer to show the actual price
to retailers so that they may know their cost and determine markups
that will allow them to operate competitively and at a profit. A
trade discount is applied by the seller to the list price and is
independent of a cash or time discount. Discounts may also be used
by manufacturers to adjust prices charged to retailers without
changing list prices. This is usually done by series discounting
and is expressed as a series of percentages. To compute a series
discount, such as 40%, 20%, 10%, first apply the 40% discount to
the list price, then apply the 20% discount to the remainder, and
finally apply the 10% discount to the second remainder.

13. According to the above paragraph, trade discounts are   13.____
     A. applied by the buyer
     B. independent of cash discounts
     C. restricted to cash sales
     D. used to secure rapid payment of bills

14. According to the above paragraph, if the sales terms   14.____
     5/10, Net 60 appear on a bill in the amount of $100
     dated December 5, 1984 and the buyer submits his payment
     on December 15, 1984, his PROPER payment should be
       A. $60   B. $90   C. $95   D. $100

15. According to the above paragraph, if a manufacturer gives   15.___
    a trade discount of 40% for an item with a list price of
    $250 and the terms are Net Cash, the price a retail mer--
    chant is required to pay for this item is
       A. $250   B. $210   C. $150   D. $100

16. According to the above paragraph, a series discount of   16.___
    25%, 20%, 10% applied to a list price of $200 results
    in an ACTUAL price to the buyer of
       A. $88   B. $90   C. $108   D. $110

17. According to the above paragraph, if a manufacturer gives   17.___
    a trade discount of 50% and the terms are 6/10, Net 30,
    the cost to a retail merchant of an item with a list price
    of $500 and for which he takes the time discount, is
       A. $220   B. $235   C. $240   D. $250

Questions 18-22.

DIRECTIONS: Questions 18 through 22 are to be answered SOLELY on
               the basis of the following paragraph.

The city may issue its own bonds or it may purchase bonds as an
investment. Bonds may be issued in various denominations, and the
face value of the bond is its par value. Before purchasing a bond,
the investor desires to know the rate of income that the investment
will yield. In computing the yield on a bond, it is assumed that the
investor will keep the bond until the date of maturity, except for
callable bonds which are not considered in this passage. To compute
exact yield is a complicated mathematical problem, and scientifically
prepared tables are generally used to avoid such computation. However, the approximate yield can be computed much more easily. In
computing approximate yield, the accrued interest on the date of
purchase should be ignored, because the buyer who pays accrued
interest to the seller receives it again at the next interest date.
Bonds bought at a premium (which cost more) yield a lower rate of
income than the same bonds bought at par (face value), and bonds
bought at a discount (which cost less) yield a higher rate of income
than the same bonds bought at par.

18. An investor bought a $10,000 city bond paying 6% interest.   18.___
    Which of the following purchase prices would indicate that
    the bond was bought at a PREMIUM?
       A. $9,000   B. $9,400   C. $10,000   D. $10,600

19. During 1974, a particular $10,000 bond paying 7½% sold   19.___
    at fluctuating prices.
    Which of the following prices would indicate that the
    bond was bought at a DISCOUNT?
       A. $9,800   B. $10,000   C. $10,200   D. $10,750

20. A certain group of bonds was sold in denominations of   20.___
    $5,000, $10,000, $20,000, and $50,000.
    In the following list of four purchase prices, which
    one is MOST likely to represent a bond sold at par value?
       A. $10,500   B. $20,000   C. $22,000   D. $49,000

8

21. When computing the approximate yield on a bond, it is   21.____
DESIRABLE to
    A. assume the bond was purchased at par
    B. consult scientifically prepared tables
    C. ignore accrued interest on the date of purchase
    D. wait until the bond reaches maturity

22. Which of the following is MOST likely to be an exception   22.____
to the information provided in the above paragraph?
Bonds
    A. purchased at a premium   B. sold at par
    C. sold before maturity   D. which are callable

Questions 23-25.

DIRECTIONS: Questions 23 through 25 are to be answered SOLELY on
                the basis of the following passage.

There is one bad habit of drivers that often causes chain collisions at traffic lights. It is the habit of keeping one foot poised over the accelerator pedal, ready to step on the gas the instant the light turns green. A driver who is watching the light, instead of watching the cars in front of him, may *jump the gun* and bump the car in front of him, and this car in turn may bump the next car. If a driver is resting his foot on the accelerator, his foot will be slammed down when he bumps into the car ahead. This makes the collision worse and makes it very likely that cars further ahead in the line are going to get involved in a series of violent bumps.

23. Which of the following conclusions can MOST reasonably be   23.____
drawn from the information given in the above passage?
    A. American drivers have a great many bad driving habits.
    B. Drivers should step on the gas as soon as the light
       turns green.
    C. A driver with poor driving habits should be arrested
       and fined.
    D. A driver should not rest his foot on the accelerator
       when the car is stopped for a traffic light.

24. From the information given in the above passage, a reader   24.____
should be able to tell that a chain collision may be
defined as a collision
    A. caused by bad driving habits at traffic lights
    B. in which one car hits another car, this second car
       hits a third car, and so on
    C. caused by drivers who fail to use their accelerators
    D. that takes place at an intersection where there is
       a traffic light

25. The above passage states that a driver who watches the   25.____
light instead of paying attention to traffic may
    A. be involved in an accident
    B. end up in jail
    C. lose his license
    D. develop bad driving habits

TEST 2

Questions 1-4.

DIRECTIONS: Each of the statements in this section is followed by several labeled choices. In the space at the right, write the letter of the sentence which means MOST NEARLY what is stated or implied in the passage.

1. It may be said that the problem in adult education seems to be not the piling up of facts but practice in thinking. This statement means MOST NEARLY that   1.___
   A. educational methods for adults and young people should differ
   B. adults seem to think more than young people
   C. a well-educated adult is one who thinks but does not have a store of information
   D. adult education should stress ability to think

2. Last year approximately 19,000 fatal accidents were sustained in industry. There were approximately 130 non-fatal injuries to each fatal injury.   2.___
   According to the above statement, the number of non-fatal accidents was
   A. 146,000   B. 190,000   C. 1,150,000 D. 2,500,000

3. No employer expects his stenographer to be a walking encyclopedia, but it is not unreasonable for him to expect her to know where to look for necessary information on a variety of topics.   3.___
   The above statement means MOST NEARLY that the stenographer should
   A. be a college graduate
   B. be familiar with standard office reference books
   C. keep a scrapbook of all interesting happenings
   D. go to the library regularly

4. For the United States, Canada has become the most important country in the world, yet there are few countries about which Americans know less. Canada is the third largest country in the world; only Russia and China are larger. The area of Canada is more than a quarter of the whole British Empire.   4.___
   According to the above statement, the
   A. British Empire is smaller than Russia or China
   B. territory of China is greater than that of Canada
   C. Americans know more about Canada than they do about China or Russia
   D. Canadian population is more than one-quarter the population of the British Empire

Questions 5-8.

DIRECTIONS: Questions 5 through 8 are to be answered SOLELY on the basis of the following paragraph.

A few people who live in old tenements have the bad habit of throwing garbage out of their windows, especially if there is an empty lot near their building. Sometimes the garbage is food; sometimes the garbage is half-empty soda cans. Sometimes the garbage is a little bit of both mixed together. These people just don't care about keeping the lot clean.

5. The above paragraph states that throwing garbage out of windows is a   5.___
     A. bad habit   B. dangerous thing to do
     C. good thing to do   D. good way to feed rats

6. According to the above paragraph, an empty lot next to an   6.___
old tenement is sometimes used as a place to
     A. hold local gang meetings   B. play ball
     C. throw garbage   D. walk dogs

7. According to the above paragraph, which of the following   7.___
throw garbage out of their windows?
     A. Nobody   B. Everybody
     C. Most people   D. Some people

8. According to the above paragraph, the kinds of garbage   8.___
thrown out of windows are
     A. candy and cigarette butts
     B. food and half-empty soda cans
     C. fruit and vegetables
     D. rice and bread

Questions 9-12.

DIRECTIONS: Questions 9 through 12 are to be answered SOLELY on the basis of the following paragraph.

The game that is recognized all over the world as an all-American game is the game of baseball. As a matter of fact, baseball heroes like Joe DiMaggio, Willie Mays, and Babe Ruth were as famous in their day as movie stars Robert Redford, Paul Newman, and Clint Eastwood are now. All these men have had the experience of being mobbed by fans whenever they put in an appearance anywhere in the world. Such unusual popularity makes it possible for stars like these to earn at least as much money off the job as on the job. It didn't take manufacturers and advertising men long to discover that their sales of shaving lotion, for instance, increased when they got famous stars to advertise their product for them on radio and television.

9. According to the above paragraph, baseball is known every-   9.___
where as a(n) _____ game.
     A. all-American   B. fast
     C. unusual   D. tough

10. According to the above paragraph, being so well known   10.____
     means that it is possible for people like Willie Mays
     and Babe Ruth to
         A. ask for anything and get it
         B. make as much money off the job as on it
         C. travel anywhere free of charge
         D. watch any game free of charge

11. According to the above paragraph, which of the following   11.____
     are known all over the world?
         A. Baseball heroes   B. Advertising men
         C. Manufacturers   D. Basketball heroes

12. According to the above paragraph, it is possible to sell   12.____
     much more shaving lotion on television and radio if
         A. the commercials are in color instead of black and white
         B. you can get a prize with each bottle of shaving lotion
         C. the shaving lotion makes you smell nicer than usual
         D. the shaving lotion is advertisied by famous stars

Questions 13-15.

DIRECTIONS: Questions 13 through 15 are to be answered SOLELY on
              the basis of the following passage.

That music gives pleasure is axiomatic. Because this is so, the
pleasures of music may seem a rather elementary subject for discussion.
Yet the source of that pleasure, our musical instinct, is not at all
elementary. It is, in fact, one of the prime puzzles of consciousness. Why is it that we are able to make sense out of these nerve
signals so that we emerge from engulfment in the orderly presentation
of sound stimuli as if we had lived through an image of life?

If music has impact for the mere listener, it follows that it
will have much greater impact for those who sing it or play it themselves with proficiency. Any educated person in Elizabethan times
was expected to read musical notation and take part in a madrigal-
sing. Passive listeners, numbered in the millions, are a comparatively recent innovation.

Everyone is aware that so-called serious music has made great
strides in general public acceptance in recent years, but the term
itself still connotes something forbidding and hermetic to the mass
audience. They attribute to the professional musician a kind of
initiation into secrets that are forever hidden from the outsider.
Nothing could be more misleading. We all listen to music, profes-
sionals, and non-professionals alike in the same sort of way, in a
dumb sort of way, really, because simple or sophisticated music
attracts all of us in the first instance, on the primordial level
of sheer rhythmic and sonic appeal. Musicians are flattered, no
doubt, by the deferential attitude of the layman in regard to what
he imagines to be our secret understanding of music. But in all
honesty, we musicians know that in the main we listen basically as
others do, because music hits us with an immediacy that we recognize
in the reactions of the most simple minded of music listeners.

13. A suitable title for the above passage would be
    A. HOW TO LISTEN TO MUSIC
    B. LEARNING MUSIC APPRECIATION
    C. THE PLEASURES OF MUSIC
    D. THE WORLD OF THE MUSICIAN

13.____

14. The author implies that the passive listener is one who
    A. cannot read or play music
    B. does not appreciate serious music
    C. does not keep time to the music by hand or toe tapping
    D. will not attend a concert if he has to pay for the privilege

14.____

15. The author of the above passage is apparently inconsistent when he discusses
    A. the distinction between the listener who pays for the privilege and the one who does not
    B. the historical development of musical forms
    C. the pleasures derived from music by the musician
    D. why it is that we listen to music

15.____

Questions 16-18.

DIRECTIONS: Questions 16 through 18 are to be answered SOLELY on the basis of the following passage.

Who are the clerisy? They are people who like to read books. The use of a word so unusual, so out of fashion, can only be excused on the ground that it has no familiar synonym. The word is little known because what it describes has disappeared, though I do not believe it is gone forever. The clerisy are those who read for pleasure, but not for idleness; who read for pasttime, but not to kill time; who love books, but do not live by books.

Let us consider the actual business of reading -- the interpretative act of getting the words off the page and into your head in the most effective way. The most effective way is not the quickest way of reading; and for those who think that speed is the greatest good, there are plenty of manuals on how to read a book which profess to tell how to strip off the husk and guzzle the milk, like a chimp attacking a coconut. Who among today's readers would whisk through a poem, eyes aflicker, and say that he had read it? The answer to that last question must unfortunately be: far too many. For reading is not respected for the art it is.

Doubtless there are philosophical terms for the attitude of mind of which hasty reading is one manifestation, but here let us call it *end-gaining*, for its victims put ends before means; they value not reading, but having read. In this, the end-gainers make mischief and spoil all they do; end-gaining is one of the curses of our nervously tense, intellectually flabby civilization. In reading, as in all arts, it is the means, and not the end, which gives delight and brings the true reward. Not straining forward toward the completion, but the pleasure of every page as it comes, is the secret of reading. We must desire to read a book, rather than to have read it. This change in attitude, so simple to describe, is by no means simple to achieve, if one has lived the life of an end-gainer.

16. A suitable title for the above passage would be   16.____
    A. READING FOR ENLIGHTENMENT
    B. THE ART OF RAPID READING
    C. THE WELL-EDUCATED READER
    D. VALUES IN READING

17. The author does NOT believe that most people read because   17.____
    they
    A. are bored
    B. have nothing better to do
    C. love books
    D. wish to say that they have read certain books

18. The *change in attitude* to which the author refers in the   18.____
    last sentence of the above passage implies a change from
    A. dawdling while reading so that the reader can read a
       greater number of books
    B. reading light fiction to reading serious fiction and
       non-fiction
    C. reading works which do not amuse the reader
    D. skimming through a book to reading it with care

Questions 19-22.

DIRECTIONS: Questions 19 through 22 are to be answered SOLELY on
              the basis of the following passage.

Violence is not new to literature. The writings of Shakespeare and Cervantes are full of it. But those classic writers did not condone violence. They viewed it as a just retribution for sins against the divine order or as a sacrifice sanctioned by heroism. What is peculiar to the modern literature is violence for the sake of violence. Perhaps our reverence for life has been dulled by mass slaughter, though mass slaughter has not been exceptional in the history of mankind. What is exceptional is the boredom that now alternates with war. The basic emotion in peacetime has become a horror of emptiness: a fear of being alone, of having nothing to do, a neurosis whose symptoms are restlessness, an unmotivated and undirected rage, sinking at times into vapid listlessness. This neurotic syndrome is intensified by the prevailing sense of insecurity. The threat of atomic war has corrupted our faith in life itself.

This universal neurosis has developed with the progress of technology. It is the neurosis of men whose chief expenditure of energy is to pull a lever or push a button, of men who have ceased to make things with their hands. Such inactivity applies not only to muscles and nerves but to the creative processes that once engaged the mind. If one could contrast visually, by time-and-motion studies, the daily actions of an eighteenth-century carpenter with a twentieth-century machinist, the latter would appear as a <u>confined, repetitive clot</u>, the former as a free and even fantastic pattern. But the most significant contrast could not be visualized - the contrast between

14

a mind suspended aimlessly above an autonomous movement and a mind consciously bent on the shaping of a material substance according to the persistent evidence of the senses.

19. A suitable title for the above passage would be
    A. INCREASING PRODUCTION BY MEANS OF SYSTEMATIZATION
    B. LACK OF A SENSE OF CREATIVENESS AND ITS CONSEQUENCE
    C. TECHNOLOGICAL ACHIEVEMENT IN MODERN SOCIETY
    D. WHAT CAN BE DONE ABOUT SENSELESS VIOLENCE

    19.____

20. According to the author, Shakespeare treated violence as a
    A. basically sinful act not in keeping with religious thinking
    B. just punishment of transgressors against moral law
    C. means of achieving dramatic excitement
    D. solution to a problem provided no other solution was available

    20.____

21. According to the author, boredom may lead to
    A. a greater interest in leisure-time activities
    B. chronic fatigue
    C. senseless anger
    D. the acceptance of a job which does not provide a sense of creativity

    21.____

22. The underlined phrase refers to the
    A. hand movements made by the carpenter
    B. hand movements made by the machinist
    C. relative ignorance of the carpenter
    D. relative ignorance of the machinist

    22.____

23. The concentration of women and female-headed families in the city is both cause and consequence of the city's fiscal woes. Women live in cities because it is easier and cheaper for them to do so, but because fewer women are employed, and those that are receive lower pay than men, they do not make the same contribution to the tax base that an equivalent population of men would. Concomitantly, they are more dependent on public resources, such as transportation and housing. For these reasons alone, urban finances would be improved by increasing women's employment opportunities and pay. Yet nothing in our current urban policy is specifically geared to improving women's financial resources. There are some proposed incentives to business to create more jobs, but not necessarily ones that would utilize the skills women currently have. The most innovative proposal was a tax credit for new hires from certain groups with particularly high unemployment rates. None of the seven targeted groups were women.
    Which sentence is BEST supported by the above paragraph?
    A. Innovative programs are rapidly improving conditions for seven targeted groups with traditionally high unemployment rates.

    23.____

   B. The contribution of women to a city's tax base reflects
      their superior economic position.
   C. Improving the economic position of women who live in
      cities would help the financial conditions of the
      cities themselves.
   D. Most women in this country live in large cities.

24. None of this would be worth saying if Descartes had been   24.____
    right in positing a one-to-one correspondence between
    stimuli and sensations. But we know that nothing of the
    sort exists. The perception of a given color can be evoked
    by an infinite number of differently combined wavelengths.
    Conversely, a given stimulus can evoke a variety of sensa-
    tions, the image of a duck in one recipient, the image of
    a rabbit in another. Nor are responses like these entirely
    innate. One can learn to discriminate colors or patterns
    which were indistinguishable prior to training. To an
    extent still unknown, the production of data from stimuli
    is a learned procedure. After the learning process, the
    same stimulus evokes a different datum. I conclude that,
    though data are the minimal elements of our individual
    experience, they need be shared responses to a given stimu-
    lus only within the membership of a relatively homogeneous
    community: educational, scientific, or linguistic.
    Which sentence is BEST supported by the above paragraph?
    A. One stimulus can give rise to a number of different
       sensations.
    B. There is a one-to-one correspondence between stimuli
       and sensations.
    C. It is not possible to produce data from stimuli by
       using a learned procedure.
    D. It is not necessary for a group to be relatively
       homogeneous in order to share responses to stimuli.

25. Workers who want to move in the direction of participative   25.____
    structures will need to confront the issues of power and
    control. The process of change needs to be mutually shared
    by all involved, or the outcome will not be a really parti-
    cipative model. The demand for a structural redistribution
    of power is not sufficient to address the problem of change
    toward a humanistic, as against a technological, workplace.
    If we are to change our institutional arrangements from
    hierarchy to participation, particularly in our workplaces,
    we will need to look to transformations in ourselves as
    well. As long as we are imbued with the legitimacy of
    hierarchical authority, with the sovereignty of the status
    quo, we will never be able to generate the new and original
    participative forms that we week. This means if we are
    to be equal to the task of reorganizing our workplaces, we
    need to think about how we can reeducate ourselves and
    become aware of our own assumptions about the nature of
    our social life together. Unless the issue is approached
    in terms of these complexities, I fear that all the
    worker participation and quality of work life efforts will
    fail.

According to the above paragraph, which of the following is NOT true?
 A. Self-education concerning social roles must go hand in hand with workplace reorganization.
 B. The structural changing of the workplace, alone, will not bring about the necessary changes in the quality of work life.
 C. Individuals can easily overcome their attitudes towards hierarchical authority.
 D. Changing the quality of work life will require the participation of all involved.

KEY (CORRECT ANSWERS)

TEST 1	TEST 2
1. B	1. D
2. B	2. D
3. B	3. B
4. A	4. B
5. C	5. A
6. B	6. C
7. B	7. D
8. D	8. B
9. D	9. A
10. C	10. B
11. D	11. A
12. A	12. D
13. B	13. C
14. C	14. A
15. C	15. C
16. C	16. D
17. B	17. C
18. D	18. D
19. A	19. B
20. B	20. B
21. C	21. C
22. D	22. B
23. D	23. C
24. B	24. A
25. A	25. C

INTERPRETATION OF READING MATERIALS

IN THE SOCIAL STUDIES

DIRECTIONS: In the passage that follows, each question or incomplete
statement below is followed by several suggested answers
or completions. Select the one that BEST answers the
question or completes the statement. Base your choice
in each case on the materials given and on your own
understanding of the subject matter.

PASSAGE

*Well, easily the most obvious badge of class in Britain is the
accent of spoken language. Sociologists used to predict that the
influence of radio would iron out regional accents and pronunciations
and convert everyone into a passable imitation of a B.B.C. announcer.
They have been proved wrong. In some strange ways, the standard
London voices emerging from the wireless set have stiffened the resolution of the regions to maintain their regionalism. The old accents,
the broad vowels of Yorkshire and Lancashire, the rich brogues of the
West Country and the tortured staccato tones of the Cockney are heard
as often as ever they were - and what's more they have more or less
ousted spoken B.B.C. from the influential "telly." Most of our TV
commercials use lower-middle class inflexions and strong regional
accents to put across their message.*

*Quality and more value for money are clearly associated in the
LMC mind with rugged, down-to-earth, nonsense language. During the
war, the most effective broadcasters were Winston Churchill and J.B.
Priestley, neither of whom used public-school accents. Churchill went
out of his way to mispronounce such words as Nazi and Montevideo and
spoke simply even when at his most rhetorical. Priestley employed a
strong "Bruddersford" accent, as he has always done, and once again
the message was strongly reinforced by the mode of delivery. The
voice of authority is still that of John Citizen, the Man in the Street.*

1.   The advent of the B.B.C.   1.____
     A. standardized speech
     B. made people aware of the differences in accents
     C. revised the standards of English speech
     D. converted regional accents
     E. encouraged predictions from sociologists

In paragraph 1, it is mentioned that sociologists used to
predict that regional accents would be influenced by the speech
of the B.B.C. Therefore, Item E is correct. The paragraph
further states that these predictions were proven wrong; therefore, Items A, B, and C must be incorrect. It is stated throughout the passage that regional accents were rather reinforced by
the B.B.C. standard. Item B is not mentioned in the passage;
however, it is safe to assume that people were always aware of
the differences in accents.

2. The regional accent called *Yorkshire*   2.___
   A. stiffened the resolution of this region to change
      its speech habits
   B. is a kind of brogue
   C. has disappeared
   D. contains broad vowels
   E. is staccato

Item A is false because the passage states that the resolution
was stiffened to MAINTAIN their speech habits. Item B refers
to the West Country accent. Item E refers to Cockney. Item C
is false because ...*Yorkshire...*, *Lancashire...the West Country*
...*the Cockney are heard as often as ever they were.* The
passage also mentions the *broad vowels of Yorkshire.* Therefore,
Item D is correct.

3. Most B.B.C. commercials are   3.___
   A. prohibited by the government
   B. considered contrary to the principles of B.B.C. broad-
      casting
   C. referred to as *telly*
   D. using upper-middle class accents
   E. using lower-middle class inflexions

The passage states (end of paragraph one), *Most of our TV com-*
mercials use lower-middle class inflexions.... Therefore, Item E
is correct. Items A and B are not mentioned in the passage.
Item C refers to an English colloquialism for television. Item
D is false.

4. Why did Churchill occasionally mispronounce words?   4.___
   Because
   A. he rose from the lower classes
   B. he didn't have an extensive education
   C. he wanted the majority of the people to heed him
   D. English pronunciation is often unlike American
   E. he used a public-school accent

Items A and B are false, aside from not being mentioned in the
passage. The last paragraph of the passage explains why Item C
is the correct one. It states that the voice of authority is
the man in the street, that is, a voice which would use simple
speech, a regional accent, and occasionally mispronounce words.
Item D has nothing to do with the question. Item E is false:
a public-school accent, in England, designates a higher standard
of speech.

5. J.B. Priestley was   5.___
   A. a prominent member of Parliament
   B. a prominent industrialist
   C. the head of the B.B.C.
   D. a novelist
   E. an ambassador

J.B. Priestley was a prominent English playwright and novelist.
Therefore, Item D is correct. Items A, B, C, and E are false.

6. The opposite of a *Bruddersford* accent (the combining of   6.___
the names of two Yorkshire mill towns) might be called
   A. Oxford   B. Cockney   C. Exeter   D. Oxbridge   E. Cambridge

There is an *Oxbridge* accent, also a portmanteau word (PORTMANTEAU
WORD, a word made by telescoping or blending two other words,
as BRUNCH for BREAKFAST and LUNCH), signifying the accents of
Oxford and Cambridge. It is upper-class and, therefore, the
opposite of the accent which derives its name from the two mill
towns. Therefore, Item D is correct. Items A, B, C, and E
are false.

———

TEST 1

PASSAGE

Secretary of State Richard Olney in 1895 was only stating the truth when he insisted that all basic political power in the Caribbean was in the hands of the United States, but in asserting this view, he used the infuriating word "fiat" - which annoyed both the British and the Latin Americans. Theodore Roosevelt, in creating the Republic of Panama, behaved no worse than the great W.E. Gladstone did in occupying Egypt; but Gladstone occupied Egypt with ostensible reluctance. (Henry Labouchere, the Liberal wit, said that what he objected to in the Grand Old Man was not his having the ace of trumps up his sleeve, but his assertion that God had put it there.) Theodore Roosevelt boasted of what he had done "to take the Canal," and his unfortunate candor was very expensive in cash and credit.

Then there is the question of the Senate. An examination of Molloy's great collection of treaties will show how late the British Foreign Office was in learning that a treaty with the Unites States is valid only if the Senate gives its consent. Again and again, European powers have made what they thought were hard bargains with the executive branch of the United States, only to have them rejected by the Senate. A great deal can be said in favor of many, if not all, of the Senate's actions, but the view expressed by John Hay that a treaty sent to the Senate has as much chance as a bull sent into the bull ring still survives in Europe if it no longer survives in the same form in the United States.

QUESTIONS

1. The author seems to be citing examples of
   A. successful U.S. diplomacy
   B. the need for better statesmen
   C. how certain U.S. statesmen have been diplomatically clumsy
   D. why Europe does not like the U.S.
   E. how the U.S. consistently mishandles foreign relations

2. In John Hay's view,
   A. treaties should not be made with foreign powers
   B. treaties should not be made by the executive branch of the government
   C. treaties should not have to be sent to the Senate
   D. all treaties made with other governments should be rejected by the Senate
   E. a treaty sent to the Senate has little chance of survival

3. Theodore Roosevelt, at one time,
   A. sent W.E. Gladstone to occupy Egypt
   B. stated that all political power in the Caribbean was in the hands of the U.S.
   C. was the Grand Old Man of the Democratic Party
   D. boasted of taking the Panama Canal
   E. infuriated both the British and the Latin Americans by his use of the word *fiat*

1. ___

2. ___

3. ___

4

4. The author of this passage might be said to be writing 　　　　　　4.＿＿＿
   in a vein
      A. of acceptance regarding past American blunders
      B. of criticism tempered with humor
      C. which is extremely unflattering to Europe
      D. of ridicule
      E. of malice

5. The author seems to be suggesting that 　　　　　　　　　　　5.＿＿＿
      A. European and Latin American countries are in disagree-
         ment with the U.S.
      B. the U.S. could be more diplomatically astute
      C. treaties should not be subject to both Senate and
         Executive approval
      D. Europe does not understand the U.S. system of ratifying
         treaties
      E. Theodore Roosevelt was not one of the best Presidents
         of the U.S.

6. Theodore Roosevelt was famous for having said 　　　　　　6.＿＿＿
      A. *"The business of America is business"*
      B. (In reference to isolationalism) *"River, stay 'way
         from my door"*
      C. *"Speak softly and carry a big stick"*
      D. *"The only thing we have to fear is fear itself"*
      E. *"This generation has a rendezvous with destiny"*

―

TEST 2

PASSAGE

*The position Makarios holds in Cyprus is the result of his own
skillful maneuvers. It is a position which he has built up by
Byzantine wiliness, by clever use of other personalities, of the press,
of the emotions of the people he knows so well. When other governments,
driven to desperation by the Cyprus problem, drop hints that were
Makarios to be overthrown the problem could quickly be solved, they
are talking dangerous nonsense. Makarios is a man of his people, with
their strengths and their weaknesses. If the Cyprus problem is to be
solved, he is the man who must be convinced that the solution is just,
he is the man whose confidence must be gained, for in Cyprus he alone
will be able to convince and retain the confidence of his people.*

*Makarios explains the relationship between himself and his people
this way: "The Archbishop of Cyprus is elected by the whole people.
Ours is the only church in the world where this happens. He is elected
to be the religious and national leader. I, therefore, enjoy the
confidence of the vast majority of my people. I can convince the
people. I am not a party leader; I have no army to force them to
follow me: I express the will of the people and the people follow me.
I just do what I think right."*

Makarios does not himself dismiss the thesis that were he removed, the Cyprus problem could be more quickly solved. He admits that he is a stubborn man and that this stubbornness has already thwarted both the Americans and the British in imposing their ideas of a settlement. "I am stubborn. I cannot do what I do not believe in."

QUESTIONS

1. Makarios, President and Archbishop of Cyprus, gained his   1.____
   position
   A. by a Byzantine coup
   B. by consent of the populace
   C. through the press
   D. by playing upon emotionalism
   E. through strategic use of his armies

2. The author of the passage indicated a belief that Makarios   2.____
   A. was in danger of being overthrown
   B. was actually a dictator
   C. should not head both church and state
   D. was representative of the average Cypriote
   E. did not enjoy the confidence of his people

3. The British had been thwarted in imposing their ideas by   3.____
   A. the Americans   B. the Cypriote army
   C. party leadership   D. Makarios
   E. NATO

4. The Cypriote Orthodox Church is unique in that it(s)   4.____
   A. has its own army
   B. is not wholly separate from affairs of state
   C. head is appointed
   D. Archbishop is elected by the whole people
   E. religious leader is not its national leader

5. Cyprus is an island which belongs to (the)   5.____
   A. Greece   B. Turkey
   C. Malta   D. British Commonwealth
   E. Enosis

6. Corcyra, an adjacent Grecian island, is acknowledged to   6.____
   be immortalized in the literary work of
   A. THE TEMPEST   B. ELECTRA
   C. MEDEA   D. ETRUSCAN PLACES
   E. OEDIPUS REX

TEST 3

PASSAGE

The old argument about the respective merits of career and non-career appointments has little relevance. Today and in the future, most ambassadors will come from the career service - the proportion is now about two out of three - but there will still be room for candidates with special qualifications brought in from outside - as witness General Taylor. There is no place, however, as Ambassador Samuel Berger, recent envoy to Korea, has said, for a "non-career man who brings neither interest, nor aptitude, nor professional skills" to the job.

Over the years, successful ambassadors have come from many different backgrounds and occupations. If any generalization is valid, it may be that a solid foundation in some specialty is an asset, for mastery of a particular field often seems to lend a person added depth and confidence. The Foreign Service has tried to give young officers opportunities to specialize, but, on the whole, too few have been allowed to spend enough time in one place or in one type of work or to take advanced studies. Today, qualifications in the social sciences, in economics or in military affairs are highly desirable.

Yet, when all is said and done, the important thing is that an ambassador be a cultivated man who, in the best sense, is wise in the ways of the world, with the maturity of judgment that comes from varied experience, and with reserves of know-how and courage to call upon in a pinch.

QUESTIONS

1. It is found to be an asset that an ambassador have   1.____
    A. interest   B. depth
    C. some specialization   D. as many languages as possible
    E. confidence

2. One reason the officers of the foreign service have NOT   2.____
   become proficient in any one field is
    A. the concentration required is incompatible with the
       temperament of the typical ambassador
    B. they have too much to do
    C. their work demands a general knowledge
    D. they concentrate on one type of work
    E. they move around too much

3. An ambassador should be   3.____
    A. highly civilized B. well-liked   C. reliable
    D. a linguist   E. courageous

4. Successful ambassadors, prior to their appointment, are   4.____
   enlisted from
    A. the best universities   B. varied backgrounds
    C. men active in Washington D. Cabinet members
    E. industry

5. Fundamentally, an ambassador is   5.____
    A. totally responsible for our *image* abroad
    B. responsible for any uprisings that might occur in
       the country to which he is appointed
    C. the President's personal agent
    D. guaranteed diplomatic immunity
    E. fulfilling a social as well as political role

6. His traditional role is
   A. that of teacher
   B. to promote industry
   C. to see that people _____ the best possible impression of the U.S.
   D. that of a negotiator
   E. that of a propagandist

TEST 4

PASSAGE

Unless all the warning signals are wrong, this year we are really in for it. The mudslinging, the personal attacks, and the smears that always accompany a national election threaten in the next few weeks to submerge completely the voices of reasoned debate. Once again, as Lord Bryce declared, we are going to be treated to "the spectacle of half the honest men supporting for the leadership of the nation a person whom the other half declare to be a knave."

A knave, did he say? No mere knave. A thief, a cheat, a fixer of elections, a fake, a phony, a dodger of military duty, an inciter of riots, a coddler of Communists - and a man who is certain to be the victim of another heart attack.

Or: a crypto-Fascist, a warmonger, an extremist, a nuclear adventurer, a fool, a frustrated dictator, a simpleton, a racist, a fallout fancier, a know-nothing, a menace to little girls eating ice cream cones - and a man subject to recurrent nervous breakdowns.

All these epithets have been hurled at President Johnson or Senator Goldwater already. And the real smear season - the final frenzied few weeks of the campaign - is still to come.

Even before the cannonading began, Bruce L. Felknor, executive director of the Fair Campaign Practices Committee, the 10-year-old private agency that attempts to referee election battles, predicted that this would be an "exceptionally rough" campaign. He said that the "unusual polarization of opinion" - exemplified by Senator Goldwater's determination to provide "a choice, not an echo" - has given this campaign an encompassing emotional intensity rare in national politics.

QUESTIONS

1. The author states that mudslinging
   A. is always accompanied by warning signals
   B. is the worst sort of personal attack
   C. is dishonest
   D. was denounced by Lord Bryce
   E. always accompanies a national election

2. While Lord Bryce uses the word *knave*, the author implies 2.____
   that
   A. he really means a thief
   B. usually half the nation denounces the man running
      for office
   C. were Lord Bryce living today he would find other words
   D. today such a word would be considered mild
   E. men running for office can inspire riots

3. The *spectacle* referred to in the passage is the 3.____
   A. political campaign speeches
   B. election
   C. political parties
   D. reasoned or unreasoned debate
   E. manner in which the people express their choice

4. In which of the following comparisons made by the author 4.____
   is the parallelism of the characteristics MOST satisfactory?
   A. A cheat and an extremist
   B. The victim of a heart attack and a man subject to
      nervous breakdowns
   C. A phony and a fallout fancier
   D. An inciter of riots and a crypto-Fascist
   E. A fake and a fool

5. Why does the author feel that personal attacks threaten 5.____
   to submerge reasoned debate?
   Because
   A. they are incompatible with one another
   B. people are swayed by such attacks
   C. a man who will denounce and attack personally is
      incapable of reason
   D. valid personal attacks may disqualify an otherwise
      suitable candidate
   E. the persons seeking to defame through personal attack
      may thereby promote public sympathy for the opposition
      through vile or illogical defamation

6. What does the author mean by the term *nuclear adventurer*? 6.____
   A man who
   A. would be inclined to experiment in the search for
      more effective nuclear weapons
   B. would seek to employ nuclear discoveries to maintain
      the peace
   C. would be adventurous and imaginative in recruiting
      scientists to better our nuclear position in the arms
      race
   D. would probably spend too much of the taxpayers' money
      on the building of unnecessary planes and bombs
   E. might act without sufficient forethought and consulta-
      tion and possibly plunge the world into a nuclear war

―――――

9

TEST 5

The permanent system, which went into force in 1920, includes essentially all the elements of immigration policy that are in our law today. The immigration statutes now establish a system of annual quotas to govern immigration from each country. Under this system, 156,987 quota immigrants are permitted to enter the United States each year. The quotas from each country are based upon the national origins of the population of the United States in 1920.

The use of the year 1920 is arbitrary. It rests upon the fact that this system was introduced in 1924, and the last prior census was in 1920. The use of a national origins system is without basis in either logic or reason. It neither satisfies a national need nor accomplishes an international purpose.

In an age of interdependence among nations, such a system is an anachronism, for it discriminates among applicants for admission into the United States on the basis of accident of birth.

Because of the composition of our population in 1920, the system is heavily weighted in favor of immigration from northern Europe and severely limits immigration from southern and eastern Europe and from other parts of the world.

A qualified person born in England or Ireland who wants to emigrate to the United States can do so at any time. A person born in Italy, Hungary, Poland, or the Baltic states may have to wait many years before his turn is reached.

One writer has listed six motives behind the act of 1924. They were: (1) postwar isolationism; (2) the doctrine of the alleged superiority of Anglo-Saxon and Teutonic "races"; (3) the fear that "pauper labor" would lower wage levels; (4) the belief that people of certain nations were less law-abiding than others; (5) the fear that entrance of many people with different customs and habits would undermine our national and social unity and order.

QUESTIONS

1. The immigration quota in effect then was based upon the   1.____
    A. current population of the United States
    B. population of the United States in 1920
    C. act of 1921
    D. population of the United States in 1929
    E. nationalities living at present in the United States

2. The author of the passage seems to feel that our   2.____
   immigration system is
    A. necessary   B. illogical
    C. understandable   D. inevitable
    E. though not completely fair, the only one possible at this ti

10

3. Which of the reasons listed in parentheses at the end of the passage indicates why a person of English birth may (or may not) enter the United States?
    A. (1)   B. (2)   C. (3)   D. (4)   E. (5)

4. Why is the immigration system an anachronism? Because
    A. where it was once of value, it no longer is
    B. it dated back to 1920
    C. it favors immigration from southern and eastern Europe
    D. it limits immigration from northern Europe
    E. of our independence of other nations

4.___

5. A quota is
    A. a changing estimate
    B. a proportional part or share
    C. something that is quoted
    D. a number or amount
    E. a bid or offer so named or published

5.___

6. An emigrant is one who
    A. enters one country from another
    B. seeks residence in the United States
    C. migrates
    D. leaves a country for residence elsewhere
    E. enters and settles in another country

6.___

TEST 6

PASSAGE

In Stalin's time, a leader removed from the Soviet power pyramid was tried, imprisoned, or executed, or became an "unperson" - disappearing not only physically but from all Soviet history and reference books.

Under Nikita Khrushchev, things changed. When "Khrush" got rid of "Bulge" (Premier Bulganin) and his other rivals in 1957, the worst he did was to accuse them of being "antiparty" and send them into obscurity.

Week before last, when Mr. K's own time came, there was a throwback of sorts to the Russia of Koestler's "Darkness at Noon." Official secrecy on how he was removed remained complete. The new "B and K" team of Leonid Brezhnev, 57, party First Secretary (and hence Number One) and Aleksei Kosygin, 60, Premier, conducted itself at public functions for the three latest Soviet cosmonauts as though the "dearly beloved Nikita Sergeyevitch" of the past seven years no longer existed. Books about him disappeared from bookstores; portraits of him still remaining on store counters, could not be bought.

The rigidly controlled Soviet press rested on its brief announcement of 11 days ago that Mr. Khrushchev had been relieved of his duties at his own request due to advancing age (he was 70) and failing

*health. And, by early last week, it became clear that this way
of disposing of leaders would no longer suffice - not for the foreign
Communist parties, with their new and less subservient relationship
with Moscow, nor, possibly, for the Russian people, thawed out
partially from political terror and less susceptible to myths and
mysteries.*

QUESTIONS

1. When Khrushchev's position as Soviet leader terminated,   1.____
   A. he was imprisoned
   B. he was accused of being *antiparty*
   C. there was complete official secrecy regarding the manner
   D. Brezhnev and Kosygin spoke well of him
   E. he was sent into obscurity

2. He was replaced as First Secretary by   2.____
   A. Brezhnev   B. Kosygin
   C. Nikita Sergeyevitch   D. Bulganin
   E. Brezhnev and Kosygin

3. Books written about Khrushchev   3.____
   A. unlike those in Stalin's period, did not disappear
   B. remained, unsold, on the bookshelves
   C. are currently being rewritten
   D. disappeared from the bookstores
   E. shared the same fate as his portraits

4. The author seems to be of the opinion that, regarding   4.____
   Khrushchev,
   A. his age and health made it impossible for him to
      maintain his position
   B. the Russian people have accepted his absence without
      question
   C. foreign branches of the party will cease to ask questions
   D. the party will have to elaborate on its eleven-day-old
      statement
   E. the people are too susceptible to political terror to
      demand further information or explanation

5. Stalin, after his death, was replaced by   5.____
   A. Mikoyan and Bulganin   B. Molotov and Khrushchev
   C. Gromyko and Malenkov   D. Beria, Khrushchev, and Malenkov
   E. Aleksei Adzubei and Marshal Zhukhov

6. In 1962, Khrushchev suffered a defeat when he   6.____
   A. withdrew troops from Vietnam
   B. had to abandon his farm programs as disastrous
   C. made a diplomatic break with China
   D. had to answer charges of nepotism
   E. was forced to withdraw missiles from Cuba

___

TEST 7

He is half the size of an American soldier and twice as disciplined. He does not smoke or drink. He shuns fish and meat and shrinks from contact with women.

To many exasperated Westerners, he seems bent on losing in Saigon any advantage the soldier wins on the battlefield. He believes that only his strategy will bring peace to Vietnam, that he will succeed where soldiers are bound to fail. His religion teaches humility and reconciliation, but he is jealous of his new political power and defiant in his demands.

He is a Buddhist priest. Like some Negro clergymen in the United States, he has come to the forefront of a struggle that is recasting (1966 the shape of his country. He toppled one government in 1963. This(1965) year, he shook another until its military leader approached his temple as chastened as a novice seeking instruction.

In one sense, each priest exemplifies the movement. Since they united to overthrow President Ngo Dinh Diem, the Buddhists have spoken with a single voice.

QUESTIONS

1. In the passage, the author makes a comparison between   1.___
    A. a Negro and a clergyman
    B. a priest and a Buddhist
    C. the battlefield and Saigon
    D. a soldier and a priest
    E. the Buddhists and President Diem

2. The Buddhist priest, on matters of military strategy,   2.___
    A. looks to the United States
    B. trusts the Vietnamese soldiers
    C. trusts the American soldiers
    D. belives only in himself
    E. disbelieves in toppling governments

3. In matters of food, he is   3.___
    A. a vegetarian
    B. constantly fasting
    C. as disciplined as his countrymen
    D. disinterested
    E. a consumer of fish and meat only

4. The author indicates there is a contradiction between   4.___
    the Buddhists'
    A. religion and their political demands
    B. humility and their belief in reconciliation
    C. desire to recast the shape of their government and
       their toppling of governments
    D. strategy and their announced political aim
    E. jealousy of their political power and their new demands

5. Until 1963, Vietnam was ruled by
   A. a Buddhist, Thich Tam Chau
   B. a Roman Catholic Archbishop
   C. Nguyen Khanh
   D. *Big Minh*
   E. Ngo Dinh Diem

5.____

6. A coup d'etat refers specifically to the overthrow of an existing government by
   A. stuffing the ballot boxes
   B. civil war
   C. dynastic legitimization
   D. a decisive blow
   E. a revolutionary small group

6.____

TEST 8

PASSAGE

He won his unique place in history by what he did between the ages of 65 and 70. This is a stage of life at which most people have already retired and relaxed their grip. A lifetime's opportunity at 65! How many of us could have taken advantage of this at that age? But, at 65, Churchill was just ready to get going. In his 60's, he was what most of us are in our 40's. He was at the height of his powers.

In the trajectory of a human life, there is a brief span in which the unspent vigor of youth overlaps with the accumulated experience and wisdom of maturity. For most of us, if this brief golden moment comes at all, it comes between 40 and 50. Churchill's golden moment came 20 years farther on in life than usual. This was fortunate for Britain and for the world, and it was fatal for the Nazis and for Germany.

Some people who are famous today were virtually unknown during their lifetime. Mendel, the discoverer of the laws of genetics, had to wait till a whole generation had passed before he suddenly leaped into fame. Churchill's leap into fame was sudden, like Mendel's, but fortunately Churchill did not have to wait so long to receive his due. He had become supremely famous within a few days of taking over the Government of Britain in the dark and desperate situation in which Britain found herself in the summer of 1940. Churchill then became famous immediately, all over the world, and it is noteworthy that he became as famous in the United States as everywhere else.

This is noteworthy considering what Churchill's major achievement was. It was Churchill who foiled Germany's attempt to conquer the world, and the American people - so it seems to a European observer - have not even yet realized how near Germany came, twice within Churchill's lifetime, to accomplishing her evil ambition. Americans seem never to have taken the deadly German menace to human freedom so much to heart as they have taken the less formidable Communist menace.

14

QUESTIONS

1. Churchill had in common with Mendel   1.____
   A. a generation's wait before recognition
   B. a sudden leap into fame
   C. the fact that they both became famous within a few
      days of their accomplishments
   D. the fact that they both became famous for political
      reasons
   E. a similar attitude toward fame

2. The MOST unusual thing about Churchill's accomplishments   2.____
   in relation to his age was:
   A. In his 40's, he was what most of us are in our 60's
   B. What he had already accomplished by the time he was 65
   C. What he did between the ages of 65 and 70
   D. What he accomplished after the age of 70
   E. Churchill's *golden moment* came 20 years' earlier than
      usual

3. What was MOST striking about Churchill's career?   3.____
   A. He foiled Germany's attempt to conquer the world.
   B. He became as famous in Europe as in America.
   C. Americans never seemed to take the German menace so
      seriously as the Communist one.
   D. He became as famous in the United States as everywhere
      else.
   E. He never achieved so much fame in America as he did in
      Europe.

4. The author feels there is a brief, important span of life   4.____
   which comes
   A. when certain elements of youth and maturity merge
   B. between 40 and 50
   C. with unspent youth
   D. with accumulated experience
   E. with the wisdom of maturity

5. Since the people of America considered Churchill every bit   5.____
   as important as the people of Europe, this was probably
   because
   A. Germany was as close to domination of America as it
      was to domination of Europe
   B. America never took the German menace to freedom so
      seriously as the Europeans
   C. the Americans recognized that their destiny, too, was
      at stake
   D. he had such emotional impact
   E. Germany had gained control of all Europe except for
      Britain

6. During the Second World War, Churchill was   6.____
   A. a leading member of Parliament
   B. England's Prime Minister

15

C. First Lord of the Admiralty
D. a prominent author of several books
E. a member of the Cabinet

TEST 9

PASSAGE

In the long, fabled history of China, many of her leaders have, like Mao Tse-tung, pushed their way by iron will and shrewdness from humble beginnings to supreme power. In one of his poems, Mao implied that none who has ruled China in the past, not even the pitiless Chin Emperor, Shih Huang Ti, nor the great Han Wu Ti, is his equal. Mao's estimate of himself was an index to the vanity and self-confidence of this one-time country bumpkin who not only wielded more power over China's swarming millions than any of his predecessors but aspired as well to power on a world scale.

The success that was to be his seemed already in Mao's sharp, reflective eyes and assured manner when this writer last saw him in Yenan in the winter of 1945. He received visiting foreign correspondents in the rustic building that was headquarters in bleak, northwest China for the Chinese Communist party. A big man with a round face, high cheekbones, and a shock of black hair combed straight back, he was dressed in a long-sleeved padded gown. Pictures showed him older, a little heavier, but with the same sharp, distant, dreamy look in his eyes that he had in Yenan. Aloofly, politely, he greeted us and then excused himself for more pressing duties, leaving the tedious details of explaining Chinese Communist views to Liu Shao-chi, then, as now, his right-hand man.

QUESTIONS

1. In 1945, Mao Tse-tung gave the impression of   1.____
   A. a man from humble beginnings
   B. a poet
   C. realistic self-confidence
   D. a man who had no wish for domination beyond China
   E. self-assurance

2. Mao felt himself to be the equal of   2.____
   A. Liu Shao-chi
   B. no one
   C. any of China's past Emperors
   D. Han Wu Ti
   E. Shih Huang Ti

3. The passage was taken from an article containing an   3.____
   interview with Mao.
   This interview took place in
      A. Cambodia   B. Manchuria   C. Yenan
      D. Canton   E. southwest China

16

4. A rather surprising disclosure, considering Mao's position, 4.____
was that he
   A. was not humble
   B. did not feel himself greater than Han Wu Ti
   C. received visitors in a rustic building
   D. had written poems
   E. wore a long-sleeved padded gown

5. A part of China within his jurisdiction was   5.____
   A. Macao   B. Kunming   C. Hong Kong
   D. Formosa   E. Laos

6. Mao's political philosophy of government was   6.____
   A. socialistic
   B. capitalistic
   C. that of a representative republic
   D. communistic
   E. democratic

TEST 10

PASSAGE

On Sunday morning, November 24, arrangements were made for Oswald's transfer from the city jail to the Dallas County jail, about 1 mile away. The news media had been informed on Saturday night that the transfer of Oswald would not take place until after 10 A.M. on Sunday. Earlier on Sunday, between 2:30 and 3 A.M., anonymous telephone calls threatening Oswald's life had been received by the Dallas office of the FBI and by the office of the county sheriff. Nevertheless, on Sunday morning, television, radio, and newspaper representatives crowded into the basement to record the transfer. As viewed through television cameras, Oswald would emerge from a door in front of the cameras and proceed to the transfer vehicle. To the right of the cameras was a "down" ramp from Main Street on the north. To the left was an "up" ramp leading to Commerce Street on the south.

The armored truck in which Oswald was to be transferred arrived shortly after 11 A.M. Police officials then decided, however, that an unmarked police car would be preferable for the trip because of its greater speed and maneuverability. At approximately 11:20 A.M., Oswald emerged from the basement jail office flanked by detectives on either side and at his rear. He took a few steps toward the car and was in the glaring light of the television cameras when a man suddenly darted out from an area on the right of the cameras where newsmen had been assembled. The man was carrying a Colt .38 revolver in his right hand and, while millions watched on television, he moved quickly to within a few feet of Oswald and fired one shot into Oswald's abdomen. Oswald groaned with pain as he fell to the ground and quickly lost consciousness. Within 7 minutes, Oswald was at Parkland Hospital where, without having regained consciousness, he was pronounced dead at 1:07 P.M.

1. The news media were
   A. not informed of the transfer
   B. given the wrong time
   C. not present
   D. informed of the transfer
   E. informed that the transfer would take place on Saturday

   1. ____

2. To facilitate maneuverability, the police
   A. barred the press
   B. used an unmarked car
   C. used an armored truck
   D. flanked Oswald as he emerged from the basement
   E. announced the time of the transfer

   2. ____

3. Oswald died of
   A. a succession of shots fired
   B. one shot in the head
   C. one shot in the abdomen
   D. one shot from a Colt .32 revolver
   E. one shot fired from a rifle

   3. ____

4. The armored truck arrived
   A. at 11:20 A.M.
   B. before Oswald emerged from the basement jail office
   C. about 10:00 A.M.
   D. at exactly 1:07 P.M.
   E. shortly before 2:30 A.M.

   4. ____

5. In relation to the television cameras, Commerce Street was
   A. to the left of the *up* ramp
   B. leading from Main Street
   C. leading from a *down* ramp
   D. to the left
   E. to the right

   5. ____

6. Oswald was shot when he
   A. had left the glaring light of the TV cameras
   B. took a few steps toward the car
   C. emerged from the basement
   D. entered the car
   E. emerged from the jail office

   6. ____

7. Oswald was
   A. an assassin
   B. an alleged assassin
   C. a murderer in the first degree
   D. a murderer in the second degree
   E. insane

   7. ____

8. The report containing the passage is popularly known as the ____ Report.
   A. Kennedy   B. Dallas   C. Oswald
   D. Warren   E. Presidential

   8. ____

18

KEYS (CORRECT ANSWERS)

TEST 1

1.	C	4.	B
2.	E	5.	B
3.	D	6.	C

EXPLANATION OF ANSWERS

1. The CORRECT ANSWER IS C. The author is not making any general statement, but citing certain cases. Therefore, B, D, and E must be considered too general. And since the author is citing cases of an unsuccessful nature, A is, of course, false.

2. In the last sentence of the last paragraph occurs John Hay's comparison of the Senate and the bull ring. This view indicates that E MUST BE THE CORRECT ANSWER. He did not comment on the treatment of treaties by either branch of the government.

3. The CORRECT ANSWER IS D, as shown in the last sentence of Paragraph 1. Items B and E refer to Richard Olney. While he is referred to in the passage as the Grand Old Man, he was not a Democrat..

4. Closer to the tone of the passage than the possibilities of A, D, or E is the answer stated in B. D and E are rather strong as descriptions of the passage, while A is too weak. C is completely false. The CORRECT ANSWER, THEN, IS B.

5. Items C and E are not stated or suggested at all in the passage. Items A and D are too extreme in their conclusions. B, THEN, WOULD SEEM TO BE THE MOST FITTING ANSWER.

6. A was said by President Coolidge; D and E by Franklin Delano Roosevelt; C WAS SAID BY THEODORE ROOSEVELT AND IS THE CORRECT ANSWER.

TEST 2

1.	B	4.	D
2.	D	5.	D
3.	D	6.	A

EXPLANATION OF ANSWERS

1. The passage states Makarios is a *man of his people* and retains the confidence of his people. The passage further states, *"The Archbishop of Cyprus is elected by the whole people."* Therefore, though C and D may have influenced their decision, he holds his office by consent of the people. THE CORRECT ANSWER, THEN, IS B.

2. Towards the end of the first paragraph, Makarios is deemed to be *a man of his people.....with their strengths and weaknesses,* WHICH WOULD MAKE ITEM D CORRECT. The writer refers to the talk of his being overthrown as *dangerous nonsense.* He does not express any opinion on Items B and C, and refutes Item E.

3. The passage states that both the Americans and the British have been thwarted in imposing their ideas, and, we must presume, have been so thwarted by Makarios. THEREFORE, THE ANSWER IS D. He says, in the passage, *"I am not a party leader...,"* discounting C as a possible answer. B and E are not mentioned.

4. D IS THE CORRECT ANSWER and is stated in the quotation in Paragraph 2, where Makarios says, *"...Ours is the only church in the world where this happens."* Item B is a correct statement regarding the Church, but is not a unique fact; Items A, C, and E are false.

5. The Cypriotes elected in 1961 to become members of the British Commonwealth of Nations. It has rejected its political ties with Greece; THEREFORE, THE CORRECT ANSWER WOULD BE D. (Enosis, Item E, is the Greek word for *union,* referring, in this case, to the union of Greece and Cyprus.)

6. Shakespeare's THE TEMPEST is said to have derived its locale from Corcyra, WHICH RENDERS ITEM A CORRECT. (And there exists in THE TEMPEST a name which is an anagram for Corcyra.) D is a travelogue about Greece written by D.H. Lawrence but is not specifically related to Corcyra; nor are answers B, C, and E.

TEST 3

1.	C	4.	B
2.	E	5.	C
3.	A	5.	D

EXPLANATION OF ANSWERS

1. *"A solid foundation in some specialization is an asset,"* states the author. Answers B and E are mentioned as beneficial, but they are the by-products of NUMBER C, WHICH IS THE CORRECT ANSWER.

2. The ANSWER IS CONTAINED IN PARAGRAPH 2, SENTENCE 3. B and C might be considered valid answers were it not for the more specific inclusion of Answer E, which is taken directly from the passage.

3. The last paragraph describes a cultivated man: wise, mature, experienced, courageous. It states that this is *the important thing.* Such a man would be termed highly civilized. THUS, THE ANSWER IS A. The other items, particularly E, courageous, are assets but are merely parts of the whole—*cultivated* or civilized.

4. THE OPENING SENTENCE OF PARAGRAPH 2 CONTAINS THE ANSWER: IT IS ITEM B. While any of the other answers presented may count as factors in the selection of an ambassador, no particular one is favored.

5. C IS THE CORRECT ANSWER. For any one man to fulfill the requirements of Answers A and B would be impossible. D and E are true factually regarding ambassadors, but hardly describe their fundamental role.

6. D IS THE ANSWER HERE. He is not a teacher nor is he that which is stated in B. C and E are superficial duties compared to the vital act of negotiator or arbiter.

———

TEST 4

1. E	4. B
2. D	5. A
3. E	6. E

EXPLANATION OF ANSWERS

1. This is a common sense question answered directly in the passage. It is also the theme of the article. THE CORRECT ANSWER IS E. While C and D might be considered indirectly correct through deduction, they are not stated in the passage.

2. The author uses the quotation in Paragraph 1 directly to contrast with the stronger terminology of Paragraph 2. The clue to the correct answer is contained in the second sentence of Paragraph 2, THE ONLY POSSIBLE ANSWER THEN BEING D. C is misleading because the author's attention is focused on the changes in the times and in words, not in conjecture on the words Lord Bryce might use today.

3. The *spectacle* referred to in the quotation is concerned with ....*half the honest men....leadership of the nation-....to be a knave.* Therefore, THE CORRECT ANSWER IS E. While A and C seek to condition the response of the people, they, themselves, are not the *spectacle*.

4. THE ONLY ANSWER WHICH STATES SIMILAR CHARACTERISTICS IS B. The other pairs of epithets bears no relationship to one another.

5. The author implies that the smear personal attack is unreasonable and absurd, thus making it impossible to stem from, or to exist alongside, reasonable argument. A, THEN, IS THE ONLY POSSIBLE CORRECT ANSWER. While B and E may be true, they are not in direct relation to the question.

6. Though this information is not specifically contained in the passage, it should be reasonably surmised that the term stated is an epithet, which disqualifies A, B, and C. The threat contained in E is far stronger and more extreme than the description in D. THEREFORE, E IS THE CORRECT ANSWER.

TEST 5

1.	B		4.	B
2.	B		5.	B
3.	B		6.	D

EXPLANATION OF ANSWERS

1. At the end of Paragraph 1, the passage states, *"The quotas from each country are based upon the population of the United States in 1920."* THEREFORE, THE CORRECT ANSWER IS B. Since Items A, C, D, and E refer to events that have taken place since 1920, they are false. Item D indicates the year the permanent system went into force. Item C is not mentioned. Item A is not mentione in relation to the immigration quota and what it is based upon; nor is item E.

2. The author states (Paragraph 2), *"The use of a national origins system is without basis in either logic or reason."* THEREFORE, THE CORRECT ANSWER IS B. From the quotation, the reader may assume that Items A, C, and E are false. Nowhere is Item D mentioned.

3. THE CORRECT ANSWER IS B. The passage states: *"(2) the doctrine of the alleged superiority of the Anglo-Saxon and Teutonic 'races'* this statement immediately follows the flat declaration that *"A qualified person born in England....who wants to emigrate to the United States can do so at any time."* Items C, D, and E are contr dictory to Item B. Item A is contradictory and irrelevant.

4. The author states, in Paragraph 3, that our present system is an anachronism because it is based on what was true of our populatio in 1920. THEREFORE, B IS THE CORRECT ANSWER. Item A is not correct because the author does not indicate that it was ever of value. Items C and D are false statements. And in Paragraph 3, the author speaks of the *interdependence* among nations, discounti E.

5. Item C refers to a quotation. Item E refers to a quotation of another kind, i.e., the stock market. Item D is incomplete and incorrect. THE CORRECT ANSWER, THEN, IS B. Item A is false because a quota is unchanging in its percentage effect.

6. An emigrant is one who leaves a country for residence elsewhere. THEREFORE, THE ANSWER IS D, as opposed to immigrant, which is defined in Answer E, and, partly, in Item A. Item C is insufficient. Item B is false because neither immigration nor emigration is limited to the United States alone in today's world.

TEST 6

1.	C	4.	D
2.	A	5.	D
3.	D	6.	E

EXPLANATION OF ANSWERS

1. Item A relates to the Stalinist period, and Items B and E relate to the Khrushchev period. Item D is inaccurate because he was not spoken of by these men. And in Paragraph 3, it is stated that *"official secrecy on how he was removed remained complete."* THE ANSWER, THEN, IS C.

2. Khrushchev held two positions, that of First Secretary and Premier. He was replaced as First Secretary by Brezhnev (Paragraph 3, sentence 3), and as Premier by Kosygin (Item B). THEREFORE, THE CORRECT ANSWER IS A. Item D, Bulganin, was his predecessor, and Item C, Nikita Sergeyevitch, are actually Khrushchev's first two names.

3. In the last sentence of Paragraph 3, the author states: *Books about him disappeared from bookstores...."* THIS INDICATES THAT D IS THE CORRECT ANSWER. Portraits of him (reference to Item E) remained in the stores but could not be bought (last clause of the last sentence of Paragraph 3), thus indicating that Item E is false. Item A is false because the books DID disappear. There is no mention made in the passage of their being rewritten, thus eliminating Item C. And the passage further indicates that they did NOT remain on the bookshelves, thus discounting B.

4. The last portion of the final paragraph makes clear the author's opinion that *this way of disposing of leaders would no longer suffice.* The final paragraph clearly refutes the acceptability of Items A, B, C, and E. THE CORRECT ANSWER HERE IS D.

5. Item E, Adzubei, was Khrushchev's son-in-law and the former editor of IZVESTIA, the official government newspaper. THE CORRECT ANSWER IS D, the *troika* of Beria, Khrushchev, and Malenkov. Beria was soon thereafter put to death, and Malenkov was deposed after approximately two years in power.

6. THE CORRECT ANSWER IS ITEM E. In the *nuclear crisis* of November, 1962, President Kennedy, of the United States, demanded the removal of all missiles from Cuba by the Russians. In a gigantic test of nerves, Khrushchev gave in. One year later, Kennedy was

dead, the victim of an assassin's bullet. Two years later, Khrushchev was out of power, peacefully deposed by the other party leaders. Items A, B, C, and D are not true.

TEST 7

1.	D	4.	A
2.	D	5.	E
3.	A	6.	E

EXPLANATION OF ANSWERS

1. The passage begins with a comparison between an American soldier and a Buddhist priest. THUS, D IS THE PROPER COMPLETION OF THE STATEMENT. The battlefield and Saigon (Item C) are not compared but, rather, the soldier and the priest in relation to them. There is a comparison made between a Negro clergyman and a Buddhist priest, but not in the vein of Items A and B. There is no comparison such as Item E suggests in the passage.

2. In Paragraph 2 of the passage, the author states, *"He believes that only his strategy will bring peace to Vietnam"*; and further that *"he will succeed where soldiers are bound to fail."* In Paragraph 3, the reader finds *"....he toppled one government in 1963."* Therefore, Items A, B, C, and E may be discarded, and D IS THE CORRECT ANSWER.

3. The reader is told (in Paragraph 1) that, *"....he shuns fish and meat."* This means he must be a consumer of such other foods as fruits, vegetables, etc., ESTABLISHING A AS THE CORRECT ANSWER. There is no mention made of the eating habits of his countrymen. And his diet, though disciplined, is not referred to as one of *constantly fasting* (Item B). Items C and D are not mentioned in the passage, and Item E is denied.

4. The last sentence in Paragraph 2 states, *"His religion teaches humility and reconciliation but he is jealous of his new political power and defiant in his demands."* THIS CONTRADICTION WOULD INDICATE THAT A IS THE CORRECT ANSWER. The other combinations of answers (Items B, C, D, and E) are actually consistent with one another, and not contradictory.

5. The rule of Vietnam by President Ngo Dinh Diem, a Catholic layman, was overthrown in 1963 by a bloody military coup led by General Minh and General Khanh. ITEM E IS, THEREFORE, THE CORRECT ANSWER. Item A refers to the present (1965) Buddhists' chief political spokesman. Items A, B, C, and D are false. Item B refers to President Diem's brother, who was the Roman Catholic Archbishop of Vietnam.

6. A *coup d'etat* is the violent overthrow of an existing government by a small group. That is, it signifies the overthrow and displacement of the leaders, rather than that of the system of government itself. E IS, THEREFORE, THE CORRECT ANSWER. Item D refers to a *coup de grace*, administering the final blow (or death) to a losing cause (or a dying person). Items A, B, and C are incorrect. General Khanh (Item C), a military leader, was apparently the real power in Vietnam then in 1965. *Big Minh* (Item D) refers to General Minh, who served briefly in a primary role after the deposition of Diem but who has now been relegated to a secondary place by General Khanh.

TEST 8

1.	B	4.	A
2.	C	5.	C
3.	D	6.	B

EXPLANATION OF ANSWERS

1. Paragraph 3 states that *"Churchill's leap into fame was sudden, like Mendel's..."* And this was, apparently, the only thing they had in common. THEREFORE, B IS THE CORRECT ANSWER. Item A applies to Mendel alone, NOT to Churchill. Items C, D, and E are false.

2. *"He won his unique place in history by what he did between the ages of 65 and 70"* begins the passage. THEREFORE, C IS CLEARLY THE CORRECT ANSWER. Item A is incorrect because the reverse is actually stated in the passage. Items B, D, and E are false.

3. The author points out (at the end of Paragraph 3) how noteworthy it was that Churchill became as famous in the United States as he did everywhere else, albeit this was NOT his major achievement. THEREFORE, THE CORRECT ANSWER IS D. Item A is, according to the author, Churchill's major achievement, but it is not the correct answer here because it is not what the question calls for. Item B is incorrect. It is actually a reversal of Item A. Item E is false. Item C is stated in the passage but is not related to the question.

4. THE CORRECT ANSWER IS A and is explained at the beginning of Paragraph 3. This is a better answer than B because it is more specific. Items C, D, and E are only part of the correct answer and so are incomplete.

5. THE CORRECT ANSWER IS C. Item A is incorrect; Germany was not so close to the domination of America. Item E is true but is not the reason for, or the answer to, the statement. Item D is irrelevant. Item B is possibly true but does not satisfactorily complete the statement.

6. During World War II, Churchill was Prime Minister of England. He did hold all the other posts mentioned in Items A, C, and E, but PRIOR to World War II. He was a journalist and writer of books, Item D, but that was not his primary function during the war. THE CORRECT ANSWER, THEN, IS B.

TEST 9

1.	E	4.	D
2.	B	5.	B
3.	C	6.	D

EXPLANATION OF ANSWERS

1. The author seems to feel that Mao had an excess of self-confidence which was not realistic. Also, the reader is told he "...*aspires as well to power on a world scale*" (end of Paragraph 1). The answer is contained in the first sentence of Paragraph 2 where the author speaks of Mao's *self-assured manner*. Obviously, he did not give the impression of a man from humble beginnings (Item A). THE CORRECT ANSWER, THEN, IS E. Item C is incorrect because a wish for such power does not seem realistic. Item D is false because the reverse is true. Item B is neither mentioned nor implied in relation to the impression Mao gave.

2. The passage states, "*In one of his poems, Mao implied that none who has ruled China in the past.....is his equal.*" This leads us to discard Item C. THEREFORE, THE CORRECT ANSWER IS B. Liu Shao-chi (Item A) is his right-hand man. The other men (Items D and E) are past Emperors of China.

3. In Paragraph 2, the author states, *"He received visiting foreign correspondents.....in Yenan."* THEREFORE, C IS THE CORRECT ANSWER, and Items A, B, and D are false. Yenan is in northwest China, states the passage, discounting E.

4. The rustic building was headquarters for the Chinese Communist party, and is, therefore, not the correct answer. This discounts Item C. However, the reader is told in the first paragraph that Mao DOES write poems. THEREFORE, THE CORRECT ANSWER IS D. Items A and B are false statements. Item E is true but hardly a surprising disclosure.

5. THE CORRECT ANSWER TO QUESTION 5 IS B. Kunming is a city in China. Item A, Macao, is a Portuguese possession. Item C, Hong Kong, is a British Crown Colony. Laos is an independent country, discounting E. Item D, Formosa, is not within the jurisdiction of Mao, and so is false.

6. China is now under Communist rule. THEREFORE, THE CORRECT ANSWER IS D. Items A, B, C, and E are false.

TEST 10

1. D
2. B
3. C
4. B
5. D
6. B
7. B
8. D

EXPLANATION OF ANSWERS

1. The news media were informed of the transfer on Saturday, discounting Items A and E. They were given the correct time, discounting B. Also, they were present at the transfer, eliminating Item C. ITEM D IS THE CORRECT ONE, as stated in the second sentence of the first paragraph.

2. The passage states (second sentence, second paragraph), *"Police officials decided...an unmarked car would be preferable...because of its greater speed and maneuverability."* THEREFORE, ITEM B IS CORRECT. Item A is false. Item C indicates a discarded choice. Items D and E are true in themselves but had nothing to do with facilitating maneuverability; therefore, they are incorrect in this context.

3. The passage states that (second paragraph, third sentence from end), *"....he...fired one shot into Oswald's abdomen."* THEREFORE, ITEM C IS CORRECT. Item D is incorrect because, actually, *"The man was carrying a Colt .38 revolver...."* Items A, B, and E are false.

4. *"The armored truck arrived shortly after 11:00..."* states the passage in Paragraph 2, sentence one. Item A is the time Oswald emerged from the basement. Item C was the announced time of the transfer. Item D was the time of his death. Item E is the time the police received anonymous telephone calls. ITEM B IS, THEREFORE, CORRECT.

5. Item A is false because the street was not to the left of the ramp. Item B is false because Main St. and Commerce St. are not mentioned as connecting. Item C is false because the *down* ramp led from the cameras to Main St. ITEM D IS CORRECT as found in the last sentence of Paragraph 1. Item E is false; the right led to Main St.

6. Item A is false because the cameras were still on him. ITEM B IS CORRECT because it is the last moment referred to in the passage before the description of the shooting. Item C is false, as is Item E, because movements are detailed beyond that point. Item D is false because Oswald was shot before he got to the car.

7. Oswald did not live to stand trial. In view of this and because of the absence of complete proof, Oswald must be technically termed the ALLEGED assassin of President Kennedy. THEREFORE, ITEM B IS CORRECT. Items A, C, and D are false. Item E can now neither be proved nor disproved.

8. The report was issued by a commission headed by Earl Warren, Chief Justice of the Supreme Court. ITEM D IS CORRECT. Items A, B, C, and E are incorrect.

———

EXAMINATION SECTION

TEST 1
PASSAGE

By far, the best-known industry in Steuben County is the manufacture of glass. Just after the Civil War, the Flint Glass Company moved from Brooklyn to Corning. One reason why the company chose to settle in Corning was that the railroad from Pennsylvania to Corning brought coal for fuel at a low cost. In the early days, the company made lantern chimneys, bottles, and such familiar products. Later, it began making electric light bulbs. Now it manufactures all kinds of glass products. It makes Pyrex, a kind of glass that resists heat so well that it is used for cooking and baking. The company also makes glass wool, which is used for insulation and other purposes, and glass bricks, out of which the walls of some modern buildings are built.

1. The Flint Glass Company moved to Corning because it 1.___
  A. would be exempt from local taxes
  B. had been promised free land for its buildings
  C. could obtain coal cheaply
  D. could make glass bricks there

2. Glass wool, made in Corning, is used for 2.___
  A. insulation
  B. low cost fuel
  C. manufacturing lantern chimneys
  D. making electric blankets

3. Since its early days in Corning, the number and variety of 3.___
  the products of the glass industry have
  A. decreased   B. remained about the same
  C. increased slightly   D. increased greatly

4. The county in which Corning is located is 4.___
  A. Chautauqua B. Cortland   C. Seneca   D. Steuben

5. Pyrex is used for 5.___
  A. antifreeze   B. cooking utensils
  C. curtain material   D. refrigeration

___

TEST 2
PASSAGE

While Admiral Dewey was waiting in Manila Bay, exciting events were happening in the Atlantic. Soon after the start of the war, a Spanish fleet under Admiral Pascual Cervera set sail from the coast of Spain. An American fleet under Admiral William T. Sampson set out to give battle to Cervera's fleet. On May 19, Cervera's fleet came to anchor in the Cuban harbor of Santiago. Sampson's fleet quickly took up its position just outside the channel in order to blockade the *harbor, which was too well defended by forts for the Americans to sail in. An American army was landed on the coast a few miles south of Santiago. On July 1-2, this force captured the outer defenses of the city at San Juan Hill and began a siege of Santiago. One of the regiments of volunteers that took part in the charge at San Juan Hill had been recruited by Theodore Roosevelt, who was second in command. The victory of the American army caused the Spaniards to give up hope. The Spanish commander in Cuba ordered Admiral Cervera to put to sea and save his fleet if he could. On July 3, Cervera, with his ships under full steam, started out of Santiago Harbor.*

1. The paragraph describes a campaign in the   1.____
    A. War of 1812   B. Mexican War
    C. Civil War   D. Spanish-American War

2. At the time of the Cuban campaign, a new regiment was   2.____
   recruited by
    A. Cervera   B. Dewey   C. Roosevelt   D. Sampson

3. The American victory at San Juan Hill caused the enemy to   3.____
    A. lose confidence   B. surrender unconditionally
    C. retreat to San Juan Hill D. enter Santiago

4. The war was fought   4.____
    A. only in the Atlantic Ocean
    B. only in the Pacific Ocean
    C. on both land and sea
    D. off the coast of Tripoli

5. Sampson's fleet tried to   5.____
    A. keep Cervera's fleet from entering the harbor
    B. blockade Santiago Harbor
    C. attack San Juan Hill
    D. prevent the United States regiment from entering the battle

TEST 3

PASSAGE

In the generation after Appomattox, the pattern of our present society and economy took shape. Growth - in area, numbers, wealth, power, social complexity, and economic maturity - was the one most arresting fact. The political divisions of the republic were drawn in their final form, a dozen new states were admitted to the Union, and an American empire was established. In a space of forty years, population increased from thirty-one to seventy-six million, fifteen million immigrants - an ever-increasing proportion of them from southern and eastern Europe - poured into the Promised Land, and great cities like New York, Chicago, Pittsburgh, Cleveland, and Detroit doubled and redoubled their size. In swift succession, the Indians were harried out of their ancient haunts on the high plains and in the mountains and valleys beyond and herded into reservations, the mining and cattle kingdoms rose and fell, the West was peopled and farmed, and by the end of the century, the frontier was no more. Vast new finds of iron ore, copper, and oil created scores of great industries; small business grew into big business.

1. Which one of the following terms BEST describes the period discussed? 1.___
    A. Expansion B. Conservation C. Regulation .D. Isolation

2. The policy of the Federal government toward the Indians was to 2.___
    A. break up the tribal governments
    B. disenfranchise the Indians
    C. educate all Indian children in public schools
    D. remove them to reservations

3. An IMPORTANT factor in the industrial development that followed the Civil War was the 3.___
    A. diversification of agriculture
    B. development of new mineral resources
    C. rapid transformation of farmers into industrial workers
    D. development of a colonial empire

4. The last stage in the development of the West was accomplished by 4.___
    A. Indians   B. farmers   C. ranchers   D. miners

5. Which one of the following statements is made concerning the United States during the period described in the paragraph? The United States 5.___
    A. established an empire
    B. secured special interests in the oil wells and copper mines of Mexico
    C. developed a policy of dollar diplomacy
    D. advocated the open-door policy

6. Which one of the following statements concerning the frontier is made in the paragraph? 6.___
    A. After the admission of twelve states, expansion ceased.
    B. An outstanding characteristic of the frontier people was their intense nationalism.
    C. At the end of the 19th century, the frontier came to an end.
    D. The frontier was most important in shaping our present society.

———

TEST 4

PASSAGE

If George Washington could have visited the United States in the 1840's, his thoughts might have run somewhat like this:

"I find it hard to believe that over 20,000,000 people now live in the United States, and that towns have been built beyond the

Mississippi River. In my day, there were only 4,000,000 people, and most of these lived along the Atlantic Coast. Can this great city be New York, where I took the oath of office as President? The city I knew had 60,000 inhabitants; today, they tell me, it is the largest city in the New World and has a population of 500,000. What is this engine belching smoke and sparks which carries people across the countryside? When I traveled from Mount Vernon to New York in 1789, I depended on horses. I see factories where machines spin thread to weave it into cloth. Who ever heard in my day of a machine that could spin eighty threads at one time? Here is a boat run by steam which travels against the current of a river! In my time, we depended on the wind to drive our boats. Who would have believed that this country could change so greatly in fifty years!"

1. How much GREATER was the population of the United States   1.___
    in 1840 than in 1789?
    A. Twice as great   B. Five times as great
    C. Twelve times as great   D. Twenty times as great

2. George Washington was inaugurated in   2.___
    A. Boston   B. Mount Vernon
    C. New York   D. Philadelphia

3. A method of transportation used in the 1840's but not   3.___
    in Washington's time was the
    A. airplane   B. automobile   C. sailboat   D. railroad

4. The changes described in the paragraph took place within   4.___
    a period of about ____ years.
    A. 10   B. 20   C. 50   D. 70

5. In Washington's time, MOST of the people in the United   5.___
    States lived
    A. beyond the Mississippi   B. along the eastern seaboard
    C. in the deep South   D. in the Northwest

TEST 5

PASSAGE

In philosophy, the New Deal was democratic, in method evolutionary. Because for fifteen years legislative reforms had been dammed up, they now burst upon the country with what seemed like violence but when the waters subsided, it was clear that they ran in familiar channels. The conservation policy of the New Deal had been inaugurated by Theodore Roosevelt; railroad and trust regulation went back to the eighties; banking and currency reforms had been advocated by Bryan and partially achieved by Wilson; the farm-relief program borrowed much from the Populists, labor legislation from the practices of such states as Wisconsin and Oregon. Even judicial reform, which caused such a mighty stir, had been anticipated by Lincoln and Theodore Roosevelt. And in the realm of international relations, the policies of the New Deal were clearly continuations of the traditional policies of strengthening national security, maintaining freedom of the seas, supporting law and peace, and championing democracy in the Western world

1. All of the following are suitable titles for the selection   1.___
   EXCEPT
   A. The New Deal - an Evolution
   B. The Radical Program of the New Deal
   C. Precedents for the New Deal
   D. Conservatism in the New Deal

2. Many students of history do not agree that legislative   2.___
   reforms had been *dammed up* during the fifteen-year period
   preceding the New Deal.
   All of the following legislative measures were passed
   during this fifteen-year period EXCEPT the ____ Act.
   A. Norris-LaGuardia
   B. Reconstruction Finance Corporation
   C. Sherman Antitrust
   D. Agricultural Marketing

3. This selection traces the origin of many of the policies   3.___
   of the New Deal to all of the following EXCEPT
   A. former Presidents
   B. legislation of the Western states
   C. minority parties
   D. the Supreme Court

4. All of the following were indications of isolationism in   4.___
   the New Deal period EXCEPT the
   A. *cash-and-carry* policy   B. Johnson Debt-Default Act
   C. Lima Conference   D. *America First* organization

5. Abraham Lincoln, Theodore Roosevelt, and Franklin   5.___
   Roosevelt had all of the following policies in common EXCEPT
   A. trust regulation
   B. expansion of executive powers
   C. land reforms
   D. economic betterment of the common man

6. According to the selection legislative reforms of the   6.___
   New Deal are characterized by all of the following adjectives
   EXCEPT
   A. democratic   B. evolutionary
   C. reactionary   D. traditional

7. All of the following Presidents were associated with   7.___
   banking reforms EXCEPT
   A. Warren Harding   B. Andrew Jackson
   C. Abraham Lincoln   D. Woodrow Wilson

8. According to the selection, some legislative precedents   8.___
   for the New Deal were furthered in the United States by
   all of the following Presidents EXCEPT
   A. Abraham Lincoln   B. Theodore Roosevelt
   C. Calvin Coolidge   D. Woodrow Wilson

9. The student seeking primary source material on the New
   Deal farm program should consult
   A. THE WORLD ALMANAC
   B. the CONGRESSIONAL RECORD
   C. an encyclopedia of the social studies
   D. WHO'S WHO IN AMERICA ____

9.____

TEST 6

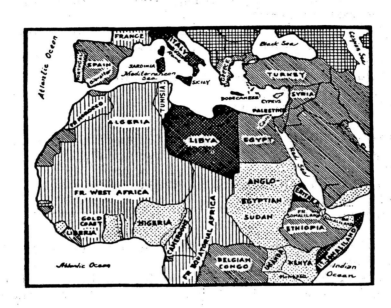

PASSAGE

London, August 14, 1948. A bankrupt empire was put for disposal
in London this week. Although the empire, once the property of Italy,
has few assets, bidding for the properties was spirited. Italy,
despite her present domestic problems, was bidding strongly. Only
Italy seemed to want the whole lot; others were angling for bits and
pieces and odd parcels of the colonies. On the other hand, Great
Britain, which wants the properties almost as badly as Italy, was
bidding timidly as if she were afraid of running up the price too fast
and too far.

The international auction sale was arranged last year when the
winning powers in the recent war settled accounts with Italy. In the
Italian peace treaty, Italy renounced all rights to her colonies. The
Dodecanese promptly were ceded to Greece. In an annex to the treaty,
the Big Four agreed that their Foreign Ministers should decide on the
disposal of the other three colonies - Eritrea and Italian Somaliland
on the east coast of Africa and Libya in North Africa. Failing a
decision within one year, that is, by September 15, 1948, the Big Four
agreed that they would hand over the problem to the United Nations
General Assembly and abide by its verdict.

That year was nearly out when the deputies of the Big Four
Foreign Ministers met, not to decide finally the future of the colonies,
but merely to pass on recommendations to the Council of Foreign Minis-

ters. When these deputies met last October, they sent out a four-power commission to investigate the situation in the colonies and the wishes of the inhabitants. Reports of that commission were in the hands of the deputies when they met this week.

1. The writer believes that the former Italian colonies 1.___
   A. have many fine resources
   B. are desired by some of the great powers
   C. are financially sound
   D. are strategically important to Russia

2. The Italian colonies in Africa include 2.___
   A. Ethiopia, Eritrea, Libya
   B. Italian Somaliland, Eritrea, Libya
   C. Eritrea, Libya, and the Dodecanese
   D. Ethiopia, Tripoli, and the Dodecanese

3. Italy's African colonies bordered on the 3.___
   A. Mediterranean Sea
   B. Indian Ocean
   C. Atlantic Ocean and Red Sea
   D. Red Sea, Mediterranean Sea, and Indian Ocean

4. The MOST appropriate title for the article would be 4.___
   A. PROBLEMS OF WORLD EMPIRES
   B. FATE OF ITALY'S AFRICAN EMPIRE UNDECIDED
   C. FOUR POWERS INVESTIGATE ITALY'S COLONIES
   D. ITALY'S WEALTH IN AFRICA

5. Libya lies 5.___
   A. east of Algeria   B. east of Egypt
   C. north of Egypt   D. west of Tunisia

6. The author of the article 6.___
   A. thinks that the colonies will be restored to the natives
   B. says the colonies will be given to the Arabs
   C. predicts that the colonies will be returned to Italy
   D. makes no prediction as to the action of the United Nations Assembly

7. MOST of Libya's boundaries bordered on 7.___
   A. possessions of the French Empire
   B. possessions of the British Empire
   C. the sea
   D. independent countries

8. If the Big Four cannot agree upon the disposition of the 8.___
   Italian colonies, they will refer the problem to the
   A. International Court of Justice
   B. Trusteeship Council
   C. General Assembly of the United Nations
   D. Security Council of the United Nations

9. The author of the article states that
    A. the colonies were disposed of in the Italian peace treaty
    B. Greece received all the Italian colonies
    C. the Big Four were first assigned disposal of the colonies
    D. the United Nations Assembly would have to approve the disposal of the colonies

9.____

10. The author names the following countries as bidders in the disposal of the remaining colonies
    A. France and the Netherlands
    B. Great Britain and France
    C. Italy and Portugal
    D. Great Britain and Italy

10.____

11. By a study of this map, a student could determine the
    A. number of air miles from Rome to Cairo
    B. most densely populated areas
    C. notable topographic features of Ethiopia
    D. boundaries and comparative areas

11.____

12. Of the following statements selected from the article, the one that is CLEARLY a statement of opinion is that
    A. the Dodecanese were ceded to Greece
    B. the Big Four agreed to hand over the problem to the United Nations under certain conditions
    C. the deputies met in October, 1947
    D. Great Britain was afraid of running the price up too fast and too far

12.____

TEST 7

PASSAGE

"We hold these truths to be self-evident: that all men and women are created equal; that they are endowed by their Creator with certain inalienable rights; that among these are life, liberty, and the pursuit of happiness...

"The history of mankind is a history of repeated injuries and usurpations on the part of man toward woman, having in direct object the establishment of an absolute tyranny over her. To prove this, let facts be submitted to a candid world.

"He has never permitted her to exercise her inalienable right to the elective franchise.

"He has compelled her to submit to laws, in the formation of which she had no voice...

"He has so framed the laws of divorce, as to what shall be the proper causes, and in case of separation, to whom the guardianship of the children shall be given, as to be wholly regardless of the *happiness of women - the law, in all cases, going upon a false supposition of the supremacy of man, and giving all power into his hands...*

"*He has monopolized nearly all the profitable employments, and from those she is permitted to follow, she receives but a scanty remuneration. He closes against her all the avenues to wealth and distinction which he considers most honorable to himself. As a teacher of theology, medicine, or law, she is not known.*

"*He has denied her the facilities for obtaining a thorough education, all colleges being closed against her...*"

RESOLUTIONS ADOPTED AT THE SENECA FALLS CONVENTION, 1848

1. This selection appeals for support of the movement for   1.____
   A. temperance   B. women's rights
   C. social security   D. child labor legislation

2. Which served as a model for this selection?   2.____
   A. Federal Bill of Rights   B. Emancipation Proclamation
   C. Mayflower Compact   D. Declaration of Independence

3. An *inalienable right* is BEST defined as a right that   3.____
   A. cannot be taken away
   B. is granted to women only
   C. is granted to all except aliens
   D. is guaranteed by the preamble to the Federal Constitution

4. Which right did women enjoy at the time of the Seneca Falls 4.____
   Convention?
   A. The right to serve on juries
   B. The right of assembly
   C. Equal vocational opportunities
   D. Equal rights before the law

5. Which problem of the Seneca Falls Convention remains a   5.____
   legal issue in the United States today?
   A. A voice in making laws
   B. College admission
   C. Equal pay for equal work in industry
   D. Exclusion from the practice of medicine

6. About how long after the Seneca Falls Convention was the   6.____
   right to the elective franchise (referred to in the selection) achieved by a constitutional amendment? ____ years.
   A. 5   B. 50   C. 75   D. 100

_____

TEST 8

1. The cartoon suggests that in the 82nd Congress
   A. harmony prevailed
   B. more agreement existed on domestic issues than on foreign policy
   C. only the reactionary Democrats opposed Truman's foreign policy
   D. there was disagreement within both the Democratic and the Republican parties

   1.____

2. The cartoon specifically refers to division within the Republican party over
   A. foreign policy   B. inflation
   C. civil rights   D. taxation

   2.____

3. Which of the following are leaders of the two Republican groups represented in the cartoon?
   A. Taft and Acheson   B. Dewey and Hoover
   C. Austin and Dulles   D. Stassen and Lehman

   3.____

4. We can conclude from the cartoon that in the 82nd Congress, there was
   A. little prospect that either group in the Democratic party will take a world-minded view
   B. no possibility of any important legislation
   C. no possibility that the President's recommendations will receive favorable consideration
   D. little likelihood of settling significant foreign policy issues on strict party lines

   4.____

5. Which of the following conclusions drawn from the cartoon   5.___
   can be readily proved?
   A. There was a reaction group in the Democratic party.
   B. All isolationists came from the same part of the
      country.
   C. The 82nd Congress was evenly divided between Republicans
      and Democrats.
   D. The Republicans were more interested in foreign policy
      than in domestic issues.

   _____

TEST 9

FAMILY INCOME BEFORE TAXES
United States,   1946 and 1953

PERCENT OF FAMILIES

1. In 1953, the percent of families with incomes between   1.___
   $3000 and $3,999 was APPROXIMATELY
   A. 5%   B. 10%   C. 15%   D. 20%

2. In 1946, which income bracket included the largest   2.___
   percentage of families?
   A. $1,000 to $1,999   B. $2,000 to $2,999
   C. $3,000 to $3,999   D. $4,000 to $4,999

3. Which of these income brackets included a larger   3.___
   percentage of families in 1953 than in 1946?
   A. $1,000 to $1,999   B. $2,000 to $2,999
   C. $3,000 to $3,999   D. $4,000 to $4,999

4. In 1953, the percent of families with incomes less than   4.___
   $3,000 was about
   A. 30   B. 45   C. 60   D. 75

5. The average family income in 1953 was CLOSEST TO   5.___
   A. $1,500   B. $2,500   C. $4,500   D. $6,000

   _____

TEST 10

1. For the year 1948, the chart shows a _____ period.   1.___
   A. two-month   B. six-week   C. seven-week   D. eight-week

2. Throughout the period from October 1945 to February 1948,   2.___
   stock market prices
   A. rose sharply
   B. declined sharply
   C. remained comparatively steady
   D. fluctuated greatly

3. A comparison of wholesale food prices at the end of the   3.___
   second week in February 1948 with wholesale food prices
   in October 1945 shows an increase of APPROXIMATELY _____
   points.
   A. 50   B. 100   C. 200   D. 300

4. In the period covered by the graph, wholesale food prices   4.___
   declined sharply
   A. once   B. twice   C. three times D. four times

5. The prices of non-food items reached their highest peak   5.___
   in
   A. March 1946   B. December 1946
   C. March 1947   D. December 1947

6. For the period shown in 1948, all items   6.___
   A. rose   B. remained the same
   C. declined   D. fluctuated greatly

7. The month in which the GREATEST increase in wholesale   7.___
   food prices occurred was
   A. July 1946   B. October 1946
   C. September 1947   D. December 1947

8. The same wholesale order of groceries that cost $100 in   8.___
   August 1939 cost approximately $450 in
   A. November 1946   B. March 1947
   C. December 1947   D. January 1948

_____

KEYS (CORRECT ANSWERS)

TEST 1	TEST 2	TEST 3	TEST 4	TEST 5
1. C	1. D	1. A	1. B	1. B
2. A	2. C	2. D	2. C	2. C
3. D	3. A	3. B	3. D	3. D
4. D	4. C	4. B	4. C	4. C
5. B	5. B	5. A	5. B	5. A
		6. C		6. C
				7. A
				8. C
				9. B

TEST 6	TEST 7	TEST 8	TEST 9	TEST 10
1. B	1. B	1. D	1. C	1. C
2. B	2. D	2. A	2. B	2. C
3. D	3. A	3. B	3. D	3. C
4. B	4. B	4. D	4. A	4. B
5. A	5. C	5. A	5. C	5. D
6. D	6. C			6. C
7. A				7. A
8. C				8. D
9. C				
10. D				
11. D				
12. D				

INTERPRETATION OF LITERARY MATERIALS

EXAMINATION SECTION

DIRECTIONS: In the passages that follow, each question or incomplete statement that follows each passage is followed by several suggested answers or completions. Select the one that BEST answers the question or completes the statement. Base your choice in each case on the materials given and on your own understanding of the subject matter.

TEST 1

What things there are to write, if one could only write them! My mind is full of gleaming thoughts; gay moods and mysterious, mothlike meditations hover in my imagination, fanning their painted wings. They would make my fortune if I could catch them; but always the rarest, those freaked with azure and the deepest crimson, flutter away beyond my reach. The ever-baffled chase of these filmy nothings often seems, for one of sober years in a sad world, a trifling occupation. But have I not read of the great Kings of Persia who used to ride out to hawk for butterflies, nor deemed this pastime beneath their royal dignity?

1. The author believes that striving to write well is
   A. inappropriate for a mature person
   B. unappreciated
   C. unnecessary
   D. a trifling occupation
   E. a worthy occupation

   1.___

2. The author finds that
   A. there are few subjects to write about
   B. he cannot capture the pictures of his imagination
   C. he is too old for writing gay trifles
   D. he cannot keep his mind on his writing
   E. it is easy to write

   2.___

3. The theme of this paragraph is
   A. thoughts about butterflies
   B. the sport of kings
   C. the pursuit of ideas
   D. fortune out of reach
   E. the joy of writing

   3.___

_____

TEST 2

The single business of Henry Thoreau, during forty-odd years of eager activity, was to discover an economy calculated to provide a satisfying life. His one concern, that gave to his ramblings in Concord fields a value of high adventure, was to explore the true meaning of wealth. As he understood the problem of economics, there were three possible solutions open to him: to exploit himself, to exploit his fellows, or to reduce the problem to its lowest denominator. The first was quite impossible - to imprison oneself in a treadmill when the morning called to great adventure. To exploit one's fellows seemed to Thoreau's sensitive social conscience an even greater infidelity. Freedom with abstinence seemed to him better than serfdom with material well-being, and he was content to move to Walden Pond and to set about the high business of living, "to front only the essential facts of life and to see what it had to teach." He did not advocate that other men should build cabins and live isolated. He had no wish to dogmatize concerning the best mode of living - each must settle that for himself. But that a satisfying life should be lived, he was vitally concerned. The story of his emancipation from the lower economics is the one romance of his life, and WALDEN is his great book. It is a book in praise of life rather than of Nature, a record of calculating economies that studied saving in order to spend more largely. But it is a book of social criticism as well, in spite of its explicit denial of such a purpose. In considering the true nature of economy, he concluded, with Ruskin, that the cost of a thing is the amount of life which is required in exchange for it, immediately or in the long run. In WALDEN, Thoreau elaborated the text: "The only wealth is life."

1. In Thoreau's opinion, the price of a thing should always   1.___
    be measured in terms of
       A. time   B. effort   C. money
       D. romance   E. life

2. According to Thoreau, the wealth of an individual is   2.___
    measured by
       A. the money he makes
       B. the experience he gains
       C. the amount he saves
       D. the books he writes
       E. his social standing

3. Thoreau's solution to the problem of living was to   3.___
       A. study Nature
       B. make other men work for him
       C. work in a mill
       D. live in a simple way
       E. write for a living

4. Thoreau was very   4.___
       A. active   B. lazy   C. dissatisfied
       D. unsociable   E. stingy

5. Thoreau's CHIEF aim in life was to
    A. discover a satisfactory economy
    B. do as little work as possible
    C. convert others to his way of life
    D. write about Nature
    E. live in isolation

5.___

6. The theme of this paragraph is
    A. problems of economics
    B. Thoreau's philosophy of life
    C. WALDEN, Thoreau's greatest work
    D. how Thoreau saved money
    E. life at Walden Pond

6.___

_____

TEST 3

A moment's reflection will make it clear that one can not live a full, free, influential life in America without argument. No doubt, people often argue on insufficient evidence and for insufficient reasons; no doubt, they often argue on points about which they should rather be thinking and studying; no doubt, they sometimes fancy they are arguing when they are merely wrangling and disputing. But this is only proof that argument is employed badly, that it is misused rather than used skillfully. Argument, at the right moment and for the right purpose and in the right way, is undoubtedly one of the most useful instruments in American life; it is an indispensable means of expressing oneself and impressing others.

1. The theme of this paragraph is
    A. the usefulness of argument
    B. principles of argument
    C. how to win arguments
    D. misuses of argument
    E. need for evidence in argument

1.___

2. Argument is an important factor in American life because it gives people a chance to
    A. talk about things of which they know little
    B. influence the ideas of others
    C. develop sufficient evidence
    D. have friendly conversations
    E. use argument at the right time and in the right way

2.___

3. Argumentation is being used unwisely when it results in
    A. understanding   B. compromise
    C. deliberation   D. bickering
    E. differences of opinion

3.___

_____

3

TEST 4

The characteristic American believes, first, in justice as the foundation of civilized government and society, and, next, in freedom for the individual, so far as that freedom is possible without interference with the equal rights of others. He conceives that both justice and freedom are to be secured through popular respect for the laws enacted by the elected representatives of the people and through the faithful observance of those laws. It should be observed, however, that American justice in general keeps in view the present common good of the vast majority, and the restoration rather than the punishment of the exceptional malignant or defective individual. It is essentially democratic; and especially it finds sufferings inflicted on the innocent unintelligible and abhorrent.

Blind obedience and implicit submission to the will of another do not commend themselves to characteristic Americans. The discipline in which they believe is the voluntary cooperation of many persons in the orderly and effective pursuit of common ends. Thus, they submit willingly to any restrictions on individual liberty which can be shown to be necessary to the preservation of the public health, and they are capable of the most effective cooperation at need in business, sports, and war.

1. The American people believe in   1.____
      A. unquestioning obedience to their laws
      B. strict discipline
      C. liberty without restraint
      D. subservience to the President
      E. working together for a necessary purpose

2. American justice emphasizes   2.____
      A. the welfare of the minority
      B. retaliation for disobedience
      C. rehabilitation of wrongdoers
      D. the sufferings of the innocent
      E. punishment of criminals

3. The PRIMARY element in the American way of life is   3.____
      A. the right to vote
      B. freedom
      C. willingness to follow leaders
      D. justice
      E. popular respect for laws

4. The theme of this selection is   4.____
      A. American justice
      B. a plea for cooperation
      C. the basis of American democracy
      D. the American government
      E. liberty as the foundation of government

_____

4

TEST 5

The change in the treatment of his characters is a significant index to Shakespeare's growth as a dramatist. In the earlier plays, his men and women are more engaged with external forces than with internal struggles. In as excellent an early tragedy as ROMEO AND JULIET, the hero fights more with outside obstacles than with himself. In the great later tragedies, the internal conflict is more emphasized, as in the cases of HAMLET and MACBETH. He grew to care less for mere incident, for plots based on mistaken identity, as in the COMEDY OF ERRORS; he became more and more interested in the delineation of character, in showing the effect of evil on Macbeth and his wife, of jealousy on OTHELLO, of indecision on Hamlet, as well as in exploring the ineffectual attempts of many of his characters to escape the consequences of their acts.

1. The development of Shakespeare as a dramatist is MOST   1.___
    clearly revealed in his
    A. improved treatment of complications
    B. increased use of involved plots
    C. handling of emotional conflicts
    D. increased variety of plot
    E. decreased dependency on historical characters

2. In his later plays, Shakespeare became interested in   2.___
    A. plots based on mistaken identity
    B. great characters from history
    C. the history of his country
    D. the study of human nature
    E. the struggle of the hero with external forces

3. The theme of this paragraph is   3.___
    A. comedies and tragedies of Shakespeare
    B. Shakespeare's best plays
    C. Shakespeare's development as a dramatist
    D. the moral aspects of Shakespeare's later plays
    E. Shakespeare's interest in good and evil

TEST 6

Solitude is a great chastener when once you accept it. It quietly eliminates all sorts of traits that were a part of you - among others, the desire to pose, to keep your best foot forever in evidence, to impress people as being something you would like to have them think you are even when you aren't. Some men I know are able to pose even in solitude; had they valets they no doubt would be heroes to them. But I find it the hardest kind of work myself; and as I am lazy, I have stopped trying. To act without an audience is so tiresome and profitless that you gradually give it up and at last forget how to act at all. For you become more interested in making the acquaintance of yourself as you really are, which is a meeting that, in the haunts of men, rarely takes place. It is gratifying, for example, to discover that you prefer to be clean rather than dirty even when there is no one but God to care which you are; just as it is amusing to note, however, that for scrupulous cleanliness, you are not inclined to make superhuman sacrifices, although you used to believe you were. Clothes, you learn, with something of a shock, have for you no interest whatsoever....You learn to regard dress merely as covering, a precaution. For its color and its cut you care nothing.

1. The activities of everyday life seldom give us the chance   1.___
   to
     A. learn our own peculiarities
     B. keep our best foot forward
     C. impress people
     D. dress as we would like
     E. be immaculately clean

2. The desire to appear well-dressed USUALLY depends upon   2.___
     A. an audience   B. industriousness
     C. personal pride   D. the need for cleanliness
     E. a fondness for acting

3. In solitude, clothes   3.___
     A. constitute one item that pleases the valet
     B. make one careless
     C. are part of acting
     D. are valued for their utility only
     E. are tiresome

4. A desire to appear at your best is a trait that   4.___
     A. goes with laziness
     B. may disappear when you are alone
     C. depends primarily on clothes
     D. is inhuman
     E. is evil

5. The theme of this paragraph is   5.___
     A. carelessness in clothes
     B. acting without an audience
     C. discoveries through solitude
     D. showing off to best advantage
     E. being a hero to yourself

TEST 7

In width of scope, Yeats far exceeds any of his contemporaries. He is the only poet since the 18th century who has been a public man in his own country and the only poet since Milton who has been a public man at a time when his country was involved in a struggle for political liberty. This may not seem an important matter, but it is a question whether the kind of life lived by poets for the last two hundred years or so has not been one great reason for the drift of poetry away from the life of the community as a whole, and the loss of touch with tradition. Once the life of contemplation has been divorced from the life of action, or from real knowledge of men of action, something is lost which it is difficult to define; but which leaves poetry enfeebled and incomplete. Yeats responded with all his heart as a young man to the reality and the romance of Ireland's struggle, but he lived to be completely disillusioned about the value of the Irish rebellion. He saw his dreams of liberty blotted out in horror by "the innumerable clanging wings that have put out the moon." It brought him to the final conclusion of the futility of all discipline that is not of the whole being, and of "how base at moments of excitement are minds without culture"; but he remained a man to whom the life of action always meant something very real.

1. According to the writer of the paragraph, great poetry is   1.____
   MOST often produced by poets who
   A. are involved in the problems of life around them
   B. spend their time in contemplation
   C. drift away from the community
   D. break away from tradition
   E. take part in war

2. The writer implies that, as compared with older poetry,   2.____
   present-day poetry is more
   A. complete   B. romantic   C. alive
   D. ineffectual   E. comprehensive

3. Yeats was PRIMARILY a
   A. soldier   3.____
   C. dreamer   B. man of action
   E. politician   D. rigid disciplinarian

4. The theme of this paragraph is   4.____
   A. basis of true poetry
   B. the necessity of culture
   C. action versus contemplation
   D. Yeats as a poet and patriot
   E. Yeats' part in the Irish rebellion

TEST 8

Only twice in literary history has there been a great period of tragedy, in the Athens of Pericles and in Elizabethan England. What these two periods had in common, two thousand years and more apart in time, that they expressed themselves in the same fashion, may give us some hint of the nature of tragedy, for far from being periods of darkness and defeat, each was a time when life was seen exalted, a time of thrilling and unfathomable possibilities. They held their heads high, those men who conquered at Marathon and Salamis and those who fought Spain and saw the Great Armada sink. The world was a place of wonder; manking was beauteous; life was lived on the crest of the wave. More than all, the poignant joy of heroism had stirred men's hearts. Not stuff for tragedy, would you say? But on the crest of the wave, one must feel either tragically or joyously; one cannot feel tamely. The temper of mind that sees tragedy in life has not for its opposite the temper that sees joy. The opposite pole to the tragic view of life is the sordid view. When humanity is seen as devoid of dignity and significance, trivial, mean, and sunk in dreary hopelessness, then the spirit of tragedy departs.

1. In an age of glory, one   1.____
    A. is not indifferent
    B. usually feels tragic
    C. feels happy
    D. is apathetic
    E. feels mean and hopeless

2. The two periods in which great tragedies were written   2.____
    were periods of
    A. gloom   B. serenity   C. defeat
    D. confusion   E. valor

3. The mental attitude that finds tragedy in life is charac-   3.____
    terized by
    A. sordidness   B. indifference   C. exaltation
    D. triviality   E. hopelessness

4. The theme of this paragraph is   4.____
    A. two thousand years of tragedy
    B. Periclean Athens
    C. the tragedy of war
    D. the psychology of happiness
    E. mainsprings of tragic drama

8

TEST 9

There are few books which go with midnight, solitude, and a candle. It is much easier to say what does not please us then than what is exactly right. The book must be, anyhow, something benedictory by a sinning fellow man. Cleverness would be repellent at such an hour. Cleverness, anyhow, is the level of mediocrity today; we are all too infernally clever. The first witty and perverse paradox blows out the candle. Only the sick mind craves cleverness, as a morbid body turns to drink. The late candle throws its beams a great distance; and its rays make transparent much that seemed massy and important. The mind at rest beside that light, when the house is asleep, and the consequential affairs of the urgent world have diminished to their right proportions because we seem them distantly from another and a more tranquil place in the heavens, where duty, honor, witty arguments, controversial logic on great questions, appear such as will leave hardly a trace of fossil in the indurated mud which will cover them - the mind then smiles at cleverness. For though at that hour the body may be dog-tired, the mind is white and lucid, like that of a man from whom a fever has abated. It is bare of illusions. It has a sharp focus, small and starlike, as a clear and lonely flame left burning by the altar of a shrine from which all have gone but one. A book which approaches that light in the privacy of that place must come, as it were, with open and honest pages.

1. At midnight in the solitude of one's room, the mind is   1.___
   A. tired   B. keen   C. sick
   D. troubled   E. clever

2. The author considers the average book of today   2.___
   A. inane   B. sinful   C. benedictory
   D. restful   E. open and honest

3. Naming the qualities of a book suitable for reading when   3.___
   one retires is
   A. logical   B. a clever job
   C. difficult   D. like lighting a candle
   E. tiresome

4. To make good reading at bedtime, a book must be   4.___
   A. light   B. witty   C. controversial
   D. historical   E. straightforward

5. The theme of this paragraph is   5.___
   A. reading by candlelight
   B. books for convalescents
   C. not a time to read
   D. books for tired minds
   E. books for midnight reading

TEST 10

Few things are more stimulating than the sight of the forceful wings of large birds cleaving the vagueness of air and making the piled clouds a mere background for their concentrated life. The peregrine falcon, becalmed in the blue depths, cruises across space without a tremor of his wide wings. Wild geese beat up in the sky in a compact wedge. Primeval force is in their strongly moving wings and their beautiful, outstretched necks, in their power of untiring effort, and the eager search of their wild hearts for the free spaces they love. The good fellowship of swift, united action, the joy of ten thousand that move as one, is in the flight of flocks of birds. When seagulls flash up from the water with every wing at full stretch, there is no deliberation; it is as if each bird saw a sweeping arc before it and followed its individual way faithfully. The unerring judgment of the grand curve when the wings are so near and yet never collide, the speed of the descent, are pure poetry.

1. He admires the ability of seagulls to   1.____
    A. coordinate their flight   B. reach great heights
    C. stretch their wings   D. rise from the water
    E. dive swiftly

2. The flight of the wild goose, as compared with that of   2.____
    the falcon, is MORE
    A. active   B. beautiful   C. poetic
    D. deliberate   E. graceful

3. The author finds the sight of flying birds   3.____
    A. inspiring   B. awesome   C. joyful
    D. consoling   E. primitive

4. The author admires the falcon's   4.____
    A. wild freedom   B. effortless flight
    C. united action   D. primitive force
    E. unerring judgment

5. The theme of this paragraph is   5.____
    A. our wild birds   B. the superb falcon
    C. the beauty of flight   D. citizens of the sky
    E. the lure of the wild

TEST 11

As we know the short story today, it is largely a product of the nineteenth and twentieth centuries and its development parallels the rapid development of industrialism in America. We have been a busy people, busy principally in evolving a production system supremely efficient. Railroads and factories have blossomed almost overnight; mines and oil fields have been discovered and exploited;

mechanical inventions by the thousand have been made and perfected. Speed has been an essential element in our endeavors, and it has affected our lives, our very natures. Leisurely reading has been, for most Americans, impossible. As with our meals, we have grabbed bits of reading standing up, cafeteria style, and gulped down cups of sentiment on the run. We have had to read while hanging on to a strap in a swaying trolley car or in a rushing subway or while tending to a clamoring telephone switchboard. Our popular magazine has been our literary automat, and its stories have often been no more substantial than sandwiches.

1. From this selection, one would assume that the author's
   attitude toward short stories is one of   1.___
   A. approval   B. indifference   C. contempt
   D. impartiality   E. regret

2. The short story has developed because of Americans'   2.___
   A. reactions against the classics
   B. need for reassurance
   C. lack of culture
   D. lack of education
   E. taste for speed

3. The short story today owes its popularity to its   3.___
   A. settings   B. plots   C. style
   D. length   E. characters

4. The theme of this paragraph is   4.___
   A. *quick-lunch* literature
   B. life in the machine age
   C. culture in modern life
   D. reading while traveling
   E. the development of industrialism

TEST 12

If Shakespeare needs any excuse for the exuberance of his language (the high key in which he pitched most of his dramatic dialogue), it should be remembered that he was doing on the plastic stage of his own day what on the pictorial stage of our day is not so much required. Shakespeare's dramatic figures stood out on a platform-stage, without background, with the audience on three sides of it. And the whole of his atmosphere and environment had to come from the gestures and language of the actors. When they spoke, they provided their own scenery, which we now provide for them. They had to do a good deal more (when they spoke) than actors have to do today in order to give the setting. They carried the scenery on their backs, as it were, and spoke it in words.

1. The nature of the stage for which Shakespeare wrote made   1.____
    it necessary for him to
        A. employ only highly dramatic situations
        B. depend on scenery owned by the actors themselves
        C. have the actors shift the scenery
        D. create atmosphere through the dialogue
        E. restrict backgrounds to familiar types of scenes

2. In comparison with actors of Shakespeare's time, actors   2.____
    of today
        A. carry the settings in their words
        B. pitch their voices in a lower key
        C. depend more on elaborate settings
        D. have to do more to make the setting clear
        E. use many gestures

3. The theme of this paragraph is   3.____
        A. the scenery of the Elizabethan stage
        B. the importance of actors in the Shakespearean drama
        C. the influence of the Elizabethan stage on Shakespeare's
           style
        D. the importance of words
        E. suitable gestures for the Elizabethan stage

                            _____

TEST 13

It is no secret that I am not one of those naturalists who suffer
from cities, or affect to do so, nor do I find a city unnatural or
uninteresting, or a rubbish heap of follies. It has always seemed to
me that there is something more than mechanically admirable about a
train that arrives on time, a fire department that comes when you
call it, a light that leaps into the room at a touch, and a clinic
that will fight for the health of a penniless man and mass for him
the agencies of mercy, the x-ray, the precious radium, the anes-
thetics and the surgical skill. For, beyond any pay these services
receive, stands out the pride in perfect performance. And above all,
I admire the noble impersonality of civilization that does not
inquire where the recipient stands on religion or politics or race.
I call this beauty, and I call it spirit - not some mystical soul-
fulness that nobody can define, but the spirit of man, that has
been a million years a-growing.

1. The author implies that efficient operation of public   1.____
    utilities is
        A. expensive
        B. of no special interest
        C. admired by most naturalists
        D. mechanically commendable
        E. spiritual in quality

2. The aspect of city life MOST commendable to this author is its 2.___
   A. punctuality
   B. free benefits
   C. impartial service
   D. mechanical improvement
   E. health clinics

3. The author makes a defense of 3.___
   A. cities
   B. prompt trains
   C. rural life
   D. nature
   E. free clinics

4. The services rendered by city agencies are given 4.___
   A. only for pay
   B. on time
   C. only to people having a certain political allegiance
   D. to everybody
   E. to the spirit of man

5. The theme of this paragraph is 5.___
   A. the spirit of the city
   B. advantages of a city home
   C. disagreement among naturalists
   D. admirable characteristics of cities
   E. tolerance in the city

_____

TEST 14

The annual survey of chemistry published by the American Chemical Society attributes the vast change in warfare to the airplane and, above all, to the motor fuels of today. We never think of gasoline as an explosive, yet it has to some extent taken the place of the artillery propellants of a quarter of a century ago. A bomber is hardly a gun, but it certainly performs the function of one, with a range of many hundred miles.

About fifteen years ago, we began to hear of iso-octane, a fuel used to measure antiknock qualities of high-compression gasoline. It was ideal for airplanes but quantity production was not practical. Now we make lakes of it. Its performance is so remarkable that the planes propelled by it can carry loads that would have been inconceivable only ten years ago. As a result, octane numbers and indexes of antiknock properties have lost much of their former significance. It will probably be necessary to adopt some new standard. If we relate size and weight of engine to octane number, a truer picture of what aviation fuels really are is obtained. For each pound of weight, aviation engines of today produce, respectively, 100 percent and 50 percent more power than could those of 1918 and 1930.

13

1. The writer suggests that gasoline may be considered an
   explosive because
      A. it produces high compression
      B. modern bombing planes are essentially long-range guns
      C. guns now have greater range
      D. iso-octane is now manufactured in quantity
      E. it has replaced explosives in cannons

   1.___

2. The proposed standard for measuring the quality of motor
   fuels is the
      A. ratio of power to weight
      B. antiknock index
      C. iso-octane number
      D. load-carrying ability
      E. relation of engine weight and size to octane number

   2.___

3. Per pound of weight, the average engine now produces
      A. very much iso-octane
      B. high compression
      C. twice as much power as in 1930
      D. double the power of 1918
      E. 100 percent efficiency

   3.___

4. The theme of this selection is
      A. the chemist speeds the airplane
      B. mass production of iso-octane
      C. improving the gasoline engine
      D. changing methods in warfare
      E. gasoline as an explosive

   4.___

TEST 15

*Once the rivers of America slid undisturbed between their banks,
save when a birch canoe, manned by stolid Indians, sewed a narrow
seam in the water. Then came a day when our rivers were broad high-
ways filled with packets, lumber rafts, and houseboats. There were
years when the rivers languished, deserted by the great commerce
they had carried; years, too, of floods and devastation. Today,
there is a difference. Efforts are being made to tame the untamed,
to yoke the slow-sliding rivers to useful purpose. Dams are being
built that will end the tragic flooding of the lowlands. Wasteful
torrents are being taught economy, taught to irrigate the lands that
lie fallow, needing only water to bring them to fruitfulness. The
life-giving fluid to renewed utility is being fed into these rivers
of ours, and they are again becoming a vital and integral part of
our economy.*

1. A MAJOR reason for flood control is
      A. provision of suitable streams for the Indians
      B. profits for the public utilities
      C. conservation of farming areas
      D. relief of unemployment
      E. restoring river commerce

   1.___

14

2.   America's rivers have
      A. been a steady commercial asset
      B. helped protect us against invasion
      C. brought serious destruction through floods
      D. alternated frequently between periods of usefulness
         and of destruction or neglect
      E. suffered complete neglect as railroads developed

2.___

3.   Failing to utilize a country's rivers
      A. is economically wasteful
      B. makes the rivers sluggish
      C. restores their scenic beauty
      D. renews their picturesque traffic
      E. causes wasteful torrents

3.___

4.   For the safety of property and people, rivers must be
      A. made into highways
      B. used for irrigation
      C. allowed to lie fallow
      D. utilized for commerce
      E. brought under control

4.___

5.   The theme of this paragraph is
      A. from Indian canoe to modern boat
      B. conservation and our rivers
      C. the utility of water
      D. changing river traffic
      E. rivers, dams, and the public utilities

5.___

KEY (CORRECT ANSWERS)

TEST 1	TEST 2	TEST 3	TEST 4	TEST 5
1. E	1. E	1. A	1. E	1. C
2. B	2. B	2. B	2. C	2. D
3. C	3. D	3. D	3. D	3. C
	4. A		4. C	
	5. A			
	6. B			

TEST 6	TEST 7	TEST 8	TEST 9	TEST 10
1. A	1. A	1. A	1. B	1. A
2. A	2. D	2. E	2. A	2. A
3. D	3. B	3. C	3. C	3. A
4. B	4. D	4. E	4. E	4. B
5. C			5. E	5. C

TEST 11	TEST 12	TEST 13	TEST 14	TEST 15
1. E	1. D	1. E	1. B	1. C
2. E	2. C	2. C	2. E	2. C
3. D	3. C	3. A	3. D	3. A
4. A		4. D	4. A	4. E
		5. D		5. B

———

EXAMINATION SECTION

TEST 1

PASSAGE

The higher forms of plants and animals, such as seed plants and vertebrates, are similar or alike in many respects but decidedly different in others. For example, both of these groups of organisms carry on digestion, respiration, reproduction, conduction, growth, and exhibit sensitivity to various stimuli. On the other hand, a number of basic differences are evident. Plants have no excretory systems comparable to those of animals. Plants have no heart or similar pumping organ. Plants are very limited in their movements. Plants have nothing similar to the animal nervous system. In addition, animals cannot synthesize carbohydrates from inorganic substances. Animals do not have special regions of growth, comparable to terminal and lateral meristems in plants, which persist throughout the life span of the organism. And finally, the animal cell *wall* in only a membrane, while plant cell walls are more rigid, usually thicker, and may be composed of such substances as cellulose, lignin, pectin, cutin, and suberin. These characteristics are important to an understanding of living organisms and their functions and should, consequently, be carefully considered in plant and animal studies.

1. Which of the following do animals lack?
    A. Ability to react to stimuli
    B. Ability to conduct substances from one place to another
    C. Reproduction by gametes
    D. A cell membrane
    E. A terminal growth region

    1.___

2. Which of the following statements is FALSE?
    A. Animal cell *walls* are composed of cellulose.
    B. Plants grow as long as they live.
    C. Plants produce sperms and eggs.
    D. All vertebrates have hearts.
    E. Wood is dead at maturity.

    2.___

3. Respiration in plants take place
    A. only during the day
    B. only in the presence of carbon dioxide
    C. both day and night
    D. only at night
    E. only in the presence of certain stimuli

    3.___

4. An example of a vertebrate is the
    A. earthworm   B. starfish   C. amoeba
    D. cow   E. insect

    4.___

5. Which of the following statements is TRUE?
    A. All animals eat plants as a source of food.
    B. Respiration, in many ways, is the reverse of photosynthesis.
    C. Man is an invertebrate animal.

    5.___

D. Since plants have no hearts, they cannot develop high pressures in their cells.
E. Plants cannot move.

6. Which of the following do plants lack?   6._
    A. A means of movement
    B. Pumping structures
    C. Special regions of growth
    D. Reproduction by gametes
    E. A digestive process

7. A substance that can be synthesized by green plants but not   7._
   by animals is
    A. protein   B. cellulose   C. carbon dioxide
    D. uric acid   E. water

TEST 2

PASSAGE

The discovery of antitoxin and its specific antagonistic effect upon toxin furnished an opportunity for the accurate investigation of the relationship of a bacterial antigen and its antibody. Toxin-antitoxin reactions were the first immunological processes to which experimental precision could be applied, and the discovery of principles of great importance resulted from such studies. A great deal of the work was done with diphtheria toxin and antitoxin and the facts elucidated with these materials are in principle applicable to similar substances.

The simplest assumption to account for the manner in which an antitoxin renders a toxin innocuous would be that the antitoxin destroys the toxin. Roux and Buchner, however, advanced the opinion that the antitoxin did not act directly upon the toxin, but affected it indirectly through the mediation of tissue cells. Ehrlich, on the other hand, conceived the reaction of toxin and antitoxin as a direct union, analogous to the chemical neutralization of an acid by a base.

The conception of toxin destruction was conclusively refuted by the experiments of Calmette. This observer, working with snake poison found that the poison itself (unlike most other toxins) possessed the property of resisting heat to 100°C, while its specific antitoxin, like other antitoxins, was destroyed at or about 70°C. Nontoxic mixtures of the two substances, when subjected to heat, regained their toxic properties. The natural inference from these observations was that the toxin in the original mixture had not been destroyed, but had been merely inactivated by the presence of the antitoxin and again set free after destruction of the antitoxin by heat.

1. Both toxins and antitoxins ordinarily   1.___
   A. are completely destroyed at body temperatures
   B. are extremely resistant to heat
   C. can exist only in combination
   D. are destroyed at 180°F
   E. are products of nonliving processes

2. MOST toxins can be destroyed by   2.___
   A. bacterial action   B. salt solutions
   C. boiling   D. diphtheria antitoxin
   E. other toxins

3. Very few disease organisms release a true toxin into the   3.___
   bloodstream.
   It would follow, then, that
   A. studies of snake venom reactions have no value
   B. studies of toxin-antitoxin reactions are of little
      importance
   C. the treatment of most diseases must depend upon informa-
      tion obtained from study of a few
   D. antitoxin plays an important part in the body defense
      against the great majority of germs
   E. only toxin producers are dangerous

4. A person becomes susceptible to infection again immediately   4.___
   after recovering from
   A. mumps   B. tetanus   C. diphtheria
   D. smallpox   E. tuberculosis

5. City people are more frequently immune to communicable   5.___
   diseases than country people are because
   A. country people eat better food
   B. city doctors are better than country doctors
   C. the air is more healthful in the country
   D. country people have fewer contacts with disease carriers
   E. there are more doctors in the city than in the country

6. The substances that provide us with immunity to disease are   6.___
   found in the body in the
   A. blood serum   B. gastric juice
   C. urine   D. white blood cells
   E. red blood cells

7. A person ill with diphtheria would MOST likely be treated   7.___
   with
   A. diphtheria toxin   B. diphtheria toxoid
   C. dead diphtheria germs D. diphtheria antitoxin
   E. live diphtheria germs

8. To determine susceptibility to diphtheria, an individual   8.___
   may be given the _____ test.
   A. Wassermann   B. Schick   C. Widal
   D. Dick   E. Kahn

9. Since few babies under six months of age contract diphtheria, 9.__
   young babies PROBABLY
   A. are never exposed to diphtheria germs
   B. have high body temperatures that destroy the toxin if
      acquired
   C. acquire immunity from their mothers
   D. acquire immunity from their fathers
   E. are too young to become infected

10. Calmette's findings   10.__
    A. contradicted both Roux and Buchner's opinion and
       Ehrlich's conception
    B. contradicted Roux and Buchner, but supported Ehrlich
    C. contradicted Ehrlich, but supported Roux and Buchner
    D. were consistent with both theories
    E. had no bearing on the point at issue

TEST 3

PASSAGE

Sodium chloride, being by far the largest constituent of the
mineral matter of the blood, assumes special significance in the
regulation of water exchanges in the organism. And, as Cannon has
emphasized repeatedly, these latter are more extensive and more
important than may at first thought appear. He points out *there are
a number of circulations of the fluid out of the body and back again,
without loss.* Thus, for example, it is estimated that from a quart
and one-half of water daily *leaves the body* when it enters the mouth
as saliva, another one or two quarts are passed out as gastric juice,
and perhaps the same amount is contained in the bile and the secretions
of the pancreas and the intestinal wall. This large volume of water
enters the digestive processes; and practically all of it is reabsorbed through the intestinal wall, where it performs the equally
important function of carrying in the digestive foodstuffs. These
and other instances of what Cannon calls *the conservative use of
water in our bodies* involve essentially osmotic pressure relationships
in which the concentration of sodium chloride plays an important part.

1. This passage implies that   1.__
   A. the contents of the alimentary canal are not to be
      considered within the body
   B. sodium chloride does not actually enter the body
   C. every particle of water ingested is used over and over
      again
   D. water cannot be absorbed by the body unless it contains
      sodium chloride
   E. substances can pass through the intestinal wall in
      only one direction

2. According to this passage, which of the following processes   2.___
   requires most water?
   The
   A. absorption of digested foods
   B. secretion of gastric juice
   C. secretion of saliva
   D. production of bile
   E. concentration of sodium chloride solution

3. A body fluid that is NOT saline is   3.___
   A. blood   B. urine   C. bile
   D. gastric juice   E. saliva

4. An organ that functions as a storage reservoir from which   4.___
   large quantities of water are reabsorbed into the body is
   the
   A. kidney   B. liver   C. large intestine
   D. mouth   E. pancreas

5. Water is reabsorbed into the body by the process of   5.___
   A. secretion   B. excretion   C. digestion
   D. osmosis   E. oxidation

6. Digested food enters the body PRINCIPALLY through the   6.___
   A. mouth   B. liver   C. villi
   D. pancreas   E. stomach

7. The metallic element found in the blood in compound form   7.___
   and present there in larger quantities than any other
   metallic element is
   A. iron   B. calcium   C. magnesium
   D. chlorine   E. sodium

8. An organ that removes water from the body and prevents its   8.___
   reabsorption for use in the body processes is the
   A. pancreas   B. liver   C. small intestine
   D. lungs   E. large intestine

9. In which of the following processes is sodium chloride   9.___
   removed MOST rapidly from the body?.
   A. Digestion   B. Breathing   C. Oxidation
   D. Respiration   E. Perspiration

10. Which of the following liquids would pass from the   10.___
    alimentary canal into the blood MOST rapidly?
    A. A dilute solution of sodium chloride in water
    B. Gastric juice
    C. A concentrated solution of sodium chloride in water
    D. Digested food
    E. Distilled water

11. The reason why it is unsafe to drink ocean water even   11.___
     under conditions of extreme thirst is that it
       A. would reduce the salinity of the blood to a dangerous
          level
       B. contains dangerous disease germs
       C. contains poisonous salts
       D. would greatly increase the salinity of the blood
       E. would cause salt crystals to form in the bloodstream

TEST 4

PASSAGE

In the days of sailing ships, when voyages were long and uncertain provisions for many months were stored without refrigeration in the holds of the ships. Naturally, no fresh or perishable foods could be included. Toward the end of particularly long voyages, the crews of such ships became ill and often many died from scurvy. Many men, both scientific and otherwise, tried to devise a cure for scurvy. Among the latter was John Hall, a son-in-law of William Shakespeare, who cured some cases of scurvy by administering a sour brew made from scurvy grass and watercress.

The next step was the suggestion of William Harvey that scurvy could be prevented by giving the men lemon juice. He thought that the beneficial substance was the acid contained in the fruit.

The third step was taken by Dr. James Lind, an English naval surgeon, who performed the following experiment with 12 sailors, all of whom were sick with scurvy: Each was given the same diet, except that four of the men received small amounts of dilute sulfuric acid, four others were given vinegar, and the remaining four were given lemons. Only those who received the fruit recovered.

1. Credit for solving the problem described above belongs to   1.___
       A. Hall, because he first devised a cure for scurvy
       B. Harvey, because he first proposed a solution of the
          problem
       C. Lind, because he proved the solution by means of an
          experiment
       D. both Harvey and Lind, because they found that lemons
          are more effective than scurvy grass or watercress
       E. all three men, because each made some contribution

2. A good substitute for lemons in the treatment of scurvy is   2.___
       A. fresh eggs   B. tomato juice
       C. cod-liver oil   D. liver
       E. whole-wheat bread

3. The number of control groups that Dr. Lind used in his experiment was 3.____
   A. one   B. two   C. three   D. four   E. none

4. A substance that will turn blue litmus red is 4.____
   A. aniline   B. lye   C. ice
   D. vinegar   E. table salt

5. The hypothesis tested by Lind was: 5.____
   A. Lemons contain some substance not present in vinegar
   B. Citric acid is the most effective treatment for scurvy
   C. Lemons contain some unknown acid that will cure scurvy
   D. Some specific substance, rather than acids in general, is needed to cure scurvy
   E. The substance needed to cure scurvy is found only in lemons

6. A problem that Lind's experiment did NOT solve was: 6.____
   A. Will citric acid alone cure scurvy?
   B. Will lemons cure scurvy?
   C. Will either sulfuric acid or vinegar cure scurvy?
   D. Are all substances that contain acids equally effective as a treatment for scurvy?
   E. Are lemons more effective than either vinegar or sulfuric acid in the treatment of scurvy?

7. The PRIMARY purpose of a controlled scientific experiment is to 7.____
   A. get rid of superstitions
   B. prove a hypothesis is correct
   C. disprove a theory that is false
   D. determine whether a hypothesis is true or false
   E. discover new facts

TEST 5

PASSAGE

Photosynthesis is a complex process with many intermediate steps. Ideas differ greatly as to the details of these steps, but the general nature of the process and its outcome are well established. Water, usually from the soil, is conducted through the xylem of root, stem, and leaf to the chlorophyl-containing cells of a leaf. In consequence of the abundance of water within the latter cells, their walls are saturated with water. Carbon dioxide, diffusing from the air through the stomata and into the intercellular spaces of the leaf, comes into contact with the water in the walls of the cells which adjoin the intercellular spaces. The carbon dioxide becomes dissolved in the water in these walls, and in solution diffuses through the walls and the plasma membranes into the cells. By the agency of chlorophyl in

the chloroplasts of the cells, the energy of light is transformed
into chemical energy. This chemical energy is used to decompose the
carbon dioxide and water, and the products of their decomposition are
recombined into a new compound. The compound first formed is
successively built up into more and more complex substances until
finally a sugar is produced.

1. The union of carbon dioxide and water to form starch results   1.__
    in an excess of
        A. hydrogen   B. carbon
        C. oxygen   D. carbon monoxide
        E. hydrogen peroxide

2. Synthesis of carbohydrates takes place   2.__
        A. in the stomata
        B. in the intercellular spaces of leaves
        C. in the walls of plant cells
        D. within the plasma membranes of plant cells
        E. within plant cells that contain chloroplasts

3. In the process of photosynthesis, chlorophyl acts as a   3.__
        A. carbohydrate   B. source of carbon dioxide
        C. catalyst   D. source of chemical energy
        E. plasma membrane

4. In which of the following places are there the GREATEST   4.__
    number of hours in which photosynthesis can take place
    during the month of December?
        A. Buenos Aires, Argentina   B. Caracas, Venezuela
        C. Fairbanks, Alaska   D. Quito, Ecuador
        E. Calcutta, India

5. During photosynthesis, molecules of carbon dioxide enter   5.__
    the stomata of leaves because
        A. the molecules are already in motion
        B. they are forced through the stomata by the sun's rays
        C. chlorophyl attracts them
        D. a chemical change takes place in the stomata
        E. oxygen passes out through the stomata

6. Besides food manufacture, another useful result of photo-   6.__
    synthesis is that it
        A. aids in removing poisonous gases from the air
        B. helps to maintain the existing proportion of gases in
           the air
        C. changes complex compounds into simpler compounds
        D. changes certain waste products into hydrocarbons
        E. changes chlorophyl into useful substances

7. A process that is almost the exact reverse of photosynthesis   7.__
    is the
        A. rusting of iron   B. burning of wood
        C. digestion of starch   D. ripening of fruit
        E. storage of food in seeds

8. The leaf of the tomato plant will be unable to carry on
   photosynthesis if the
   A. upper surface of the leaf is coated with vaseline
   B. upper surface of the leaf is coated with lampblack
   C. lower surface of the leaf is coated with lard
   D. leaf is placed in an atmosphere of pure carbon dioxide
   E. entire leaf is coated with lime

8.____

TEST 6

PASSAGE

The British pressure suit was made in two pieces and joined around the middle in contrast to the other suits, which were one-piece suits with a removable helmet. Oxygen was supplied through a tube, and a container of soda lime absorbed carbon dioxide and water vapor. The pressure was adjusted to a maximum of 2½ pounds per square inch (130 millimeters) higher than the surrounding air. Since pure oxygen was used, this produced a partial pressure of 130 millimeters, which is sufficient to sustain the flier at any altitude.

Using this pressure suit, the British established a world's altitude record of 49,944 feet in 1936 and succeeded in raising it to 53,937 feet the following year. The pressure suit is a compromise solution to the altitude problem. Full sea-level pressure cannot be maintained, as the suit would be so rigid that the flier could not move arms or legs. Hence, a pressure one-third to one-fifth that of sea level has been used. Because of these lower pressures, oxygen has been used to raise the partial pressure of alveolar oxygen to normal.

1. The MAIN constituent of air not admitted to the pressure
   suit described was
   A. oxygen   B. nitrogen   C. water vapor
   D. carbon dioxide   E. hydrogen

1.____

2. The pressure within the suit exceeded that of the surround-
   ing air by an amount equal to 130 millimeters of
   A. mercury   B. water   C. air
   D. oxygen   E. carbon dioxide

2.____

3. The normal atmospheric pressure at sea level is _____ mm.
   A. 130   B. 250   C. 760   D. 1000   E. 1300

3.____

4. The water vapor that was absorbed by the soda lime came
   from
   A. condensation
   B. the union of oxygen with carbon dioxide
   C. body metabolism
   D. the air within the pressure suit
   E. water particles in the upper air

4.____

5. The HIGHEST altitude that has been reached with the
   British pressure suit is about _____ miles.
   A. 130   B. 2½   C. 6   D. 10   E. 5

5.__

6. If the pressure suit should develop a leak, the
   A. oxygen supply would be cut off
   B. suit would fill up with air instead of oxygen
   C. pressure within the suit would drop to zero
   D. pressure within the suit would drop to that of the
      surrounding air
   E. suit would become so rigid that the flier would be
      unable to move arms or legs

6.__

7. The reason why oxygen helmets are unsatisfactory for use
   in efforts to set higher altitude records is that
   A. it is impossible to maintain a tight enough fit at
      the neck
   B. oxygen helmets are too heavy
   C. they do not conserve the heat of the body as pressure
      suits do
   D. if a parachute jump becomes necessary, it cannot be
      made while such a helmet is being worn
   E. oxygen helmets are too rigid

7.__

8. The pressure suit is termed a compromise solution because
   A. it is not adequate for stratosphere flying
   B. aviators cannot stand sea-level pressure at high
      altitudes
   C. some suits are made in two pieces, others in one
   D. other factors than maintenance of pressure have to be
      accommodated
   E. full atmospheric pressure cannot be maintained at high
      altitudes

8.__

9. The passage implies that
   A. the air pressure at 49,944 feet is approximately the
      same as it is at 53,937 feet
   B. pressure cabin planes are not practical at extremely
      high altitudes
   C. a flier's oxygen requirement is approximately the same
      at high altitudes as it is at sea level
   D. one-piece pressure suits with removable helmets are
      unsafe
   E. a normal alveolar oxygen supply is maintained if the
      air pressure is between one-third and one-fifth that
      of sea level

9.__

TEST 7

PASSAGE

The formed elements of the blood are the red corpuscles or erythrocytes, the white corpuscles or leucocytes, the blood platelets, and the so-called blood dust or hemoconiae. Together, these constitute 30-40 percent by volume of the whole blood, the remainder being taken up by the plasma. In man, there are normally 5,000,000 red cells per cubic millimeter of blood; the count is somewhat lower in women. Variations occur frequently, especially after exercise or a heavy meal, or at high altitudes. Except in camels, which have elliptical corpuscles, the shape of the mammalian corpuscle is that of a circular, nonnucleated, bi-concave disk. The average diameter usually given is 7.7 microns, a value obtained by examining dried preparations of blood and considered by Ponder to be too low. Ponder's own observations, made on red cells in the fresh state, show the human corpuscle to have an average diameter of 8.8 microns. When circulating in the blood vessels, the red cell does not maintain a fixed shape but changes its form constantly, especially in the small capillaries. The red blood corpuscles are continually undergoing destruction, new corpuscles being formed to replace them. The average life of red corpuscles has been estimated by various investigators to be between three and six weeks. Preceding destruction, changes in the composition of the cells are believed to occur which render them less resistant. In the process of destruction, the lipids of the membrane are dissolved and the hemoglobin which is liberated is the most important, though probably not the only, source of bilirubin. The belief that the liver is the only site of red cell destruction is no longer generally held. The leucocytes, of which there are several forms, usually number between 7000 and 9000 per cubic millimeter of blood. These increase in number in disease, particularly when there is bacterial infection.

1. Leukemia is a disease involving the   1.___
   A. red cells   B. white cells   C. plasma
   D. blood platelets   E. blood dust

2. *The erythrocytes in the blood are increased in number after*   2.___
   a heavy meal.
   The paragraph implies that this
   A. is true
   B. holds only for camels
   C. is not true
   D. may be true
   E. depends on the number of white cells

3. When blood is dried, the red cells   3.___
   A. contract
   C. disintegrate   B. remain the same size
   E. become elliptical   D. expand

4. Ponder is PROBABLY classified as a professional   4.___
   A. pharmacist   B. physicist   C. psychologist
   D. physiologist   E. psychiatrist

5. The term *erythema*, when applied to skin conditions, signifies   5.__
    A. redness   B. swelling   C. irritation
    D. pain   E. roughness

6. Lipids are insoluble in water and soluble in such solvents   6.__
as ether, chloroform, and benzene.
It may be inferred that the membranes of red cells MOST
closely resemble
    A. egg white   B. sugar   C. bone
    D. butter   E. cotton fiber

7. Analysis of a sample of blood yields cell counts of   7.__
4,800,000 erythrocytes and 16,000 leucocytes per cubic
millimeter.
These data suggest that the patient from whom the blood
was taken
    A. is anemic
    B. has been injuriously invaded by germs
    C. has been exposed to high-pressure air
    D. has a normal cell count
    E. has lost a great deal of blood

8. Bilirubin, a bile pigment, is   8.__
    A. an end product of several different reactions
    B. formed only in the liver
    C. formed from the remnants of the cell membranes of
       erythrocytes
    D. derived from hemoglobin exclusively
    E. a precursor of hemoglobin

9. Bancroft found that the blood count of the natives in the   9.__
Peruvian Andes differed from that usually accepted as normal.
The blood PROBABLY differed in respect to
    A. leucocytes   B. blood platelets
    C. cell shapes   D. erythrocytes
    E. hemoconiae

10. Hemoglobin is probably NEVER found   10.__
    A. free in the bloodstream
    B. in the red cells
    C. in women's blood
    D. in the blood after exercise
    E. in the leucocytes

TEST 8

Chemical investigations show that during muscle contraction, the store of organic phosphates in the muscle fibers is altered as energy is released. In doing so, the organic phosphates (chiefly adenosine triphosphate and phospho-creatine) are transformed anaerobically to organic compounds plus phosphates. As soon as the organic phosphates begin to break down in muscle contraction, the glycogen in the muscle fibers also transforms into lactic acid plus free energy; this energy the muscle fiber uses to return the organic compounds plus phosphates into high-energy organic phosphates ready for another contraction. In the presence of oxygen, the lactic acid from the glycogen decomposition is changed also. About one-fifth of it is oxidized to form water and carbon dioxide and to yield another supply of energy. This time the energy is used to transform the remaining four-fifths of the lactic acid into glycogen again.

1. The energy for muscle contraction comes directly from the   1.___
   A. breakdown of the organic phosphates
   B. resynthesis of adenosine triphosphate
   C. breakdown of glycogen into lactic acid
   D. oxidation of lactic acid

2. Lactic acid does not accumulate in a muscle that is(has)   2.___
   A. in a state of lacking oxygen
   B. an ample supply of oxygen
   C. in a state of fatigue
   D. repeatedly being stimulated

3. The energy for the resynthesis of adenosine triphosphate   3.___
  and phosphocreatine comes from the
   A. oxidation of lactic acid
   B. synthesis of organic phosphates
   C. change from glycogen to lactic acid
   D. resynthesis of glycogen

4. The energy for the resynthesis of glycogen comes from the   4.___
   A. breakdown of organic phosphates
   B. resynthesis of organic phosphates
   C. change occurring in one-fifth of the lactic acid
   D. change occurring in four-fifths of the lactic acid

5. The breakdown of the organic phosphates into organic   5.___
  compounds plus phosphates is an _____ reaction.
   A. anabolic   B. aerobic
   C. endothermic   D. anaerobic

TEST 9

← DROP OF COLORED WATER
← AIR
← GLASS TUBE, SMALL BORE
← ONE-HOLE STOPPER

← THERMOS BOTTLE

1. The device shown in the diagram above indicates changes   1.__
   that are measured more accurately by a(n)
   A. thermometer   B. hygrometer   C. anemometer
   D. hydrometer   E. barometer

2. If the device is placed in a cold refrigerator for 72 hours,   2.__
   which of the following is MOST likely to happen?
   A. The stopper will be forced out of the bottle.
   B. The drop of water will evaporate.
   C. The drop will move downward.
   D. The drop will move upward.
   E. No change will take place.

3. When the device was carried in an elevator from the first   3.__
   floor to the sixth floor of a building, the drop of colored
   water moved about ¼ inch in the tube.
   Which of the following is MOST probably true?
   The drop moved
   A. downward because there was a decrease in the air
      pressure
   B. upward because there was an increase in the air pressure
   C. downward because there was an increase in the air
      temperature
   D. upward because there was an increase in the air
      temperature
   E. downward because there was an increase in the air
      temperature and a decrease in the pressure

4. The part of a thermos bottle into which liquids are poured   4.__
   consists of
   A. a single-walled, metal flask coated with silver
   B. two flasks, one of glass and one of silvered metal
   C. two silvered-glass flasks separated by a vacuum
   D. two silver flasks separated by a vacuum
   E. a single-walled, glass flask with a silver-colored
      coating

5. The thermos bottle is MOST similar in principle to
    A. the freezing unit in an electric refrigerator
    B. radiant heaters
    C. solar heating systems
    D. storm windows
    E. a thermostatically controlled heating system

        5.___

6. In a plane flying at an altitude where the air pressure is only half the normal pressure at sea level, the plane's altimeter should read approximately ____ feet.
    A. 3000   B. 9000   C. 18000   D. 27000   E. 60000

        6.___

7. Which of the following is the POOREST conductor of heat?
    A. Air under a pressure of 1.5 pounds per square inch
    B. Air under a pressure of 15 pounds per square inch
    C. Unsilvered glass
    D. Silvered glass
    E. Silver

        7.___

TEST 10

The latitude of any point on the earth's surface is the angle between a plumb line dropped to the center of the earth from that point and the plane of the earth's equator. Since it is impossible to go to the center of the earth to measure latitude, the latitude of any point may be determined indirectly as shown in the accompanying diagram.

It will be recalled that the axis of the earth, if extended outward, passes very near the North Star. Since the North Star is, for all practical purposes, infinitely distant, the line of sight to the North Star of an observer on the surface of the earth is virtually parallel with the earth's axis. Angle 1, then, in the diagram represents the angular distance of the North Star above the horizon.

Angle 2 is equal to angle 3, because when two parallel lines are
intersected by a straight line, the corresponding angles are equal.
Angle 1 plus angle 2 is a right angle and so is angle 3 plus angle 4.
Therefore, angle 1 equals angle 4 because when equals are subtracted
from equals, the results are equal.

1. If an observer finds that the angular distance of the North   1.__
    Star above the horizon is 30°, his latitude is _____°N.
        A. 15   B. 30   C. 60   D. 90   E. 120

2. To an observer on the equator, the North Star would be   2.__
    _____ the horizon.
        A. 30° above   B. 60° above   C. 90° above
        D. on   E. below

3. To an observer on the Arctic Circle, the North Star would be   3.__
        A. directly overhead   B. 23½° above the horizon
        C. 66½° above the horizon   D. on the horizon
        E. below the horizon

4. The distance around the earth along a certain parallel of   4.__
    latitude is 3600 miles.
    At that latitude, how many miles are there in one degree
    of longitude?
    _____ mile(s).
        A. 1   B. 10   C. 30   D. 69   E. 100

5. At which of the following latitudes would the sun be   5.__
    directly overhead at noon on June 21?
        A. 0°   B. 23½°S   C. 23½°N   D. 66½°N   E. 66½°S

6. On March 21, the number of hours of daylight at places on   6.__
    the Arctic Circle is
        A. none   B. 8   C. 12   D. 16   E. 24

7. The distance from the equator to the 45th parallel,   7.__
    measured along a meridian, is APPROXIMATELY _____ miles.
        A. 450   B. 900   C. 1250   D. 3125   E. 6250

8. The difference in time between the meridians that pass   8.__
    through longitude 45°E and longitude 105°W is _____ hours.
        A. 6   B. 2   C. 8   D. 4   E. 10

9. Which of the following is NOT a great circle or part of a   9.__
    great circle?
        A. Arctic Circle
        B. 100th meridian
        C. equator
        D. shortest distance between New York and London
        E. Greenwich meridian

10. At which of the following places does the sun set EARLIEST   10.__
    on June 21?
        A. Montreal, Canada   B. Santiago, Chile
        C. Mexico City, Mexico   D. Lima, Peru
        E. Manila, P.I.

KEY (CORRECT ANSWERS)

TEST 1	TEST 2	TEST 3	TEST 4	TEST 5
1. E	1. D	1. A	1. E	1. C
2. A	2. C	2. A	2. B	2. E
3. C	3. C	3. D	3. B	3. C
4. D	4. E	4. C	4. D	4. A
5. B	5. D	5. D	5. D	5. A
6. B			6. A	6. B
7. B	6. A	6. C	7. D	7. B
	7. D	7. E		8. C
	8. B	8. D		
	9. C	9. E		
	10. D	10. E		

TEST 6	TEST 7	TEST 8	TEST 9	TEST 10
1. B	1. B	1. A	1. A	1. B
2. A	2. D	2. B	2. C	2. D
3. C	3. A	3. C	3. B	3. C
4. C	4. D	4. C	4. C	4. B
5. D	5. A	5. D	5. D	5. C
6. D	6. D		6. C	6. C
7. D	7. B		7. A	7. D
8. E	8. A			8. E
9. C	9. D			9. A
	10. E			10. B

TEST 1

<u>PASSAGE</u>

Less than twenty years ago, a fabulous *new era* of medicine – or so it was supposed to be – was ushered in by the *wonder drugs*, the germkillers extraordinary. Here, it seemed, were the ultimate weapons that could rout hordes of pestilential bugs. Once and for all, there was to be an end to the menace of dozens of infectious diseases. It was a heady dream – but it grossly underestimated the enemy.

The infections are still with us. The bugs have been fighting back. Their counter-attacks, indeed, have sometimes been so vicious that scientists have been forced to go to new lengths to try to repulse them. The battle today seesaws.

One of the latest examples of bug turnabout was noted a few weeks ago when tuberculosis experts met at an isoniazid *reunion* luncheon to take a look at that drug – ten years after it had been hailed as the conqueror of TB and after the first desperately ill patients to receive it got up out of their beds and danced exuberantly in hospital corridors. Currently, as many as 6 percent of TB patients are beyond help by isoniazid – infected with strains of tubercle bacilli impervious to the drug – and resistance to isoniazid is growing.

The trend, not yet calamitous, follows explosive epidemics produced by *hospital staph* bacteria that sneer at penicillin and many other antibiotics. There have been – and continue to be – troubles with numerous other disease organisms despite, and even because of, antibiotics.

As early as 1954, University of Michigan physicians, noting the ability, evident even then, of some germs to live with highly vaunted antibiotics, suggested that *man may be sitting on a time bomb, capable of *** shattering the illusion of medical miracles****.

1. What is meant by the statement in the passage that *man may be sitting on a time bomb*?   1.___
   A. The *bugs* may progressively develop resistances to the drugs.
   B. The idea of medical miracles is an illusion.
   C. There is a great chance that TB could develop into a more difficult disease to treat.
   D. As the *bugs* get stronger, the disease becomes more prevalent.
   E. One day the miracle drugs which have been discovered will cause more harm than good.

2. *The bugs have been fighting back*, states the passage.   2.___
   This means:
   A. Higher doses of a particular drug become required.
   B. Patients develop an immunity to the disease.
   C. The *bugs* increase in number as a result of the drug.
   D. Some people have no reaction to the antibiotics.
   E. As the drugs become stronger, so do the *bugs*.

3. *Wonder drugs* are not the ultimate weapon because   3.___
   A. it remains for a drug to be discovered which the *bugs*
      cannot fight
   B. they only treat one disease, not all
   C. they are limited to certain people, i.e., many are
      allergic
   D. they sometimes carry their own diseases, with which
      they replace the ones they cure
   E. scientists deny the existence of a foreseeable day
      when the *ultimate weapon* against disease can be evolved

4. Wonder drugs were discovered   4.___
   A. by Jonas Salk
   B. 20 years ago
   C. less than two decades ago
   D. over a generation ago
   E. as a by-product of research done in nuclear physics

5. *Animalcules* is another word for   5.___
   A. antibiotics   B. bacteria   C. drugs
   D. penicillin   E. oreomycin

6. Scientists realistically predict the day when   6.___
   A. there will be no more disease
   B. better drugs will be made
   C. the *bugs* may develop a resistance to all antibiotics
   D. antibiotics will not be needed to cure disease
   E. all bacteria will be conquered

TEST 2

PASSAGE

BILLINGS, Mont. - A 60-year-old Montanan traced on a map the other
day the boundaries of the Bob Marshall Wilderness Area. As he lifted
his finger, a smile creased his face. He said:

*That's it. It has been pretty well explored for minerals, but
you never can tell when somebody might want to try something again.
Let's hope nobody can touch it now. It's something that should have
been done long ago.*

His reference was to the creation of the National Wilderness Preservation System, as set down in Public Law 88577, which went into effect September 3. The act is the compromise of a long and bitter fight to carve out of the national forests and other Federal lands a system that will, in the words of the legislation, *secure for the American people of present and future generations the benefits of an enduring resource of wilderness.*

The compromise was between conservationists and those who would put forest resources to commercial and other-than-wilderness uses.

It pins this down by its definition that a wilderness, *in contrast with those areas where man and his own works dominate the landscape, is hereby recognized as an area where the earth and the community of life are untrammeled by man, where man himself is a visitor who does not remain.*

1. The National Wilderness Preservation System was of great interest because it
   A. went into effect September 3
   B. was a compromise
   C. preserved an important resource
   D. worked hand-in-hand with commerce
   E. allowed for other-than-wilderness uses

   1.___

2. What is meant by the statement ....*somebody might want to try something again?*
   A. It might be tapped for minerals
   B. Some party might damage the property.
   C. The property's resources might be tapped for commercial purposes.
   D. Building might take place.
   E. The general public might cause forest fires or sanitation problems.

3. *Untrammeled* means
   A. not trampled on
   B. not traveled
   C. something uninvestigated by man
   D. something abused by man
   E. something left in its original condition

   3.___

4. After reading the passage, one gets the impression that the author
   A. appreciates the beauty of nature
   B. understands the needs of commerce in relation to natural resources
   C. is engaged in a bitter fight
   D. will secure for the American people an enduring wilderness
   E. is on the side of the conservationists

   4.___

5. A good title for this passage would be
   A. THE BOUNDARIES OF THE WILDERNESS
   B. EXPLORING FOR MINERALS
   C. SAVING THE WILDS
   D. HOW COMMERCE MAKES USE OF NATURAL RESOURCES
   E. THE WILDERNESS

5.__

6. The TVA, a conservation act, was enacted during the
   Presidency of
   A. Theodore Roosevelt   B. Woodrow Wilson
   C. Dwight D. Eisenhower   D. Franklin D. Roosevelt
   E. Harry Truman

6.__

TEST 3

PASSAGE

Where others saw unrelated, individually created flowers or birds
or people, he saw a mass of altering, dissolving, and interrelated
forms flowing onward through earth's history. Living creatures were
like cloud shapes contorted by the winds of time. As it happens, the
years have proved him right.

What made Darwin a scientist? Let us ask again in particular
because by modern school standards and measurements he was not a very
good pupil, let alone a candidate for genius. His career was undecided
he dawdled and misspelled words, enraged his father and, giving up a
career in medicine, was packed off to Cambridge with the notion that
he might at least learn enough to become a country parson.

We cannot analyze Darwin's entire life, but we can say that his
quoted letter to Joseph Hooker is enormously important and revelatory.
Charles Darwin was a millionaire of facts but they happened not to be
the facts in which the schools of his day were interested. Indeed,
he spoke of his Cambridge studies as *next thing to intolerable.* As a
result, his formal educational career was no measure of his real
capacities. Later, as he remembered his experience in South America,
he was to speak of lonely desert travels in which *the whole of my
pleasure was derived from what passed in my mind.*

Yet the influences at work upon him were not all of a solitary
character. His grandfather Erasmus had entertained evolutionary ideas
about which Charles had learned as a youth; a kindly botanist, John
Henslow, had obtained for him his post as naturalist on the Beagle.
On the outward voyage to South America, Darwin had read Sir Charles
Lyell's PRINCIPLES OF GEOLOGY and been convinced by Lyell's then-
heretical views that the earth was extremely ancient - a necessary
prelude to grasping the slow pace of plant and animal evolution.

1. As opposed to the individually created flowers or birds, Darwin saw   1.___
    A. living creatures
    B. masses of altering and dissolving cloud shapes
    C. interrelated forms
    D. people
    E. winds of time

2. The reader can assume from the passage that the author feels a formal education is   2.___
    A. necessary even for a candidate for genius
    B. what made Darwin a scientist
    C. not always a measure of real capacities
    D. necessary for a scientist
    E. not able to help a pupil beyond his potential

3. His first ideas about evolution may well have come from   3.___
    A. his grandfather
    B. Joseph Hooker
    C. John Henslow
    D. PRINCIPLES OF GEOLOGY
    E. his voyage to South America

4. Sir Charles Lyell's ideas were   4.___
    A. about animal evolution
    B. about plant life
    C. unaccepted by his period
    D. Darwin's primary inspiration
    E. extremely ancient

5. A work of Darwin's is   5.___
    A. ZOOLOGY OF THE VOYAGE OF THE BEAGLE
    B. ON THE TENDENCY OF VARIETIES TO DEPART INDEFINITELY FROM THE ORIGINAL TYPE
    C. TRAVELS ON THE AMAZON AND THE RIO NEGRO
    D. THE BOTANIC GARDEN
    E. ZOONOMIA

6. The famous Scopes trial brought him into conflict with   6.___
    A. William Jennings Bryan   B. Clarence Darrow
    C. the State of Tennessee   D. J.T. Scopes
    E. the State of Kentucky

TEST 4

PASSAGE

The most fascinating thing about a greenhouse is the opportunity provided for growing unusual plants. A greenhouse gardener need not limit himself to the plants he once grew in his home. He can branch out to plants from all over the world - depending on the temperature maintained in the greenhouse.

In a greenhouse where the temperature is kept just above freezing, alpine plants can be grown. Edelweiss, bottle gentian, creeping phlox, and columbines like Aquilegia akitensis and A. flabellata are just a few of the candidates. A book on rock gardening or a catalogue from a specialist nursery will suggest many other plants. A practical advantage to growing these cold-greenhouse plants is the saving on wintertime fuel bills.

Under warmer conditions, many kinds of dwarf shrubs will be fun to grow. Do not overlook some of the berried kinds like pyracantha Victory, which is hardy outdoors only about as far north as Zone 7. Tender shrubs and trees such as kumquat, calamondin orange, and dwarf lemon are satisfying to grow, for they will often have flowers and fruit at the same time.

The charming wax plant, Hoya oarnosa, develops beautifully in a warm greenhouse. Others are hibiscus, lantana, oleander, and osmanthus or sweet olive.

1. According to the passage, kumquat is a
   A. sturdy shrub
   B. dwarfed plant
   C. tender shrub
   D. fruit
   E. form of berry

1.__

2. An oleander develops
   A. in a warm greenhouse
   B. in a cold greenhouse
   C. outdoors in a southern climate
   D. well in the home
   E. in a northern climate

2.__

3. The advantage to growing plants like edelweiss in the wintertime is
   A. they are far more attractive plants than most
   B. they are too fragile for summer cultivation
   C. temperature
   D. the saving on fuel bills
   E. that they are an alpine plant

3.__

4. A good title for the passage might be
   A. HOW TO GROW NORTHERN PLANTS
   B. HOW TO GROW TROPICAL PLANTS
   C. THE FLORIDIAN PLANTS: HIBISCUS, OLEANDER, LANTANA
   D. HOW TO GROW CITRUS IN A GREENHOUSE
   E. CANDIDATES FOR A GREENHOUSE

4.__

5. Broadly, the subject covered in the passage would come
   under the heading of
      A. botany   B. nurseries
      C. gardens   D. rock gardening
      E. pyracantha

   5.____

6. A flowering plant, discovered by an American traveling in
   Mexico, and destined to become our most popular Christmas
   plant, thanks to the temperature control of the greenhouse, is the
      A. mistletoe   B. philodendron
      C. poinsettia   D. rhododendron
      E. hibiscus

   6.____

TEST 5

PASSAGE

In a provocative series of experiments, a team of scientists at Western Reserve University in Cleveland has developed techniques to remove the brain of a monkey from its body and keep it alive for many hours. Bare except for two small bits of bone to help support it, the nerves and blood vessels that once connected it to the monkey's body severed, the brain is suspended above a laboratory table. Attached to it are the tubes of a mechanical heart to maintain its blood supply; from it run wires to recording instruments. Their measurements of its electrical activity not only show that it remains alive but even suggest that sometimes this isolated brain is conscious.

While the immediate goal of the team, headed by Dr. Robert J. White, is the development of methods for obtaining answers to basic questions related to the physiology of the brain, one cannot help being fascinated by less specifically scientific, but perhaps more profoundly philosophic, considerations. Can the truly *detached minds* of the Cleveland monkeys really be conscious? If so, conscious of what?

Sensation, for example, is an important ingredient of the conscious state. Does biological science give us any clues as to what sensations, if any, the conscious incorporeal brains of the Western Reserve monkeys could have felt? After all, the nerves that normally carry to the brain indications of touch, taste, odor, light, and sound were all cut, and the associated sensory organs were far removed. Does this mean that, during its conscious periods, the isolated monkey brain floated in a sensory void, with no flashes of touch, pain, sight, or sound to remind it of the kind of existence it once knew?

1. What is used by the scientists to support the brain?   1.__
   A. Nerves and blood vessels that once connected it to
      the monkey's body
   B. Two small bits of bone
   C. A mechanical heart
   D. A laboratory table
   E. The tubes of the mechanical heart

2. The suggestion that the brain is sometimes conscious comes   2.__
   from
   A. the measurements on the recording instruments
   B. associated sensory organs
   C. the memory of the kind of existence it once knew
   D. the maintenance of its blood supply
   E. the mechanical heart

3. By the term *incorporeal brains*, the author means   3.__
   A. brains without nerves
   B. brains with mechanical tubes
   C. brains in a sensory void
   D. that the brain, though isolated, has artificial
      support
   E. disembodied brains

4. The author states that the brain can be kept alive   4.__
   A. indefinitely
   B. until it normally expires corporeally
   C. until the mechanical heart fails
   D. a few minutes
   E. for many hours

5. Scientists, by such experiments as these, are PROBABLY   5.__
   trying to determine
   A. how certain parts of the brain can be mechanically
      replaced
   B. how the brain feels and thinks
   C. whether the brain of a monkey is superior to the
      human brain
   D. how they might duplicate this experiment with a human
      brain
   E. how long brains can be kept alive without their bodies

6. A part of the brain called the brainstem is   6.__
   A. the seat of mental activity
   B. the coordinator of muscular activity
   C. an extension of the spinal cord
   D. the mantle that fits the skull
   E. controller of voluntary action and the senses

7. The cerebral cortex is   7.__
   A. divided into two equal hemispheres
   B. that part of the brain through which all nerve impulses
      are channeled
   C. that part which controls breathing
   D. that part which controls heartbeat
   E. that part which generates feelings, i.e., hunger,
      anger, pleasure

TEST 6

PASSAGE

The highest honors bestowed in the world of science were given last Thursday to an American, two Russians, and a British woman.

The Nobel Prize in physics was shared by Dr. Charles H. Townes, now provost of the Massachusetts Institute of Technology, and Drs. N.G. Basov and A.M. Prokhorov of the Soviet Union. The three men, during the early nineteen fifties, paved the way for a major invention: the maser. Dr. Townes also helped show how the maser principle could be applied to light, resulting in discovery of the laser.

The Nobel Prize in chemistry went to Mrs. Dorothy C. Hodgkin of Great Britain for her work in deciphering the structure of such complex molecules as those of penicillin and vitamin B-12. The latter is vital in treating a fatal form of pernicious anemia. Its structure was spelled out after eight years of work. *Never before*, the award announcement said, *has it been possible to determine the precise structure of so large a molecule.*

The analyses were performed by shining x-rays through crystals of the substance in question and recording the manner in which the rays were diffracted by the crystal structure.

Applied light was first achieved by Dr. Townes and his colleagues at Columbia University at a radar or *microwave* frequency. Hence, they called it *microwave amplification by stimulated emission of radiation*, or, more briefly, the maser, from the initials of these words.

When the same principle was applied to the production of intense light, it was called an optical maser or *laser*.

One of the earliest applications of the maser was to increase many-fold the sensitivity of radar systems used to detect distant missiles.

1. The invention of the maser   1.____
   A. occurred in Great Britain
   B. made it possible to determine the precise structure of a molecule
   C. was related to the work of Drs. Basov, Townes, and Prokhorov
   D. was the work of Mrs. Dorothy C. Hodgkin
   E. was the work of Dr. Charles H. Townes

2. Vital in treating a form of pernicious anemia is   2.____
   A. deciphering the structure of complex molecules
   B. vitamin B-12
   C. the analysis performed by shining x-rays through crystals
   D. recording the manner in which the rays are defracted
   E. penicillin

3. The *laser* got its name from the
   A. microwave amplification by stimulated emission of
      radiation
   B. initials of its earliest application
   C. initials of the principle of the laser applied to
      light
   D. application of the maser to increase the sensitivity
      of radar systems
   E. optical laser

3.___

4. The Nobel Prize in physics was
   A. given for the work of deciphering the structure of
      molecules
   B. given for the invention of the laser
   C. given to Mrs. D.C. Hodgkin
   D. shared
   E. given to Drs. Basov and Prokhorov

4.___

5. The above passage might be found in a(n)
   A. scientific journal dealing with nuclear physics
   B. article on the detection of missiles
   C. brochure from the Massachusetts Institute of Technology
   D. article in a medical journal on the treatment of
      pernicious anemia
   E. article on Nobel Prize winners

5.___

6. A word MOST CLOSELY related to amplification is
   A. stimulation   B. enlargement
   C. emission   D. light
   E. radiation

6.___

TEST 7

PASSAGE

Thus for most of the earth's history, life, in the form of
primitive algae, fungi, and bacteria, had little more than a toehold
in these pools. The oldest fossil evidence of such algae dates back
two or three billion years, yet diverse, large scale life forms did
not appear in the fossil record until some 600 million years ago.

It is this sudden appearance of diverse life that has puzzled
scientists. The assumption has been that the earlier record was
destroyed or that previous life forms did not have shells or skeletons
hard enough to leave a record. Yet soft plants and animals also
leave their prints in the sands of time and they, too, were absent.

What really happened, according to the new hypothesis, was that
when volcanic growth produced continents, and hence shallow pools of
considerable extent, the pond-bottom plants slowly raised the oxygen
content of the air until, at one percent of the present level, it

was sufficient to filter out almost all the lethal ultraviolet. The latter, henceforth, could poison only the top few inches of the oceans and life, which had been hardly more than microscopic, erupted in all evolutionary directions.

The eruption of oceanic life increased photosynthesis and the oxygen level rose high enough to make the dry land habitable. This led to great forests and photosynthesis became so extensive that there was perhaps ten times as much oxygen in the air as today. The carbon dioxide of the air, that acts like the glass of a greenhouse in keeping the earth warm, was depleted, and the Permian ice ages of 250 million years ago resulted.

1. An example of algae is   1.___
        A. a form of mushroom plant   B. fossiliferous
        C. seaweed   D. a form of bacteria
        E. cryptogamous plants

2. The scientists were puzzled because   2.___
        A. of the production of shallow pools
        B. of the evidences of fossiliferous life prior to 600
           million years ago
        C. they did not feel that the oldest forms of life did
           not have hard shells or skeletons
        D. they did not think volcanic growth produced continents
        E. they did not understand how plants could lower the
           oxygen content of the air

3. Continents were produced by   3.___
        A. fermentation   B. a high level of oxygen
        C. photosynthesis   D. volcanic growth
        E. the Permian ice ages

4. How could the ultraviolet poison only the top few inches   4.___
    of the oceans and life?
    Because
        A. salt water reflects the rays
        B. ultraviolet rays are poisonous to certain ocean plants
        C. the pond-bottom plants raised the oxygen content of
           the air
        D. the pond-bottom plants acted as a filter
        E. ultraviolet cannot penetrate below the ocean's surface

5. Ultraviolet rays are   5.___
        A. the strongest rays of the sun
        B. rays within the violet of the visible spectrum
        C. the rays of the sun which promote growth
        D. rays beyond the violet of the visible spectrum
        E. those rays which are attracted by salt or fresh water

6. Photosynthesis is the   6.__
   A. growth from within plant or animal life
   B. process by which plants manufacture food for their
      growth with the aid of light
   C. impulse of fluids to mix and become diffused through
      each other
   D. tendency of elements to pass through one another with
      unequal rapidity
   E. pressures produced by osmosis

—

TEST 8

PASSAGE

The discovery and use of metals was one of the crucial steps
that put mankind on the long road to modern civilization.

New clues to the discovery were reported last week. They suggest
that men were taking the first steps toward use of metal a millennium
earlier than the dawn of real metallurgy. The clues are little bits
of copper that appear to have been cold-hammered into shape as pins,
a drill, and a sharply bent hook nearly 9,000 years ago by an
artisan in one of man's earliest villages.

The copper specimens were discovered last summer by a team
excavating an ancient village site at Cayonu, in southeastern Turkey.

Co-directors of the expedition that made the discoveries were
Prof. Hale Cambel, from the University of Istanbul, and Prof. Robert
J. Braidwood of the Oriental Institute and Department of Anthropology,
University of Chicago.

In a telephone interview last week, Professor Braidwood said all
the evidence indicates that the stone dwelling in which the tools
were found was nearly 9,000 years old.

In the Shanidar Valley of northern Iraq, scientists from
Columbia University independently have found a specimen that also
seems to be cold-hammered copper and suggests the same conclusion as
that reached by Professor Braidwood and his colleagues.

1. The discovery of the cold-hammered copper specimens was made 1.__
   A. in southwestern Turkey   B. 9,000 years ago
   C. in Istanbul   D. in the Shanidar Valley
   E. on the African continent

2. Why does the author suggest that metal was used before the   2.__
   dawn of real metallurgy?
   Because
   A. the scientists found evidences of copper

    B. the scientists found evidences of cold-hammers
    C. there was evidence of life in the site at Cayonu
    D. they assumed that people must have lived in Cayonu
       9,000 years ago
    E. the scientists found copper worked into certain forms

3. Metallurgy is the   3.___
    A. discovery of metals
    B. discovery of minerals that could be worked into metals
    C. discovery of ore
    D. art of working metals
    E. application of metals to the body

4. A millennium is _____ years.   4.___
    A. thousands of
    B. a few thousand
    C. several thousand
    D. a thousand
    E. an incalculable number of

5. The dominant religion of Turkey today is   5.___
    A. Moslem   B. Hebrew
    C. Islam   D. Buddhist
    E. Greek Orthodox

6. The capital of Turkey today is   6.___
    A. Istanbul   B. Ankara
    C. Constantinople   D. Smyrna
    E. Izmir

TEST 9

PASSAGE

    A radically new concept of evolution is being discussed in
scientific circles. As presented by two Texans, it would explain the
chief puzzle in the record of life's history on earth: the sudden
appearance, some 600 million years ago, of most basic divisions of
the plant and animal kingdoms.

    There is virtually no record of how these divisions came about.
Thus, the entire first part of evolutionary history is missing.

    The theory says that evolution of a large proportion of the diverse
species that have inhabited the earth - plants, fish, trees, and so
forth - took place in two gigantic *revolutions* of comparatively short
duration.

    There is now general agreement that the earth was born as barren
of an atmosphere as is the moon today, but volcanoes poured out gases,
including an abundance of water vapor - enough to fill the oceans and
produce an envelope of *air*.

It is agreed that the early air was radically different from that of today. Volcanoes do not produce oxygen gas, and the early air was dominated by hydrogen compounds. Hence, it was transparent to ultraviolet sunlight that no longer reaches the earth. Recent observations in space have documented the nature of sunlight before filtering by the atmosphere. It is clearly rich in wavelengths of ultraviolet that are lethal to all known forms of life.

This light not only penetrated the original air, but even pierced the top 15 to 30 feet of the oceans.

Since oceanic water circulates, any drifting life would have been carried into the layer bathed in ultraviolet. Hence, it seems unlikely to Drs. Berkner and Marshall that life could have originated in the oceans. Instead, they believe it probably sprang forth independently on the bottoms of numerous deep pools, possibly warmed by the volcanic activity widespread at that time.

1. The earth, at its beginning,   1.__
   A. contained craters like the moon
   B. was barren
   C. was fertile
   D. had animal and plant life only in its oceans
   E. had only plants, fish, and trees

2. The doctors mentioned in the passage seem to believe that   2.__
   A. life could have originated in the oceans
   B. life came about as the volcanoes poured out gases
   C. a gigantic revolution took place before a large pro-
      portion of the diverse species could inhabit the earth
   D. life sprang forth from numerous deep pools
   E. oceanic water, at the beginning, did not circulate

3. How was the volcanic air different from that of today?   3.__
   A. It did not come from volcanoes.
   B. The gases did not contain water vapor.
   C. It was dominated by oxygen.
   D. Ultraviolet light could easily penetrate it.
   E. It was not dominated by hydrogen compounds.

4. The air of today can filter ultraviolet rays because   4.__
   A. there are no more volcanoes
   B. they are absorbed by the earth
   C. of its oxygen content
   D. of its hydrogen content
   E. the ocean absorbs them

5. The BEST definition of an hypothesis is a(n)   5.__
   A. theory or formula derived by inference
   B. tentative assumption made in order to draw out and test
      its logical or empirical consequences
   C. assumption made in the form of a concession
   D. interpretation of a practical situation or condition
      taken as the ground for action
   E. statement of order and relation in nature that has been
      found to be invariable under the same conditions

6. In relation to the content of the passage, the BEST defini-   6.____
   tion of air is the(a)
   A. mixture of invisible gases which surround the earth
   B. surrounding or pervading influence
   C. medium of transmission
   D. compound of 2 parts hydrogen and 1 part oxygen
   E. volcanic gas

TEST 10
PASSAGE

Some 25,000 infants suffocate each year in the United States alone. The infants, most of them premature, turn blue and choke and die.

They die from something that is not to this day in most current medical directories, dictionaries, or guides. It is a mysterious condition called hyaline membrane disease. Many years ago this disease killed Patrick Bouvier, the younger son of John F. Kennedy, and it usually kills about half of the infants it strikes.

About 2,000 of the nation's pathologists met in Miami this week for the joint annual session of the College of American Pathologists and the American Society of Clinical Pathologists. They heard a report suggesting that a cure for hyaline membrane has been found.

It was through a series of autopsies of 150 infants who died of hyaline membrane disease that the new treatment for this disease evolved.

The study was done by a Louisville pathologist, Dr. Daniel Stowens, Director of Laboratories at Children's Hospital.

From his autopsies, Dr. Stowens determined that babies who are victims of hyaline membrane disease had too much water in their bodies. The baby's major organ systems may be all right. But they attempt to get rid of the water through the lungs. This clogs these organs and prevents the normal absorption of oxygen into the blood. So the babies die.

There are many complicated theories about how hyaline membrane disease blocks the lungs. The new simple theory had led to a simple therapy.

It is the use of two epsom salts enemas. The first enema clears away the mucus; the second, which relies on epsom salts' affinity for water, draws fluid away from the lungs.

Dr. Stowens reported that gasping and choking babies have been dramatically relieved of their symptoms in a matter of a few minutes after the treatment. In the last eight months, 28 babies suffering from hyaline membrane disease have been treated by epsom salts enemas in five Louisville hospitals, and all are reported to be alive today.

1. The babies who are victims of hyaline membrane disease die   1.__
    because they
       A. are organically defective
       B. absorb oxygen into the blood
       C. lack sufficient water in their system
       D. get rid of excess water through their lungs
       E. do not attempt to get rid of the excess water in their
          system

2. Before the new method of treating the disease was dis-   2.__
    covered, it
       A. was always fatal
       B. killed half the infants it struck
       C. killed 25,000 infants a year all over the world
       D. killed 2,000 infants in the United States every year
       E. killed 150 infants a year

3. The success of the new method seems to   3.__
       A. be unpredictable
       B. be perfected
       C. involve some risk
       D. be disapproved of in some medical circles
       E. depend on the baby treated

4. The cause of death from hyaline membrane is   4.__
       A. the bloodstream   B. the lungs
       C. the membrane   D. suffocation
       E. the heart

5. Dr. Stowens might rightfully be compared to   5.__
       A. Dr. Spock
       B. the polio vaccine
       C. Dr. Teller
       D. Dr. Salk
       E. the hyaline membrane disease

6. Prior to the discovery of the therapy,   6.__
       A. there existed a simple theory about it
       B. hyaline membrane disease was not treated
       C. there was no theory on how to treat it
       D. the theories about causes were many and recondite
       E. there was a simple therapy

7. The new theory   7.__
       A. does not use epsom salts
       B. does not use water
       C. delivers fluid to the lungs
       D. relies on the affinity between epsom salts and water
       E. use various epsom salts enemas

8. With the new therapy, babies   8.__
       A. gasp and choke
       B. have been treated over the last 12 months
       C. are relieved of their symptoms in a matter of minutes
       D. are relieved of their symptoms in a few hours
       E. have now been treated in 28 hospitals

9. A pathologist is
   A. a doctor
   B. a specialist in children's diseases
   C. usually a pediatrician
   D. one versed in the nature of respiratory ailments
   E. one versed in the nature of diseases

9.____

————

KEY (CORRECT ANSWERS)

TEST 1

1. A	4. C
2. E	5. B
3. A	6. C

EXPLANATION OF ANSWERS

1. CORRECT ANSWER: A
    B is irrelevant; C is not stated; D is not stated or implied;
    E is pure conjecture and not inferred in the passage.

2. CORRECT ANSWER: E
    Items A and D are sometimes true but bear no relation to the
    question. C is false. Patients may develop an immunity to the
    antibiotics, but never to the disease. Therefore, B is false.
    The proper answer is E: *The battle today seesaws* (last sentence
    of the second paragraph).

3. CORRECT ANSWER: A
    While B and C are factually true, they do not satisfactorily
    complete the statement. D is scientifically unknown as yet.
    Item E is false. The correct answer is A (see the last sentence
    of the first paragraph).

4. CORRECT ANSWER: C
    The opening sentence is *Less than 20 years ago....a....'new
    era'....was ushered in by the 'wonder drugs'*. Therefore, C
    is the correct answer. The other answers are false.

5. CORRECT ANSWER: B
    Animalcules is a synonym for bacteria. Therefore, B is the
    proper answer. The other answers are completely incorrect as
    they are the substances which fight bacteria.

6. CORRECT ANSWER: C
    Though scientists are working constantly to perfect superior
    drugs, it has been their experience that the *bugs* are progressing
    in strength faster than the drugs can be improved. (See,
    particularly, the last paragraph.) Therefore, the correct answer
    is C.

TEST 2

1. C	4. E
2. C	5. C
3. E	6. D

EXPLANATION OF ANSWERS

1. CORRECT ANSWER: C
Item C is the correct answer, and it is clearly delineated in the quotation contained in paragraph 3, viz., ...*secure for the American people....an enduring resource of wilderness.*

2. CORRECT ANSWER: C
When the speaker says, *It has been pretty well explored for minerals, but you never can tell when somebody might want to try something again,* he is referring to a similar possibility of an exploitation by industry. This would designate C as the proper answer. Though B, D, and E are possible occurrences, he is not, in this statement, referring to these.

3. CORRECT ANSWER: E
The last clause of the passage indicates that A, B, and C are incorrect because man can visit a wilderness area and leave it *untrammeled.* D is incorrect because it infers the opposite of the word's correct meaning.

4. CORRECT ANSWER: E
The passage is not about the author's love of nature or the needs of commerce, nor does his work match the events or aims suggested in C and D. E would be most suited to his position on natural resources, and is the correct answer.

5. CORRECT ANSWER: C
The best answer presented here would be C. The theme of the passage is in no way related to items B and D. A and E could be considered, but C is much more directly related to the passage.

6. CORRECT ANSWER: D
The correct answer is D, Franklin Roosevelt (1933).

TEST 3

1. C	4. C
2. C	5. A
3. A	6. C

EXPLANATION OF ANSWERS

1. CORRECT ANSWER: C
He saw, states the passage (sentence 1), *altering, dissolving, and interrelated forms flowing onward through earth's history.* And as he saw these things, he was envisioning the relationships of all living things. He seemed to see, implies the author, no one thing independent of another. C, then, is the proper answer.

2.   CORRECT ANSWER: C
Judging from Darwin's various failures and indecisions discussed
in paragraph 2, the reader can only accept C as the correct
completion of the statement. While A, D, and E are probably
acceptable statements in themselves, they have nothing to do
with the man about whom the author is writing. B, apparently,
is not the opinion of the author.

3.   CORRECT ANSWER: A
The evolutionary ideas about which he learned as a youth came
from his grandfather long before, presumably, his many other
influences. Therefore, A must be the correct answer.

4.   CORRECT ANSWER: C
The last paragraph mentions *Lyell's then-heretical views*....
Therefore, C is the only possible answer. Item D is not
indicated in the passage, and A, B, and E are false.

5.   CORRECT ANSWER: A
Items D and E were works of Erasmus Darwin, grandfather of Charles
Items B and C are the works of Alfred Russell Wallace. Item A is
the work of Charles Darwin - his work on the Beagle mentioned in
the passage and is the correct answer.

6.   CORRECT ANSWER: C
Scopes was charged with teaching Darwinian evolution in violation
of a state law forbidding such instruction. The state was
Tennessee, and the correct answer is C. Clarence Darrow was
attorney for the defense and William Jennings Bryan, attorney
for the prosecution.

TEST 4

1. C	4. E
2. A	5. A
3. D	6. C

EXPLANATION OF ANSWERS

1.   CORRECT ANSWER: C
Paragraph 3, sentence 3, contains the description of a kumquat as
a *tender shrub*, indicating C as the correct answer.

2.   CORRECT ANSWER: A
Paragraph 4 contains the completion of the statement. It mentions
Hoya carnosa as needing a warm greenhouse and goes on to state
that, of other plants needing the same environment, one is
oleander. Thus, the answer is A. Though an oleander will flouris
outdoors in a southern climate, this is not indicated by the
author in the passage.

3. CORRECT ANSWER: D
The last sentence of paragraph 2 states that edelweiss is a cold-greenhouse plant and such plants are a *saving on wintertime fuel bills*. Therein lies its practical advantage. C and E could be considered adequate answers if the requirements only of the plant were the consideration, but D is the better answer because of the word *advantage* in the question (inferring that which is an advantage to the grower).

4. CORRECT ANSWER: E
Though A, B, C, and D are all mentioned in the passage, the all-inclusive title in item E presents the best possible choice and is the correct answer.

5. CORRECT ANSWER: A
Botany being the science discussed in the passage is the most enveloping choice and, therefore, the best answer. Thus, the answer is A. B, C, D, and E, were they to be catagorized, would all come under the heading of A since they are all parts of the whole—botany.

6. CORRECT ANSWER: C
Joel R. Poinsett, an American diplomat, discovered the flowering plant, poinsettia, in 1851, and it has since become our most popular Christmas plant. Thus, the answer is C.

———

TEST 5

1. B	5. B
2. A	6. C
3. E	7. A
4. E	

EXPLANATION OF ANSWERS

1. CORRECT ANSWER: B
It is stated in paragraph 1 that the brain is *bare except for two small bits of bone to help support it*. The answer, then, is B. Items C and E refer to things connected to the brain but not supporting it.

2. CORRECT ANSWER: A
Item C is stated as a question in the passage and goes unanswered. However, item A is stated in the last sentence of paragraph 1 and is the correct answer. Items D and E are artificial appendages on which the recording instruments depend, but cannot, themselves, estimate or measure consciousness.

3. CORRECT ANSWER: E
Incorporeal means without a body, or a disembodied brain. Therefore, E is the correct answer. The other answers are characteristic of (or related to) the brain described in the passage but do not relate to the term *incorporeal*.

4. CORRECT ANSWER: E
In sentence 1, paragraph 1, the author states there are technique:
to *remove the brain....and keep it alive for several hours*. Item
then, is the correct answer. C is not correct because, should a
mechanical heart fail, it would be replaced, and the brain would
continue its *life course* for the prescribed length of time.

5. CORRECT ANSWER: B
The correct answer is B (see paragraph two - *basic questions
related to the physiology of the brain*). Item E, the scientists
have obviously ascertained; items A, C, and D are neither
mentioned nor implied in the passage.

6. CORRECT ANSWER: C
Items A, D, and E relate to the cerebral cortex. Item B refers
to the cerebellum.

7. CORRECT ANSWER: A
Items B, C, D, and E refer to functions of the brainstem. Item A
which describes the make-up of the cerebral cortex, is the
correct answer.

———

TEST 6

1. C	4. D
2. B	5. E
3. C	6. B

EXPLANATION OF ANSWERS

1. CORRECT ANSWER: C
Paragraph 2 states, *The three men....paved the way for a major
invention: the maser*. The correct answer, therefore, is item C.
Item B relates to the work of Mrs. Hodgkin (item D), who lives
in Great Britain (item A). Item E is incomplete and, therefore,
false.

2. CORRECT ANSWER: B
The answer is contained in paragraph 3, where it is stated, ...s
*complex molecules as those of penicillin and B-12. The latter is
vital in treating...pernicious anemia*. The correct answer, then,
is B. Item A relates to the work of Mrs. Hodgkin, as do items C
and D. Item E is incorrect.

3. CORRECT ANSWER: C
The laser is an optical maser (item E), but it got its precise
name from the initials of the principle of the maser (item A)
applied to light; that is, item C, which is the correct answer.
The earliest application of the laser (item B) was item D and
has nothing to do with the laser.

4. CORRECT ANSWER: D
The prize was given to Drs. Basov, Prokhorov, and Townes. It was shared by these three men; therefore, the correct answer is D. E is incorrect because it is incomplete. The prize in Chemistry was given to Mrs. Hodgkin, item C. As for items A and B, if the reader were to check for the reason that the prize was given, he would find that it was the invention of the maser, discounting both A and B.

5. CORRECT ANSWER: E
The correct answer, and the most inclusive one, regarding the source of the passage is item E. Item A is obviously false, as is C. B and D refer to things mentioned in the passage but not the substance or the main theme of it.

6. CORRECT ANSWER: B
Item B is the correct meaning of amplification and, thus, the correct answer for the question. Items A, B, C, and E are incorrect.

TEST 7

1. C	4. D
2. B	5. D
3. D	6. B

EXPLANATION OF ANSWERS

1. CORRECT ANSWER: C
Algae is a subaqueous plant, that is a plant growing beneath the water. Therefore, the answer would be C. Items A and E are fungi. Item B, fossiliferous, means *containing or bearing fossils*. Item D is incorrect because algae is a form of plant life.

2. CORRECT ANSWER: B
The answer to this question is to be found in paragraph 1, towards the end, and the beginning of paragraph 2. Items A and D are accepted concepts. Item E is a false statement, as is C. Item B is the correct answer.

3. CORRECT ANSWER: D
At the beginning of paragraph 3, it is mentioned that *volcanic growth produced continents*. Therefore, item D is the correct answer, aside from being the only direct statement made about the production of continents. Items A, C, and E are not mentioned in relation to the production of continents.

4. CORRECT ANSWER: D
The pond-bottom plants slowly raised the oxygen content of the air....until it was sufficient to filter out almost all the lethal ultraviolet, states the passage in paragraph 3. Therefore, item D is the correct answer. A and E are false statements. Item C is true but not pertinent. Item B is misleading.

5. CORRECT ANSWER: D
Ultraviolet rays are those short rays beyond the violet of the visible spectrum. A, B, C, and E are not applicable to ultraviolet rays.

6. CORRECT ANSWER: B
Items C and D relate to the process of osmosis. Items A and E are incorrect.

TEST 8

1. D	4. D
2. E	5. C
3. D	6. B

EXPLANATION OF ANSWERS

1. CORRECT ANSWER: D
A place, apart from Cayonu, where scientists found cold-hammered copper specimens is the Shanidar Valley, item D, which is the correct answer. Istanbul is the location of the university of one of the scientists (item C). And Cayonu is in southeastern Turkey, thus discounting item A. Item B refers to the age of the specimens. Item E is false.

2. CORRECT ANSWER: E
The evidences that the scientists found were copper that had been cold-hammered into different shapes, indicating E as the correct answer. A and B are insufficient or incomplete answers. C does not represent enough evidence, nor does D.

3. CORRECT ANSWER: D
Metallurgy is *the art of working metals*. It has nothing to do with the discovery of or the existence of metal substances, discounting items A, B, and C, but rather with such activities as smelting, refining, parting, etc. Thus, the correct answer is D. Item E is incorrect.

4. CORRECT ANSWER: D
A millennium is a thousand years. Thus, the answer is D. Items A, B, C, and E are incorrect.

5. CORRECT ANSWER: C
The dominant religion of Turkey is Islam. Moslem (item A) does
have a following in Turkey, but it is not so great. Therefore,
the correct answer is C. Items B, D, and E are false.

6. CORRECT ANSWER: B
Turkey's capital is Ankara, item B, which is the correct answer.
Constantinople, item C, was the former name and the former capital;
it was replaced by the name, Istanbul, in the 20's. Izmir is the
present-day name for Smyrna, a change which was made coincidentally
with that for Constantinople.

————

TEST 9

1. B		4. C	
2. D		5. B	
3. D		6. A	

EXPLANATION OF ANSWERS

1. CORRECT ANSWER: B
*The earth was born as barren of an atmosphere as is the moon
today*, states the passage in paragraph 4. The only difference
was that it had volcanoes which poured out gases, which in turn
produced oceans and air. But since the correct answer must
refer to the earth at its beginning (refer back to the question
stem), B is the only possible answer. Item A is not mentioned.
Item C does not refer to the earth at its beginning. Item E
took place much later, during the *revolutions* mentioned in
paragraph 3. Item D is not stated in the passage.

2. CORRECT ANSWER: D
At the end of the passage, the two doctors are mentioned as
believing that life *probably sprang forth independently on the
bottoms of numerous deep pools*. Therefore, D is the correct
answer. E is a false statement. The doctors did not believe
A or B. C is false because two *gigantic revolutions* took place,
according to paragraph 3.

3. CORRECT ANSWER: D
Volcanic air was transparent to ultraviolet sunlight because it
did not produce oxygen gas and was dominated by hydrogen
compounds (paragraph 5). Item E is false. It did contain
hydrogen compounds. C is false because the reverse is true.
Items A and B are incorrect because the opposites are true.

4. CORRECT ANSWER: C
It is the oxygen content in the air which filters out the ultraviolet rays before they reach the earth or the oceans. Therefore,
the correct answer is C, and can be found in paragraph 5. Items
A, B, and E have nothing to do with the ability of the air to
filter the rays. Hydrogen, mentioned in item D, is transparent
to ultraviolet rays.

5. CORRECT ANSWER: B
    Item E refers to a law. A and C are insufficient as definitions.
    D is a broad definition but not so precise as item B, which is
    the most accurate definition presented, and the correct answer.

6. CORRECT ANSWER: A
    Since the passage is concerned with natural science, item A is
    far superior to items B and C. Items D and E are incorrect.
    The correct answer, then, is A.

TEST 10

1. D	4. D	7. D
2. B	5. D	8. C
3. B	6. D	9. E

EXPLANATION OF ANSWERS

1. CORRECT ANSWER: D
    In the next to last sentence of paragraph 6, the reason is
    explained. The correct answer is D. Item B is incorrect because
    it is the prevention of the normal oxygen flow that leads to
    fatalities. C is incorrect because they have too much water in
    their system. Whether the baby is organically defective or not
    has nothing to do with the disease, discounting A. Item E is
    incorrect because the babies do make this attempt.

2. CORRECT ANSWER: B
    In the last sentence of paragraph 2, it is stated that the
    disease killed about half the infants it struck. Thus, the
    correct answer is B. 150 infants had autopsies performed
    (item E). 25,000 yearly in the United States died from it,
    discounting item C. Item A is false. The figure 2,000 in
    item D refers to the nation's pathologists.

3. CORRECT ANSWER: B
    It would seem, since all the babies treated are alive today, that
    Dr. Stowens' approach to the disease has been perfected and that
    the cure has been found. Therefore, the correct answer is B.
    Item D is not mentioned in the passage. And items A, C, and E
    are false.

4. CORRECT ANSWER: D
    The cause of death is suffocation. This is mentioned in the first
    sentence of the passage. The correct answer is D. Items A, B,
    C, and E are organs and parts of the body affected but not the
    cause of death. Item C refers to a part of the name of the
    disease.

5. CORRECT ANSWER: D
Dr. Spock, a specialist in child growth and development, does not pioneer in the treatment of diseases, discounting A. Item C refers to a nuclear physicist. Item E refers to the disease Dr. Stowens sought to treat. But Dr. Salk, item D, found a way to treat polio successfully and, therefore, is the correct answer. Item B refers to the method he used.

6. CORRECT ANSWER: D
The answer may be reached through paragraph 7, which ends in *The new simple therapy had led to a simple theory.* Before this, there were *many complicated theories about how....disease blocks the lungs.* Therefore, item D is correct. (*Recondite* means complex, profound.) Item A is false; it occurred after the discovery of the therapy. Item B is false because it was treated. Item C is false; there were many theories. Item E is false although it contains a repetition of part of the statement appearing in the paragraph.

7. CORRECT ANSWER: D
Item A is false because the opposite is stated in the passage. Item B is false for the same reason. Item C is false because fluid is drawn away from the lungs. Item D is correct because it is part of the second stage of the treatment (or therapy) indicated in paragraph 8. Item E is false because the two that are used do not justify the adjective *various*.

8. CORRECT ANSWER: C
Item A is false because that is what occurs before they are treated. Item B is false because they have been treated over the last 8 months. Item C is correct, as indicated in paragraph 9. Item D is false because a different length of time (*a few minutes*) is mentioned in the passage. Item E is false because the passage actually states that 28 babies have been treated in 5 hospitals.

9. CORRECT ANSWER: E
A pathologist is one versed in the nature of diseases. Therefore, E is the only possible answer and the correct one. Item A is insufficient. Items B, C, and D are false.

———

EXAMINATION SECTION

DIRECTIONS: Each question or incomplete statement is followed by
several suggested answers or completions. Select the
one that BEST answers the question or completes the
statement. *PRINT THE LETTER OF THE CORRECT ANSWER IN
THE SPACE AT THE RIGHT.*

Questions 1-5.

DIRECTIONS: Questions 1 through 5 are to be answered on the basis
of the following passage.

The Grand Canyon carves through 279 miles of northern Arizona.
No one expects what he finds here, and no one forgets what he sees
and hears.

For more than ten years, Paul Winter has come to the Grand
Canyon with his soprano saxophone. He has stood on the rim at
Shoshone Point and played to cliffs that send back a triple echo.
He has played with his fellow musicians in the side canyons, and
together they have floated down the Colorado River. *I felt put back
together on the river*, Winter says, *and I wanted to make music from
that place. I wanted to make music of the canyon rather than just
about it.*

Even when non-musicians come to these great spaces, they want
to fill the stillness with sound. John Wesley Powell, first to
describe the experience of a river trip through the canyon, wrote
in 1895: *The wonders of the Grand Canyon cannot be adequately
represented in symbols of speech, nor by speech itself....It is
the land of music.*

Winter and his group of musicians would certainly agree. On a
fall evening, they play Japanese wood flutes, improvisations in
answer to the local chorus of canyon tree frogs. Upstream the next
morning the saxophone calls, sounding like a great bird, first raven,
then great blue heron. The sounds of the wind mix with the rhythms
of a frame drum. Much of this is recorded, and a small part will
become part of a record the musicians are making.

The Grand Canyon is like a journey through time, life, Earth,
underworld: It is any reality we care to invent. Paul Winter tries
to recapture this in his music.

Adapted from PAUL WINTER'S CANYON CONSORT
by Stephen Trimble, SIERRA, March/April 1986

1. Paul Winter visits the Grand Canyon to   1.___
   A. trap ravens   B. take photographs
   C. record frogs and animals D. play his saxophone

2. In 1895, John Wesley Powell suggested that   2.___
   A. only words could describe the Grand Canyon
   B. symbols are needed for nature
   C. music can best express the canyon's beauty
   D. stillness is required in nature

3. The word <u>improvisations</u> in this passage means   3.___
   A. producing high pitched sounds
   B. performing without preparation
   C. echoing the exact sound
   D. playing melodies

4. The musicians in this passage enjoy   4.___
   A. hiking in the wilderness
   B. playing old fashioned music
   C. responding in music to nature
   D. playing their music indoors

5. The author suggests that the Grand Canyon   5.___
   A. has many meanings
   B. stands for lack of freedom
   C. will be destroyed
   D. is a poor setting for art

Questions 6-10.

DIRECTIONS: Questions 6 through 10 are to be answered on the basis of the following passage.

Write about beauty and truth. Write about life, Miss Lowy had said.

Jeanie tore a page out of her notebook and opened her pen. Pulling over a chair she rested her book on the sooty window sill. She stared out at the dusk falling sadly, sadly, thickening into darkness over the coal yards.

A crash of the kitchen door caused a reverberation in the window sill. The notebook slipped out of her hands.

Where you get that soda? She heard her mother's voice, hard and more Southern-sounding than usual.

A lady give me a nickel. She come down the street and ask me--

You lyin'! I know where you got it. Gamblin' -- that's what you was doin'!

I was pitchin' pennies, Ma. It's just a game.

Gamblin' an' stealin'! Takin' up with bad friends! I told you to stay away from them boys. Didn't I? Didn't I?

Her mother's voice rose. *I'm goin' to give you a beating you ain't goin' to forget for a good long time.*

Billy wailed on a long descending note.

Later, after the supper dishes were washed, Jeanie brought her books into the kitchen and spread them out under the glaring overhead light. Billy had been asleep, huddled in his clothes. Tears had left dusty streaks on his face.

Her mother sat in an armchair, ripping out the sides of a black dress. Her spectacles made her look strange. *Beauty is truth*, Jeanie read in her notebook. Hastily, carelessly, <u>defiantly</u> disregarding margins and doubtful spellings, letting her pen dig into the paper, she began to write: *Last night my brother Billy got a terrible beating....*

Adapted from BEAUTY IS TRUTH
by Anna Guest

6. The author suggests that Jeanie   6.___
   A. hated her mother
   B. was jealous of her brother
   C. had trouble writing at first
   D. enjoyed gambling

7. An overheard conversation serves to   7.___
   A. distract the writer
   B. inspire the writer
   C. involve the writer in a fight
   D. discourage the writer

8. The word <u>defiantly</u> as used in the passage means   8.___
   A. sadly   B. falsely
   C. fearlessly   D. carefully

9. Jeanie decides to write about   9.___
   A. life around her   B. her school experiences
   C. her secret dreams   D. an ideal family

10. The author suggests that a writer   10.___
   A. depends upon imagination
   B. finds inspiration in reality
   C. must ignore life experience
   D. needs a quiet place to work

Questions 11-15.

DIRECTIONS: Questions 11 through 15 are to be answered on the basis of the following passage.

LIFE

A crust of bread and a corner to sleep in,
A minute to smile and an hour to weep in,
A pint of joy to a peck of trouble,
And never a laugh but the moans come double:
     And that is life!

A crust and a corner that love makes precious,
With the smile to warm and the tears to refresh us;
And joy seems sweeter when cares come after,
And a moan is the finest of foils for laughter:
     And that is life!

by Paul Lawrence Dunbar

11. This poem is built on   11.___
    A. an abstract definition   B. comparisons and contrasts
    C. a view of loneliness   D. impressions of poverty

12. Lines 5 and 10 express   12.___
    A. the same meaning   B. different meanings
    C. a unique message   D. a poet's doubts

13. The rhyme schemes in stanzas 1 and 2 are   13.___
    A. totally different   B. somewhat different
    C. the same   D. difficult to identify

14. In line 4, sorrow is contrasted to   14.___
    A. suspicion B. happiness C. fear   D. insecurity

15. *And a moan is the finest of foils for laughter* means   15.___
    A. a moan is a prerequisite for happiness
    B. laughter follows tragedy
    C. sadness helps us appreciate joy
    D. unhappiness and happiness are equal

Questions 16-20.

DIRECTIONS: Read the following passage. In each question, select
the word that BEST completes the passage.

Immigration, which played an important part in America's rapid
progress, increased greatly in the 1830's and 1840's. Europe
suffered from a number of revolutions and crop failures during this
period. Most of the revolutions failed, and many people with
advanced ideas had to flee for their (16) . This was especially
true in Germany, where absolute monarchy was still strong. The
worst crop (17) occurred in Ireland. There, several million
people faced starvation during the *potato famines* of 1845 and 1846.

Large numbers of Germans, Irish, and other Europeans were
attracted to the United States by its cheap land, economic prosperity,
and democratic government. But they met with an unexpected problem,
a growing feeling among Americans of dislike for (18) . Most of
the Irish were very poor. Since they could not afford to buy farms,
they (19) in the cities. There they performed the most difficult
and unpleasant types of work for very low wages. Native American
 (20) resented the Irish for keeping wages down and for taking away
jobs. The newcomers were also disliked because they were generally
uneducated and had very low living standards.

16. A. wealth   B. safety   16.___
    C. country   D. importance

17. A. success   B. likelihood   17.___
    C. failures   D. knowledge

18. A. foreigners   B. democracy   18.___
    C. farms   D. dreams

19. A. farmed   B. met   C. bought   D. settled   19.___

20. A. standards   B. immigrants   20.___
    C. workers   D. bosses

Questions 21-35.

DIRECTIONS: Each of the following sentences may have a mistake in
it. The error may be in sentence structure, usage,
capitalization, or punctuation. If there is an error,
choose the CORRECT response, and write the letter of
your answer in the space at the right. If the sentence
is correct as it is written, choose the letter of the
answer for *correct as is*.

SAMPLE: I have always chose to follow my mother's advice.
    A. Correct as is
    B. chosen; mother's
    C. choosed; mothers
    D. chose; mothers'

CORRECT ANSWER: B

21. We <u>should of stayed</u> home.   21.___
    A. correct as is   B. should have stayed
    C. should of stay   D. should have stay

22. John and <u>I</u> are going to my <u>uncle's</u> house.   22.___
    A. correct as is   B. me; uncles
    C. me; uncle's   D. I; uncles

23. <u>"How are you,"</u> she asked.   23.___
    A. correct as is
    B. "How are you," she asked?
    C. "How are you? she asked."
    D. "How are you?" she asked.

24. If you <u>had brought</u> your homework, you <u>wouldn't needed</u> to   24.___
    do it over.
    A. correct as is
    B. have brought; wouldn't needed
    C. had brought; wouldn't need
    D. had brung; wouldn't need

25. She <u>sung</u> that song <u>worse</u> than anyone I ever heard before.   25.___
    A. correct as is   B. sung; worst
    C. sung; worser   D. sang; worse

26. <u>More people than we expected.</u>   26.___
    A. correct as is
    B. Many more people than we expected.
    C. More people than expected to the party.
    D. More people than we expected came to the party.

27. <u>You can do that problem many ways, the teacher will</u>   27.___
    <u>explain them.</u>
    A. correct as is
    B. You can do that problem many ways; The teacher will
       explain them.
    C. You can do that problem many ways. The teacher will
       explain them.
    D. You can do that problem many ways the teacher will
       explain them.

28. <u>We was born</u> in New York, but <u>we are living</u> in New Jersey   28.___
    for the last two years.
    A. correct as is
    B. we was born; we was living
    C. we were born; we are living
    D. we were born; we have been living

29. After the thief had <u>robbed</u> his wallet, he told the police   29.___
    of <u>its</u> contents.
    A. correct as is   B. robbed; it's
    C. stolen; it's   D. stolen; its

30. If you think <u>he don't do nothing carefully</u>, you're right.   30.___
    A. correct as is
    B. he don't do nothing careful
    C. he doesn't do nothing carefully
    D. he doesn't do anything carefully

31. I learned in <u>English class</u> that <u>London</u> was the home of   31.___
the <u>Globe theater</u>.
    A. correct as is
    B. English class; London; Globe Theater
    C. english class; London; Globe Theater
    D. English Class; London; Globe Theater

32. He asked each of the men for <u>their</u> dollar contribution to   32.___
the charity, <u>like</u> he had promised.
    A. correct as is   B. their; as
    C. his; like   D. his; as

33. John, as well as Mary, <u>deserves</u> credit for <u>having past</u>   33.___
advanced math.
    A. correct as is   B. deserves; having passed
    C. deserve; having passed D. deserve; having past

34. <u>The dance was lovely all the</u> students dressed in formals.   34.___
    A. correct as is
    B. The dance was lovely, all the
    C. "The dance was lovely," all the
    D. The dance was lovely. All

35. I do <u>good</u> on <u>this kind</u> of test.   35.___
    A. correct as is   B. good; these kinds
    C. well; this kind   D. well; these kinds

Questions 36-40.

DIRECTIONS: A dictionary page has been reprinted below. Use the
information on this dictionary page to answer Questions
36 through 40.

mer·ci·less \'mər-sē-ləs, 'mərs-l-əs\ *adj.* Without mercy; pitiless. — **mer·ci·less·ly,** *adv.*

mer·cu·ri·al \mər-'kyür-ē-əl\ *adj.* 1 Having qualities associated with being born under the planet Mercury or attributed to the god Mercury; swift; clever; fickle; changeable. 2 Of, relating to, containing, or caused by the element mercury; as, *mercurial* medical preparations; a *mercurial* thermometer. — *n.* A drug containing mercury.

mer·cu·ric \mər-'kyür-ik\ *adj.* Of, relating to, or containing mercury.

mer·cu·ry \'mərk-yər-ē, 'mərk-r(-)ē\ *n.; pl.* **mer·cu·ries.** 1 A messenger; a guide. 2 A heavy, silver-white metallic element, the only metal that is liquid at ordinary temperatures; quicksilver. 3 The column of mercury in a thermometer or barometer.

mer·cy \'mər-sē\ *n.; pl.* **mer·cies.** 1 Kind and gentle treatment of an offender, an opponent, or some unfortunate person. 2 A kind, sympathetic manner or disposition; a willingness to forgive, to spare, or to help. 3 The power to be merciful; as, to throw oneself on an enemy's *mercy.* 4 An act of kindness; a blessing.

— The words *clemency* and *leniency* are synonyms of *mercy: mercy* usually refers to a compassionate and forgiving attitude on the part of a person who has the power or right to impose severe punishment on another; *clemency* may indicate a habit or policy of moderation and mildness in one whose duty it is to impose punishment for offences; *leniency* often indicates a deliberate overlooking of mistakes or an overindulgent acceptance of another's faults.

mere \'mir\ *n. Archaic* or *Dial.* A sheet of standing water; a lake or pool.

mere \'mir\ *adj.; superlative* **mer·est** \'mir-əst\. Only this, and nothing else; nothing more than; simple; as, a *mere* whisper; a *mere* child.

mere·ly \'mir-lē\ *adv.* Not otherwise than; simply; only.

mer·e·tri·cious \,mer-ə-'trish-əs\ *adj.* Attracting by a display of showy but superficial and tawdry charms; falsely attractive. — **mer·e·tri·cious·ly,** *adv.*

mer·gan·ser \(,)mər-'gan(t)s-r\ *n.; pl.* **mer·gan·sers** or **mer·gan·ser.** A fish-eating wild duck with a slender, hooked beak and, usually, a crested head.

merge \'mərj\ *v.; merged; merg·ing.* 1 To be or cause to be swallowed up, combined, or absorbed in or within something else; to mingle; to blend; as, *merging* traffic. 2 To combine or unite, as two business firms into one.

merg·er \'mərj-r\ *n.* 1 The combining of business concerns or interests into one. 2 The resulting business unit.

me·rid·i·an \mə-'rid-ē-ən\ *adj.* 1 At or relating to midday. 2 Of or relating to a meridian. — *n.* 1 The highest apparent point reached by the sun or a star. 2 The highest point, as of success or importance; culmination. 3 An imaginary great circle on the earth's surface, passing through the North and South Poles and any given place between. 4 The half of such a circle included between the poles. 5 A representation of such a circle or half circle on a globe or map; any of a series of lines drawn at intervals due north and south or in the direction of the poles and numbered according to the degrees of longitude.

me·ringue \mə-'rang\ *n.* A mixture of beaten white of egg and sugar, put on pies or cakes and browned, or shaped into small cakes or shells and baked.

me·ri·no \mə-'rē-,nō\ *n.; pl.* **me·ri·nos.** 1 A fine-wooled white sheep of a breed marked by the heavy twisted horns of the male. 2 A fine soft fabric resembling cashmere and originally made of the wool from this sheep. 3 A fine wool yarn.

merino

mer·it \'mer-ət\ *n.* 1 Due reward or punishment; especially, deserved reward; a mark or token of excellence or approval. 2 The condition or fact of deserving well or ill; desert; as, each according to his *merit.* 3 Worth; excellence; as, a suggestion having considerable *merit.* 4 A quality or act worthy of praise; as, an answer that at least had the *merit* of honesty. — *v.* To earn by service or performance; to deserve; as, a man who *merited* respect.

mer·i·to·ri·ous \,mer-ə-'tōr-ē-əs, -'tòr-\ *adj.* Deserving reward or honor; praiseworthy. — **mer·i·to·ri·ous·ly,** *adv.*

mer·maid \'mər-,mād\ *n.* [From medieval English *mermaide*, a compound formed from *mere* meaning "sea" and *maide* meaning "girl", "maid".] An imaginary sea creature usually represented with a woman's body and a fish's tail.

mer·man \'mər-,man, -mən\ *n.; pl.* **mer·men** \-,men, -mən\. An imaginary sea creature usually represented with a man's body and a fish's tail.

mer·ri·ment \'mer-ē-mənt, -ə-mənt\ *n.* Gaiety; mirth; fun.

mer·ry \'mer-ē\ *adj.; mer·ri·er; mer·ri·est.* 1 Full of good humor and good spirits; laughingly gay. 2 Marked by gaiety or festivity; as, a *merry* Christmas. — **mer·ri·ly** \'mer-ə-lē\ *adv.*

mer·ry-an·drew \'mer-ē-'an-,drü\ *n.* A clown; a buffoon.

mer·ry-go-round \'mer-ē-gō-,raùnd\ *n.* 1 A circular revolving platform fitted with seats and figures of animals on which people sit for a ride. 2 Any rapid round of activities; a whirl; as, a *merry-go-round* of parties.

merry-go-round

mer·ry·mak·ing \'mer-ē-,māk-ing\ *adj.* Festive; jolly. — *n.* 1 The act of making merry; merriment. 2 A frolic; a festivity. — **mer·ry·mak·er** \-,māk-r\ *n.*

me·sa \'mā-sə\ *n.* A flat-topped hill or small plateau with steep sides.

mes·cal \mes-'kal\ *n.* 1 A small, spineless cactus

36. Which of the following groups contains ONLY adjectives?   36.___
    A. merciless, meritorious, merriment
    B. merciless, meridian, merry
    C. merit, meritorious, merry
    D. merciless, meritorious, merry

37. The word <u>clemency</u> is a synonym for   37.___
    A. mercurial   B. mercy   C. merit   D. merger

38. According to the pronunciation key for each word, the   38.___
    mark showing where the stress comes in the word occurs
    A. after the stressed syllable
    B. before the stressed syllable
    C. between stressed syllables
    D. at random

39. A word which means a sweet dessert is   39.___
    A. merge   B. meringue
    C. merit   D. merry-andrew

40. His invention was of such <u>merit</u> that the world honored   40.___
    him.
    Which is the CORRECT definition for the word <u>merit</u>, as
    used in the above sentence?
    Definition
    A. 1   B. 2   C. 3   D. 4

Questions 41-45.

DIRECTIONS: Select the BEST answer for each of the following
             media questions.

41. To find information on tonight's TV schedule, you should   41.___
    NOT look at
    A. this week's TV GUIDE
    B. this week's NEWSWEEK
    C. today's newspaper
    D. the weekend newspaper's TV section

42. An index   42.___
    A. gives an alphabetical list of topics and persons
       described in a book, with the pages listed
    B. gives the geographic location of all places in a
       book
    C. only lists the famous people mentioned in a book,
       with the appropriate page references
    D. gives the chapter headings found in the book

43. Magazines may concentrate on one particular subject such   43.___
    as
    A. sports   B. hobbies
    C. fashion   D. all of the above

44. People listen to the radio and watch television   44.____
    A. for information only
    B. for entertainment only
    C. lacking anything better to do
    D. for all of the above reasons

45. TV advertising frequently appeals to everything EXCEPT   45.____
    our desire
    A. to hear the whole truth about products
    B. to impress people
    C. to be up-to-date
    D. for the best in life

Questions 46-55.

DIRECTIONS: In each of Questions 46 through 55, only one of the
words is misspelled. In each case, write the
misspelled word CORRECTLY in the space at the right.

46. banana   46.____
    regional
    apolagize
    anticipate
    grievance

47. medicine   47.____
    interruption
    weird
    benifit
    fatigue

48. clothe   48.____
    religious
    aquarium
    brillianse
    vacuum

49. adjourn   49.____
    gorgeus
    precious
    category
    possess

50. diogram   50.____
    absence
    maturity
    pitiful
    intrusion

51. reccommend   51.____
    comparative
    assurance
    prisoner
    hilarious

52. attempt
    feminine
    independant
    orchestra
    hopeful

52.____

53. parallel
    transparent
    fantacy
    arguing
    hysterical

53.____

54. accidentally
    minimum
    cathedral
    responsable
    nuclear

54.____

55. approximatly
    committing
    fascinate
    minority
    privilege

55.____

KEY (CORRECT ANSWERS)

1. D	16. B	31. B	46. apologize
2. C	17. C	32. D	47. benefit
3. B	18. A	33. B	48. brilliance
4. C	19. D	34. D	49. gorgeous
5. A	20. C	35. C	50. diagram
6. C	21. B	36. D	51. recommend
7. B	22. A	37. B	52. independent
8. C	23. D	38. B	53. fantasy
9. A	24. C	39. B	54. responsible
10. B	25. D	40. C	55. approximately
11. B	26. D	41. B	
12. B	27. C	42. A	
13. C	28. D	43. D	
14. B	29. D	44. D	
15. C	30. D	45. A	

EXAMINATION SECTION

DIRECTIONS: Each question or incomplete statement is followed by several suggested answers or completions. Select the one that BEST answers the question or completes the statement. *PRINT THE LETTER OF THE CORRECT ANSWER IN THE SPACE AT THE RIGHT.*

Questions 1-5.

DIRECTIONS: Questions 1 through 5 are to be answered on the basis of the selection below.

The school term ended. I was selected as valedictorian of my class and assigned to write a paper to be delivered at graduation. One morning the principal summoned me to his office.

"Well, Richard Wright, here's your speech," he said with smooth bluntness and shoved a stack of stapled sheets across his desk.

"What speech?" I asked as I picked up the papers.

"The speech you're to say the night of graduation," he said.

"But, professor, I've written my speech already," I said.

He laughed confidently, indulgently.

"Listen, boy, you're going to speak to both white and colored people that night. What can you alone think of saying to them? You have no experience..."

I burned.

"I know that I'm not educated, professor," I said. "But the people are coming to hear the students, and I won't make a speech that you've written."

He leaned back in his chair and looked at me in surprise.

"You know, we've never had a boy in this school like you before," he said. "You've had your way around here. Just how you managed to do it, I don't know. But, listen, take this speech and say it. I know what's best for you. You can't afford to just say anything before those white people that night." He paused and added meaningfully: "The superintendent of schools will be there; you're in a position to make a good impression on him. I've been a principal for more years than you are old, boy. I've seen many a boy and girl graduate from this school, and none of them was too proud to recite a speech I wrote for them.

I had to make up my mind quickly; I was faced with a matter of principle. I wanted to graduate, but I did not want to make a public speech that was not my own.

"Professor, I'm going to say my own speech that night," I said.

He grew angry.

"You're just a young, hotheaded fool," he said. He toyed with a pencil and looked up at me. "Suppose you don't graduate?"

"But I passed my examinations," I said.

"Look, mister," he shot at me, "I'm the man who says who passes at this school."

I was so astonished that my body jerked. I had gone to this school for two years and I had never suspected what kind of man the principal was; it simply had never occurred to me to wonder about him.

"Then I don't graduate," I said flatly.

I turned to leave.

"Say, you. Come here," he called.

I turned and faced him; he was smiling at me in a remote superior sort of way.

"You know, I'm glad I talked to you," he said. "I was seriously thinking of placing you in the school system, teaching. But, now, I don't think that you'll fit."

He was tempting me, baiting me; this was the technique that snared black young minds into supporting the southern way of life.

"Look, professor, I may never get a chance to go to school again," I said.

"But I like to do things right. You're just a young, hot fool," he said. "Wake up, boy. Learn the world you're living in. You're smart and I know what you're after. I've kept closer track of you than you think. I know your relatives. Now, if you play safe," he smiled and winked, "I'll help you to go to school, to college."

"I want to learn, professor," I told him. "But there are some things I don't want to know."

Adapted from Black Boy, the Autobiography of Richard Wright

1. The conflict between Richard and the principal of the school concerns
   A. whose speech is better -- Richard's or the principal's
   B. whether there should be a prepared speech at graduation or informal remark
   C. whether the speech that is given should be written by Richard or the principal
   D. whether the superintendent of schools should be allowed to hear the speech

1.___

2. As used in the next to the last paragraph of the selection, the word *track* means a(n)
   A. watching or an observing
   B. athletic competition
   C. footprint
   D. route or course

2.___

3. Richard's words and actions in this incident can be BEST explained by Richard's
   A. fear of what the principal could do to him
   B. always wanting to get his own way in everything
   C. realizing that the principal knew what was best for him
   D. belief that, as a matter of principle, he had to be true to what he considered to be right

3.___

4. The principal was surprised at Richard's reaction when he handed him the speech because
   A. Richard had always been a cooperative student
   B. no other student had ever acted this way with the principal before
   C. Richard had promised to do whatever the principal told him to do
   D. Richard could barely read and write

4.___

5. The frequent use of quotation marks in this passage indicates that
   A. a conversation is going on
   B. the titles of short stories, poems, and other short works being mentioned
   C. the characters do not always mean exactly what their words are saying
   D. that writer does not understand the proper uses of quotation marks

5.___

Questions 6-10.

DIRECTIONS: Questions 6 through 10 are to be answered on the basis
              of the selection below.

       We call it Sunrise Dance. But it lasts for four days. It's
the biggest ceremony of the White Mountain Apache - when a girl
passes from childhood to womanhood. When my time came at 14, I
didn't want to have one. I felt embarrassed. All my friends would
be watching me. But my parents really wanted it. My mother - she
never had one - explained it was important, "Then you will live
strong to an old age." So I didn't say no.

       My parents prepared for a year. They asked relatives, "Help
us so our daughter's dance will be a good one." Older relatives
helped choose my sponsors; I call them Godparents. One morning
my mother and father took an eagle feather to Godmother Foster and
placed it at her foot saying, "Would you prepare a dance for my
daughter?" Mrs. Foster picked up the feather. "Yes."

       We held the dance at the fairgrounds at Whiteriver. There was
room for everyone to camp. One Friday evening Godmother dressed me
and pinned an eagle feather on my head. It will help me live until
my hair turns gray. The abalone shell pendant on my forehead is
the symbol of Changing Woman, mother of all Apache people.

       The most important thing Godmother does in the whole ceremony
is to massage my body. She is giving me all her knowledge. That
night for hours around the fire, I follow a crown dancer who
impersonates a protective spirit. We all believe the spirit is
present.

       Saturday is like an endurance test. Men begin the chants at
dawn. They are really praying. Grandmother tells me to dance
while kneeling on a buckskin pad facing the sun - the Creator. In
that position, Apache women grind corn. When the times comes for
running, I go fast around a sacred cave, so nobody evil will ever
catch up with me. Rain begins, and my costume, which weighs ten
pounds, gets heavier and heavier. But I don't fall. I don't even
get tired.

       I'm really glad I had a sunrise dance. It made me realize how
much my parents care for me and want me to grow up right. They know
my small age is past and treat me like a woman. If I have a
daughter, I want her to have a sunrise dance, too.

                              Adapted from the February 1980 issue
                              of National Geographic Magazine

6. A young Apache girl participates in the ceremony described 6.___
   above when she
   A. is born
   B. is about to enter womanhood
   C. is about to be married
   D. needs godparents

7. The speaker of this selection changed her feelings toward 7.___
   her sunrise dance from
   A. anger to resignation
   B. embarrassment to humiliation
   C. refusal to resignation
   D. embarrassment to pride

8. In paragraph four, the word *impersonates* means 8.___
   A. acts the part of   B. dances with
   C. obeys   D. challenges

9. We can conclude that the sunrise dance 9.___
   A. is performed each week
   B. brings rain for the crops
   C. will make the speaker live a long time
   D. is a traditional Apache ritual

10. The MOST important part of the ceremony, according to the 10.___
    speaker, is the
    A. eagle feather   B. massage
    C. chanting men   D. sacred cave

Questions 11-15.

DIRECTIONS: Questions 11 through 15 are to be answered on the
           basis of the following passage.

I really knew I would like New York, but I thought I'd like it
immediately, as I had liked the red brick of Venice and London's
massive, somber houses. I didn't know that, for a newly arrived
European visitor, there was a "New York sickness," like sea-
sickness, air sickness, and mountain sickness.

In Europe, you stop along the streets, meet people, drink, eat,
and linger. On Sundays, you get dressed and take a stroll for the
sole pleasure of greeting friends. These streets are filled with a
community spirit that changes from hour to hour. You do not go for
walks in New York; you fly through it. It is a city in motion.
Each street looks the same as any other. I feel like anybody, anywhere. I know nobody, nowhere.

In Europe, we become attached to a neighborhood, to a cluster
of houses or a street corner, and we are no longer free. But
hardly have you entered New York than your life is cut to New York
size. You can gaze down in the evening from the top of the Queens-
borough Bridge, in the morning from New Jersey, at noon from the
Empire State Building. Your world is much larger when you live in
New York.

I have learned to love New York, especially its sky. In European cities where roofs are low, the sky crawls close to the earth and seems tamed. The New York sky is beautiful because the skyscrapers push it back, very far over our heads. Pure and lovely as a wild beast, it guards and watches over the city. This sky stretches into the distance over all America. It is the whole world's sky.

That thought alone is enough to lend softness to the world's harshest city.

Adapted from "New York"
by Jean-Paul Sartre

11. The author's purpose in writing this passage is to   11.___
   A. criticize New York
   B. praise Europe
   C. compare New York with Europe
   D. praise New York

12. The word *stroll* in paragraph two means a   12.___
   A. nap   B. walk   C. look   D. ride

13. The author's feelings about New York change from   13.___
   A. uneasiness to love   B. love to hatred
   C. fear to shock   D. uneasiness to hatred

14. The word *it* in paragraph four refers to   14.___
   A. skyscrapers   B. the beast
   C. New York   D. the sky

15. We can conclude from this passage that the author   15.___
   A. dislikes Europe now that he has discovered New York
   B. has travelled widely
   C. left Europe permanently
   D. was seasick on his journey to New York

Questions 16-20.

DIRECTIONS: Read the passages below and select from the words in each question the one that BEST completes the passages. Study the sample below and then proceed on your own.

Sample: Jim Hawkins in TREASURE ISLAND boarded a huge ship and __1__ off that day to go in search of a hidden treasure.

   1. A. drove   B. called   C. sailed   D. nodded

The CORRECT answer is C.

The Burgos' house was a poor one with a thatched roof of palm leaves, but there was the warmth of a loving home within. Paula, the mother, kept a small __16__ nearby. She grew vegetables and grain to help feed the family, selling the produce to buy food and clothing. Since she had no one with whom to leave her small daughter, Paula would take Julia on her trips to the market. Down by the river, while the washing was done in the stream, Julia and her sisters played in the grass, smelled the flowers, climbed the trees, and bathed in a pond they called the Deep Well. It was then that the child began to recognize and love __17__.

Life was simple for the Burgos family. Their world was limited to the countryside surrounding their house. But it seemed __18__ and wondrous to Julia. Her eyes would discover the beauty of every wild flower, the living miracle of a bird's nest tucked away in a bush. Years later __19__ about her childhood, she confided, "I would cry disconsolately over the leaves of a MORIVINI because it would not awaken. The MORIVINI is a plant so sensitive that its leaves shrivel and die if someone touches it.

If Julia's childhood was poor in material wealth, it was rich in vital experiences and in emotions. Unfortunately, it also abounded in __20__. One by one she saw six of her brothers die. The first time she saw her mother cry over the loss of one of her sons, Julia was devastated. She would not accept that the dead child had to be buried. "Why don't they place him on a raft and cast him off to sea?" she asked.

16. A. factory   B. garden   C. warehouse   D. dairy   16.___

17. A. families   B. bathing   C. exercise   D. nature   17.___

18. A. enormous   B. poor   C. boring   D. small   18.___

19. A. forgetting   B. singing   19.___
     C. reminiscing   D. complaining

20. A. love   B. sorrow   C. fear   D. anger   20.___

Questions 21-35.

DIRECTIONS: The sentences numbered 21 through 35 make up the paragraph that follows. There is one error either in sentence structure, spelling, punctuation, or incorrect usage in each sentence. Find the error in each sentence and write the CORRECTION in the space at the right.

Sample: A. On the last day of our vacation, we saw men skiing down a mountain that was the best part of the vacation for me.

          B. If we go back next year I plan to take skiing lessons.

          C. They shouldnt be expensive.

Answers: A. mountain. That

B. year,

C. shouldn't <u>or</u> should not

21. You are now at the mid-point in this examination in english.   21.___

22. Have you notice anything about the test so far?   22.___

23. You should of noticed it; it is about beginnings and endings.   23.___

24. In a week, you are probably gonna experience an ending and a beginning of your own.   24.___

25. We are referring to the commencement exercises that represent your graduation from High School.   25.___

26. Commencement ceremonies can be a beginning or an ending it depends on how you look at it.   26.___

27. Some students see there graduation as the completion of their formal education.   27.___

28. Others sees it as the first step to higher education or employment.   28.___

29. Are you looking at it as a beginning or an ending.   29.___

30. Both views are probably true. Because every ending begins something else.   30.___

31. As someone once said Every exit is an entrance somewhere else."   31.___

32. It is also true that each beginning contain's its own ending.   32.___

33. For example the beginning of life also contains the beginning of the end.   33.___

34. The moment we are born we begin both living and dieing.   34.___

35. "That's life," you may be thinking, and your right.   35.___

Questions 36-40.

DIRECTIONS: A dictionary page has been reprinted below. Use the information on this dictionary page to answer Questions 36 through 40.

pan·e·gyr·ist \,pan-ə-'jir-əst\ *n.* A person who formally praises a person or event.

pan·el \'pan-l\ *n.* **1** A section or part of a wall, ceiling, or door, often sunk below the level of the frame; especially, a thin and usually rectangular board set in a frame, as in a door. **2** A thin, flat piece of wood on which a picture is painted. **3** A painting on such a surface. **4** A lengthwise strip or band sewn in a dress; as, an embroidered *panel* on a skirt. **5** A list or group of persons appointed for some service; especially, a group of persons called to serve on a jury. **6** A group of no less than three persons, often experts in various fields, conducting before an audience an unrehearsed discussion on a topic of interest, either to a special audience or to the general public; a similar group, usually of persons well-known to the public, acting as players in a quiz game or guessing game conducted by a master of ceremonies on a radio or television program. — *v.;* **pan·eled** or **pan·elled; pan·el·ing** or **pan·el·ling** \-l(-)ing\. To furnish, fit, trim, or decorate with panels; as, to *panel* a wall.

pan·el·ing or **pan·el·ling** \'pan-l(-)ing\ *n.* **1** Wood or other material made into panels. **2** Panels considered collectively.

pan·el·ist \'pan-l-əst\ *n.* A member of a panel for discussion or entertainment.

pang \'pang\ *n.* **1** A sudden sharp attack of pain; a throe. **2** A sudden sharp feeling of any emotion; as, a *pang* of regret.

pan·han·dle \'pan-,hand-l\ *n.* **1** The handle of a pan. **2** An arm or projection of land shaped like the handle of a pan.

pan·han·dle \'pan-,hand-l\ *v.;* **pan·han·dled; pan·han·dling** \-l(-)ing\. To approach people on the street and beg for money. — **pan·han·dler** \-lər\ *n.*

pan·ic \'pan-ik\ *n.* **1** A sudden, terrifying fright, especially without reasonable cause. **2** A sudden, widespread fear in financial circles, causing hurried selling of securities and a rapid fall in prices. — *v.;* **pan·icked** \-ikt\; **pan·ick·ing** \-ik-ing\. **1** To affect with panic; to be affected with panic; as, one who *panics* easily. **2** *Slang.* To call forth a show of appreciation on the part of someone. The comedian's performance *panicked* the audience. — **pan·icky** \'pan-ik-ē\ *adj.* — **pan·ic-strick·en** \'pan-ik-,strik-n\ *adj.*

pan·i·cle \'pan-ik-l\ *n.* A flower cluster, loosely branched and often in the shape of a pyramid, in which the branches of the flowerless main stem are elongated clusters in the form of a raceme, blooming from the bottom toward the top and outward, as in the oat.

pan·nier \'pan-yər, 'pan-ē-ər\ *n.* **1** A large basket, especially one of wicker, carried on the back of an animal or the shoulder of a person. **2** A framework worn by women to expand their skirts at the hips. **3** An overskirt puffed out at the sides and back.

pan·o·ply \'pan-ə-plē\ *n.; pl.* **pan·o·plies.** **1** A full suit of armor. **2** Anything defending or protecting completely by covering; anything forming a magnificent covering or environment. The automo-

biles in the parade were covered with *panoplies* of flowers and bunting. — **pan·o·plied** \-plēd\ *adj.*

pan·o·ra·ma \,pan-r-'am-ə, -'äm-, -'ȧm-\ *n.* **1** A picture that is unrolled little by little as a person looks at it. **2** A clear, complete view in every direction. **3** A complete view or treatment of any subject; as, a *panorama* of history. — **pan·o·ram·ic** \-'am-ik\ *adj.*

pan·pipe \'pan-,pīp\ *n.* A wind instrument consisting of a series of hollow reeds or pipes of different lengths, closed at one end and bound together with the mouth pieces in an even row. panpipe

pan·sy \'pan-zē\ *n.; pl.* **pan·sies.** [From medieval English *pensee,* there borrowed from medieval French *pensée,* meaning literally "thought".] A low-growing, commonly annual plant belonging to the violet group and derived from the wild pansy or Johnny-jump-up, with small purple and violet flowers and, in its various garden forms, with showy five-petaled flowers that are usually of cream, violet, or yellow.

pant \'pant\ *v.* **1** To breathe hard or quickly; to gasp; as, to *pant* from running. **2** To want intensely; to long. **3** To breathe or say quickly and with difficulty. — *n.* **1** One of a series of short, quick breaths, as after exercise; a gasp. **2** A puff, as of a steam engine.

pan·ta·lets or **pan·ta·lettes** \,pant-l-'ets\ *n. pl.* Long, loose drawers with ruffles around each ankle, worn by women and girls.

pan·ta·loon \,pant-l-'ün\ *n.* **1** A clown. **2** [in the plural] Trousers.

pan·the·ism \'pan(t)th-ē-,iz-m\ *n.* **1** Any doctrine or belief that the universe taken as a whole is God. **2** The worship of gods of various creeds or religions at one time, as at one period in ancient Rome.

pantalets

pan·ther \'pan(t)th-r\ *n.* **1** The leopard. **2** In America, the cougar.

pant·ies \'pant-ēz\ *n. pl.; sing.* **pan·tie** or **panty** \'pant-ē\. A child's or woman's undergarment covering the lower trunk, with a closed crotch and very short legs.

pan·to·mime \'pant-m-,īm\ *n.* **1** A performer skilled in the art of conveying emotions and ideas without the use of words. **2** A play in which the actors use few or no words. **3** Silent movements or facial expressions that show how a person feels about something. — *v.;* **pan·to·mimed; pan·to·mim·ing.** To represent by pantomime. — **pan·to·mim·ist** \-,ī-məst, -,im-əst\ *n.*

pan·to·then·ic ac·id \'pant-ə-,then-ik\. A substance in the vitamin-B complex that promotes growth, found especially in liver and yeast.

pan·try \'pan-trē\ *n.; pl.* **pan·tries.** A small room where food and dishes are kept.

pants \'pan(t)s\ *n. pl.* **1** Trousers. **2** Drawers; especially, panties.

36. A word that originally comes from French meaning *thought*   36.__
    is
      A. panoply   B. panicle
      C. pansy   D. pantheism

37. If I had a *panoramic* view of the countryside, I would see   37.__
      A. only those things that are moving
      B. in all directions
      C. part of the scene
      D. only the grass

38. In an illustration on the page, an example of a musical   38.__
    instrument is a
      A. pantalet   B. pantaloon
      C. pannier   D. panpipe

39. A word that has at least six different meanings as a noun   39.__
    is
      A. pant   B. pantomine   C. panel   D. panic

40. The play was performed as a ____, so that the audience   40.__
    had to watch the actors' faces and movements very care-
    fully.
    Select the word that BEST completes the above sentence.
      A. panelist   B. pantomine
      C. panegyrist   D. panic

Questions 41-43.

DIRECTIONS: Questions 41 through 43 are to be answered on the
basis of the library card reproduced below.

          Working for yourself

658.1   Hewitt, Geof
H   Working for yourself; how to be suc-
      cessfully self-employed. Photos by
      T. L. Gettings. Rodale [c1977]
      304p illus

      Features the stories and advice of
      nearly one hundred self-employed peo-
      ple as well as guidelines for select-
      ing, promoting, financing, and manag-
      ing a business or trade.

      1 Professions   2 Small business

ISBN 0-87857-162-0

              © THE BAKER & TAYLOR CO.

41. The Dewey Decimal number you would use to locate this   41.___
    book on a library shelf is
       A. 1977   B. 658.1H
       C. ISBN 0-87857-162-0   D. 304

42. All of the following questions would be answered by   42.___
    reading this book EXCEPT:
       A. How have other people started their own businesses?
       B. How do I go about financing my business?
       C. What do I need to know to become a good manager?
       D. How should my boss treat me?

43. If you wanted additional books on the same topic, you   43.___
    would look in the card catalogue under the cross-
    reference
       A. Hewitt   B. professions
       C. government service   D. Rodale

Questions 44-45.

DIRECTIONS: Questions 44 and 45 are to be answered on the basis
of the newspaper advertisement for a Broadway play
shown below.

BOX OFFICE OPENS TOM'W at 10 AM
LIMITED ENGAGEMENT! 10 WEEKS ONLY!
PREVIEWS BEGIN WED. EVG., APRIL 29th
OPENS THURS. EVG., MAY 7th at 6:15
CHARGIT : (212) 944-9300
TICKETRON: (212) 977-9020   Group Sales: (212) 398-8383

MAIL ORDERS NOW!
Monday thru Saturday Evenings at 8 and Saturday
Matinees at 2: Orchestra $30.00; Mezzanine $30.00,
27.50, 25.00. Wednesday Matinees at 2: Orchestra
$28.50; Mezzanine $28.50, 25.00, 22.50. Please enclose
a self-addressed, stamped envelope along with your
check or money order made payable to: Martin Beck
Theatre. List several alternate dates.

MARTIN BECK THEATRE 302 West 45th Street, New York, N.Y.

44. Missing from the ad is   44.___
       A. the times of the performance
       B. information on how to purchase tickets
       C. the name of the play
       D. the opening night of the play

45. For a Wednesday matinee performance, the LEAST expensive   45.__
    ticket is
       A. $30.00   B. $28.50   C. $22.50   D. $20.00

Questions 46-50.

DIRECTIONS: Questions 46 through 50 are to be answered on the
              basis of the following poem.

Summons

Keep me from going to sleep too soon
Or if I go to sleep too soon
Come wake me up. Come any hour
Of night. Come whistling up the road.
Stomp on the porch. Bang on the door.   5
Make me get out of bed and come
and let you in and light a light.
Tell me the northern lights are on -
And make me look. Or tell me clouds
Are doing something to the moon   10
they never did before, and show me
See that I see. Talk to me till
I'm half as wide awake as you
and start to dress wondering why
I ever went to bed at all.   15
Tell me the walking is superb.
Not only tell me but persuade me.
You know I'm not too hard persuaded.

                Robert Francis

46. When the speaker says he is afraid he will "go to sleep   46.__
    too soon," he is really saying that he is afraid he will
       A. die suddenly
       B. lose his interest in life
       C. miss his friend's visit
       D. forget to get undressed

47. We can conclude that the speaker's friend is   47.__
       A. a woman
       B. more alive and curious about life than the speaker
       C. less alive and curious about life than the speaker
       D. disillusioned with life

48. The last line of the poem expresses   48.__
       A. difficulty   B. hope
       C. fear   D. disappointment

49. The title of the poem refers to a   49.__
       A. written notice to appear in court
       B. refusal to cooperate
       C. call for help to another person not present in the
          poem
       D. traffic violation ticket

50. Lines 3-5 in the poem are effective because they
    A. rhyme
    B. are part of a pattern of requests for action
    C. start a new stanza
    D. make use of similes

50.____

KEY (CORRECT ANSWERS)

1. C	26. ending. It
2. A	27. their
3. D	28. see
4. B	29. ending?
5. A	30. true, because
6. B	31. said: "Every
7. D	32. contains
8. A	33. example, the
9. D	34. dying
10. B	35. you are/you're
11. D	36. C
12. B	37. B
13. A	38. D
14. D	39. C
15. B	40. B
16. B	41. B
17. D	42. D
18. A	43. B
19. C	44. C
20. B	45. C
21. English	46. B
22. noticed	47. B
23. should have	48. B
24. going to	49. C
25. high school	50. B

ARITHMETICAL REASONING

EXAMINATION SECTION

DIRECTIONS FOR THIS SECTION:
Each question or incomplete statement is followed by several suggested answers or completions. Select the one that BEST answers the question or completes the statement. *PRINT THE LETTER OF THE CORRECT ANSWER IN THE SPACE AT THE RIGHT.*

TEST 1

1. A class decided to cultivate a garden. The principal gave   1. ...
them a piece of ground 40 feet long and 30 feet wide. There
were 18 boys and 12 girls in the class. The class voted
that each pupil should be allowed an equal amount of the
space in the garden.
The number of square feet which was set aside for the *exclusive* use of the boys was
     A. 30   B. 40   C. 480   D. 720

2. The chef allowed 20 minutes cooking time per pound for a   2. ...
roast weighing 6 lbs. 12 ozs. If the roast was placed in
the oven at 4:20 P.M., it *should be done* by
     A. 6:00 P.M.   B. 6:32 P.M.   C. 6:35 P.M.   D. 7:12 P.M.

3. To check the correctness of the answer to a multiplication   3. ...
example, divide the
     A. product by the multiplier B. multiplier by the product
     C. multiplicand by the multiplier
     D. multiplier by the multiplicand

4. Of the following correct ways to solve .125 X .32, the MOST   4. ...
efficient is to
     A. write .125 under .32, multiply, point off 5 places
     B. write .32 under .125, multiply, point off 5 places
     C. multiply 125 by 32 and divide by 1000 X 100
     D. divide .32 by 8

5. If you were to eat each meal in a different restaurant in   5. ...
the city's eating places, assuming that you eat 3 meals a
day, it would take you more than 19 years to cover all of
the city's eating places.
On the basis of this information, the BEST of the following
choices is that the number of restaurants in the city
     A. exceeds 20,500   B. is closer to 21,000 than 22,000
     C. exceeds 21,000   D. does not exceed 21,500

6. The cost of electricity for operating an 875-watt toaster,   6. ...
an 1100-watt steam iron, and four 75-watt lamps, each for
one hour, at 7.5 cents per kilowatt hour (1 kilowatt equals
1000 watts) is
     A. 15 cents   B. 17 cents   C. $1.54   D. $1.71

7. Of the following, the pair that is NOT a set of equivalents 7. ...
is:
     A. .021%, .00021   B. 1/4%, .0025
     C. 1.5%, 3/200   D. 225%, .225

8. Assuming that the series will continue in the same pattern, 8. ...
the NEXT number in the series 3, 5, 11, 29. ...... is
     A. 41   B. 47   C. 65   D. 83

9. If the total area of a picture measuring 10 inches by 12   9. ...
inches plus a matting of uniform width surrounding the picture is 224 square inches, the WIDTH of the matting is
     A. 2 inches   B. 2 4/11 inches C. 3 inches D. 4 inches

10. The *net price* of a $25 item after SUCCESSIVE discounts of   10. ...
    20% and 30% is
    A. $11   B. $12.50   C. $14   D. $19

TEST 2

1. The cost of 63 inches of ribbon at 12 cents per yard is   1. ...
   A. $.20   B. $.21   C. $.22   D. $.23
2. If 1 1/2 cups of cereal are used with 4 1/2 cups of water,   2. ...
   the amount of water needed with 3/4 of a cup of cereal is
   A. 2 cups   B. 2 1/8 cups C. 2 1/4 cups D. 2 1/2 cups
3. Under certain conditions, sound travels at about 1100 ft.   3. ...
   per second. If 88 ft. per second is approximately equivalent to 60 miles per hour, the speed of sound, under the
   above conditions, is, of the following, *closest to*
   A. 730 miles per hour   B. 740 miles per hour
   C. 750 miles per hour   D. 760 miles per hour
4. Of the following, the *most nearly* accurate set of equiva-   4. ...
   lents is:
   A. 1 ft. equals 30.48 centimeters
   B. 1 centimeter equals 2.54 inches
   C. 1 rod equals 3.28 meters D. 1 meter equals 1.09 feet
5. If one angle of a triangle is three times a second angle   5. ...
   and the third angle is 20 degrees more than the second
   angle, the SECOND ANGLE is
   A. 32°   B. 34°   C. 40°   D. 50°
6. Assuming that on a blueprint 1/4 inch equals 12 inches, the   6. ...
   actual length in feet of a steel bar represented on the
   blueprint by a line 3 3/8 inches long is
   A. 3 3/8   B. 6 3/4   C. 12 1/2   D. 13 1/2
7. A plane leaves Denver, Colorado, on June 1st at 1 P.M.   7. ...
   Mountain Standard Time and arrives at New York City on
   June 2nd at 2 A.M. Eastern Daylight Saving Time. The
   actual time of flight was
   A. 10 hours   B. 11 hours   C. 12 hours   D. 13 hours.
8. Of the following, the value *closest to* that of $\frac{42.10 \times .0003}{.002}$ 8. ...
   is:
   A. .063   B. .63   C. 6.3   D. 63
9. If Mrs. Jones bought 3 3/4 yards of dacron at $1.16 per   9. ...
   yard and 4 2/3 yards of velvet at $3.87 per yard, the
   amount of change she receives from $25 is
   A. $2.12   B. $2.28   C. $2.59   D. $2.63
10. The water level of a swimming pool, 75 feet by 42 feet, is   10. ...
    to be raised 4 inches. The number of gallons of water
    needed for this purpose is (1 cubic foot equals 7 1/2
    gallons)
    A. 140   B. 7,875   C. 31,500   D. 94,500

TEST 3

1. The part of the total quantity represented by a 24-degree   1. ...
   sector of a circle graph is
   A. 6 2/3%   B. 12%   C. 13 1/3%   D. 24%

2

2. If the shipping charges to a certain point are 62 cents for   2. ...
   the first 5 oz. and 8 cents for each additional ounce, the
   weight of a package for which the charges are $1.66 is
   A. 13 ounces   B. 1 1/8 lbs. C. 1 1/4 lbs. D. 1 1/2 lbs.

3. If 15 cans of food are needed for 7 men for 2 days, the   3. ...
   number of cans needed for 4 men for 7 days is
   A. 15   B. 20   C. 25   D. 30

4. The total saving in purchasing thirty 13-cent ice cream   4. ...
   pops for a class party at a reduced rate of $1.38 per
   dozen is
   A. 35¢   B. 40¢   C. 45¢   D. 50¢

5. The quotient for the division of 36 apples among 4 chil-   5. ...
   dren may be correctly found by thinking
   A. 36 ÷ 1/4   B. 36)‾4.0   C. 1/4 of 36   D. 4/36

6. The *missing term* in the equation: 1/3 of ? = 1/2 of 90 is   6. ...
   A. 45   B. 30   C. 15   D. 135

7. The fraction *closest to* 4/5 is   7. ...
   A. 2/3   B. 7/9   C. 8/11   D. 5/8

8. Of the following, the one which may be used CORRECTLY to   8. ...
   compute the value of 4 X 22 1/2 is:
   A. (4X45) + (4X1/2)   B. (4X1/2) + (4X2) + (4X2)
   C. (1/2 of 4) + (2X4) + (2X4) D. (4X20) + (4X2) + (4X1/2)

9. 16 1/2 ÷ 1/4 may CORRECTLY be expressed as   9. ...
   A. (1/4X16) + (1/4X1/2)   B. (4X16) + (4X1/2)
   C. 4)‾16.5   D. 1/4 times 33/2

10. In computation, 3/4 may be CORRECTLY transformed into   10. ...
    6/8 for the *same* reason that
    A. 7 (3+4) = 21 + 28   B. 3 apples + 5 apples = 8
    C. .2)‾3.4 = 2)‾34   D. 3 + 4 = 4 + 3

TEST 4

1. The mathematical law of distribution is illustrated by all   1. ...
   of the following EXCEPT:
   A.   15   B.   15   C.   15   D.   15
         X12   X12   X12   X12
         ───   ───   ───   ───
         150   30   180   30
          30   150   15
         ───   ───   ───   ───
         180   180   180   180

2. Of the following series of partial sums which might arise   2. ...
   in the addition of 36 and 25, the one that is INCORRECT is:
   A. 11, 31, 61 B. 11, 4, 6, 61 C. 11, 41, 61 D. 36, 56, 61

3. Of the following, the one which equals one million is: 3. ...
   A. ten hundred thousand   B. 10^7
   C. 10X10X10X10X10X10X10   D. 1 plus 6 zeros

4. Of the following groups, the one containing four terms all   4. ...
   associated with one algorismic process is:
   A. Addend, quotient, dividend, divisor
   B. Dividend, quotient, divisor, minuend
   C. Dividend, quotient, addend, minuend
   D. Multiplicand, product, minuend, addend

5. Depreciation of a certain machine is estimated, for any   5. ...
   year, at 20% of its value at the beginning of the year. If
   the machine is purchased for $600, its estimated net value
   at the end of two years is *closest to*

A. $325   B. $350   C. $375   D. $400

6. Hats are purchased at the rate of $33 per dozen. If they   6. ...
are sold at a close-out sale for $2.50 each, the *percent loss* on the cost price is
   A. 3   B. 3 1/3   C. 9 1/11   D. 10

7. The time, 3 hours, 58 minutes after 10:56 A.M., is   7. ...
   A. 4:54 P.M.   B. 2:54 P.M.   C. 4:15 P.M.   D. 2:15 P.M.

8. Mr. Brown had $20.00 when he took his three children on a   8. ...
bus trip. He spent $7.33 for the four tickets and bought
each of the children a magazine costing 15¢, a candy bar
costing 11¢, and a 5¢ package of chewing gum.
His CHANGE from the $20.00 was
   A. $12.74   B. $11.43   C. $11.74   D. $12.84

9. The loan value on a life insurance policy at the end of   9. ...
5 years is $30.19 per $1000 of insurance. The LARGEST
amount to the *nearest* dollar that can be borrowed on a
$5500 policy at the end of five years is
   A. $17   B. $151   C. $166   D. $1660

10. Using cups that hold six ounces of milk, the number of   10. ...
cupfuls a person can obtain from 1 1/2 gallons of milk is
   A. 16   B. 24   C. 32   D. 64

TEST 5

1. A storekeeper purchased an article for $36. In order to   1. ...
include 10% of cost for overhead and to provide $9 of net
profit, the MARKUP *should be*
   A. 25%   B. 35%   C. 37 1/2%   D. 40%

2. A rectangular carton has twice the height, one-third the   2. ...
length, and four times the width of a second carton. The
ratio of the volume of the first carton to that of the
second is
   A. 16:3   B. 3:1   C. 8:3   D. 3:8

3. If a boy has a number of dimes and quarters in his pocket   3. ...
adding up to $3.10, the LARGEST possible number of dimes
he can have is
   A. 16   B. 28   C. 26   D. 21

4. In a number system using the base 10, the value represented 4. ...
by the first digit 3 reading from the left, in the number
82,364,371, is
   A. 30 times the value represented by the second digit 3
   B. 100 times the value represented by the second digit 3
   C. 1,000 times the value represented by the second digit 3
   D. 10,000 times the value represented by the second digit 3

5. The number of revolutions made by a bicycle wheel of 28-   5. ...
inch diameter in traveling 1/2 mile is *closest to*
   A. 720   B. 180   C. 360   D. 120

6. Of the following, the property which is *true* of ALL paral-   6. ...
lelograms is that the
   A. diagonals are equal
   B. diagonals meet at right angles
   C. sum of the interior angles is 180°
   D. diagonals bisect each other

7.
```
        218
  32) 6985
       64
       ‾‾
       58
       32
       ‾‾
       265
       256
       ‾‾‾
         9
```
Of the following explanations about steps in the above computation, the one which is LEAST meaningful or accurate is that the
   A. 64 represents 200 X 32
   B. 265 is the result of subtracting 320 from 585
   C. 9 is part of the quotient
   D. 256 symbolizes the subtraction of 32 eight times

8. Assuming that a system of meridians and parallels of latitude like that used on maps of the earth's surface, were designed for the moon's surface, the distance covered by a man traveling 1° on the moon, as compared to that covered in traveling 1° on the earth, would be   8. ...
   A. equal   B. less
   C. greater   D. sometimes greater and sometimes less

9. 1958 may MOST correctly be expressed in Roman numerals as   9. ...
   A. MDCDLVIII   B. CMMLVIII   C. MCMLVIII   D. MCMLIIX

10. If the *same* positive quantity is added to both the numerator and the denominator of a proper fraction, the VALUE of the new fraction as compared to that of the original fraction will be   10. ...
   A. greater   B. less
   C. equal   D. either greater or less

————

SOLUTIONS TO ARITHMETICAL REASONING

TEST 1

1. Answer: (D) 720

   40 feet
   ┌─────────────────┐
   │ 1200 square   │
   │   feet   │ 30 feet
   └─────────────────┘

   ```
       40 sq. ft. per child
   30/1200
   ```

   18 (boys) X 40 = 720 sq. ft.

2. Answer: (C) 6:35 P.M.
   20 minutes for 1 lb.
   $$\frac{12 \text{ oz.}}{16 \text{ oz.}} = \frac{3}{4} \text{ lb.}$$
   $\frac{3}{4}$ X 20 = 15 minutes
   20 X 6 = 120 minutes

   ```
        120
      +  15
       ‾‾‾‾
        135 minutes
      -120 minutes (2 hours)
       ‾‾‾‾
         15 minutes
   ```

   ```
        4:20 P.M.
      + 2:15  (2 hours, 15 minutes)
       ‾‾‾‾‾‾
        6:35 P.M.
   ```

3. Answer: (A) product by the multiplier
   12 (multiplicand)
   X 2 (multiplier)
   ‾‾24‾ (product)

4. Answer: (D) divide .32 by 8
   The most efficient way is to divide .32 by 8.
   .125 = .12 1/2 = 12 1/2% = 1/8

   $1/8 \times .32 = \dfrac{.32}{8}$

   $8\overline{)\begin{matrix}.04 \\ .32 \\ \underline{.32}\end{matrix}}$

5. Answer: (A) exceeds 20,500
   365 (days in 1 year)   4 (leap-year days)
   X   3 (meals)   X 3 (meals)
   ‾1095‾ (meals in 1 year)   ‾12‾ (leap-year meals)
   X 19 (number of years)
   20,805 (number of meals eaten in 19 years)
   +   12 (number of meals eaten in leap years)
   ‾20,817‾ (total)

6. Answer: (B) 17 cents
   875 + 1100 + 300 = 2275 watts
   2275 ÷ 1000 = 2 11/40 kilowatt hours
   2 11/40 x 7.5 cents = $.17 approximately

7. Answer: (D) 225%, .225
   Taking each alternative in turn:
   A. .021% = .00021   B. 1/4% = $\dfrac{1}{400}$ = .0025

   C. 1.5% = .015+$\dfrac{15}{1000}$ = $\dfrac{3}{200}$ D. 225% = 2.25 (*not* .225)

8. Answer: (D) 83
   SUGGESTIONS FOR SERIES PROBLEMS
   1. Find the differences between the numbers (or squares of differences).
   2. In this series, each difference is multiplied by 3 and added to the succeeding number.
      3,5: the difference is 2; this difference was multiplied by 3, giving 6, which was then added to 5, to make the next number in the series 11.
      5,11: the difference is 6; this difference was multiplied by 3, giving 18, which was then added to 11, to make the next number in the series 29.
      11,29: the difference is 18; this difference should be multiplied by 3, giving 54, which, when added to 29, will give the next number in the series, 83.

9. Answer: (A) 2 inches

6

The total area = 224 square inches (16 x 14).
If 2 inches are added to either side of the picture's width and to either side of the picture's length, we get a new width of 14 inches (10+4) and a new length of 16 inches (12+4). Therefore, 14 x 16 = 224 square inches.
Or, a uniform matting width of 2 inches.

10. Answer: (C) $14

SOLUTION

Successive discounts
20%, 30%
1. Convert to decimals .2, .3
2. Subtract from 1.0   .8, .7
3. Multiply .8 X .7 = .56
4. 1.00 - .56 = .44

$$\begin{array}{r} 25.00 \\ \times\ \ .44 \\ \hline 100 \\ 100 \\ \hline \$11.00 \end{array}$$

5. $25.00 - $11.00 = $14.00

ALTERNATE SOLUTION

$$\begin{array}{r} \$\ 25 \\ \times\ \ .20 \\ \hline \$\ 5 \end{array}$$

$25 - $5 = $20

$$\begin{array}{r} \$20 \\ \times\ .30 \\ \hline \$\ 6 \end{array}$$

$20 - $6 = $14

TEST 2

1. Answer: (B) $.21

SOLUTION

$$63"=\frac{63}{36}\text{ yds} ;\ \frac{\cancel{63}}{\cancel{36}}\ X\ \frac{.01}{\cancel{.12}} = 21¢$$
$$\frac{3}{}$$

ALTERNATE SOLUTION

12¢ per yard

$$\frac{12}{36} = \frac{1}{3}¢\text{ per inch}; \frac{63"}{1}X\frac{1}{3}¢=\frac{63}{3} = 21¢$$

2. Answer: (C) 2 1/4 cups   SOLUTION

Proportion	Cereal	Water
1st mixture	1 1/2 cups	4 1/2 cups
2nd mixture	3/4 cups	x cups

3/4 is half of 1 1/2; therefore, half of 4 1/2 is 2 1/4

ALTERNATE SOLUTION

From the data given, we form the proportion,
1 1/2(cups of cereal): 4 1/2 (cups of water)=3/4 (cup of cereal):x
∴3/2 : 9/2 = 3/4 : x
3/2x = 27/4
x = 9/4 - 2 1/4 (cups of water)

3. Answer: (C) 750 miles per hour
Speed of sound = 1100 ft. per second
88 ft. per second = 60 miles an hour
$$\frac{1100}{88}$$ = 12 1/2 (the number of times the speed of sound is greater than 60 miles an hour)
∴60 x 12 1/2 = 750 miles per hour (the speed of sound)

4. Answer: (A) 1 ft. equals 30.48 centimeters
Taking each alternative in turn:
1. A meter = 100 centimeters
A meter = 39 in. (approx.) = 3 1/4 ft. ($\frac{39}{12}$ = 3 1/4)
3 1/4 ft. = 1 meter = 100 centimeters
∴1 ft. = $\frac{100}{3\ 1/4}$ = 30.48 centimeters (approx.)

7

2. 1 meter = 39 in. = 3 1/4 ft. (approx.)
3. 1 centimeter = .39 in.
4. 1 rod = 5 1/2 yds. = 16 1/2 ft.
    .·.1 rod = 5 meters (approx.) (see Item 2 above)
5. Answer: (A) 32°
    Let x = second angle
    Let 3x = first angle
    Let x + 20° = third angle
    .·. 5x + 20 = 180°
            x = 32°

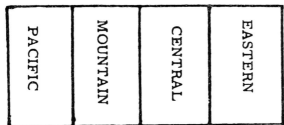

6. Answer: (D) 13 1/2
    $$\frac{1/4"}{12} = \frac{3\ 3/8"}{x}$$
    1/4 ÷ 12/1 = 27/8 ÷ x/1
    1/4 X 1/12 = 27/8 X 1/x

$$\frac{1}{4} = \frac{27}{8x}$$
8x = 48 X 27 = 1296
    x = 162 inches
      = 13 1/2 ft.

7. Answer: (A) 10 hours
        TIME BELTS

PACIFIC	MOUNTAIN	CENTRAL	EASTERN

4 A.M. 5 A.M. 6 A.M. 7 A.M. E. S. T.
8 A. M. D. S. T.

In traveling eastward we set
our clocks forward for each
time zone.

Plane left at 1 P.M.
Traveled around clock 12 hours
or 13 hours at 2 A.M.

    Subtract 2 hours' difference between Mountain Time and Eastern
    Standard Time. Subtract another hour for Daylight Saving Time.
    That is, 13 - 3 = 10 hours
8. Answer: (C) 6.3
    In 42.10, discard for practical purposes the .10 and perform as
    follows: $\frac{42 \times .0003}{.002} = \frac{.0126}{.002} = \frac{12.6}{2} = 6.3$
9. Answer: (C) $2.59
        $1.16 $3.87 $18.06 $25.00
    X   3 3/4   X   4 2/3   +   4.35   -   22.41
        $4.35 $18.06 $22.41 $ 2.59
10. Answer: (B) 7,875
    42 X 75 X 1/3 ft. (4") = 1050 cu. ft.
                        X   7 1/2
                        7,875 gallons

TEST 3

1. Answer: (A) 6 2/3%

$$\frac{24}{360} = \frac{2}{30} = \frac{1}{15} = .06\ 2/3 = 6\ 2/3\%$$

2. Answer: (B) 1 1/8 lbs.
   Total charges   = $1.66
   Charge for 1st 5 oz. =   .62
                          $1.04 (remaining charges at rate of .08/oz.)
   $1.04 ÷ .08 (oz.) = 13 oz.
      5 oz. + 13 oz. = 18 oz. (Total no. of oz. in weight of pkge.)
   OR $\frac{18}{16}$ = 1 1/8 lb.

3. Answer: (D) 30
   If 15 cans of food are needed for 7 men for 2 days, therefore,
   7 1/2 cans are needed for these same 7 men for 1 day.
   7 1/2 ÷ 7 = $\frac{15}{14}$, the no. of cans needed by 1 man for 1 day.

   4 x 7 x $\frac{15}{14}$ = 30, the number of cans needed by 4 men for 7 days.

4. Answer: (C) 45¢
   $.13 x 30 = $3.90 (regular rate)
   30 = 2 1/2 doz.; $1.38 x 2 1/2 = $3.45 (reduced rate)
   Total saving = $.45 ($3.90 - $3.45)

5. Answer: (C) 1/4 of 36 $\frac{36}{4}$ = 9

6. Answer: (D) 135   1/3 of ? = 1/2 of 90
                      1/3 x = 45
                          x = 3 X 45
                            = 135

7. Answer: (B) 7/9   4/5 = .80   8/11 = .73
                      2/3 = .66   5/8 = .63
                      7/9 = .78

8. Answer: (D) (4 X 20) + (4 X 2) + (4 X 1/2)
      22 1/2
   X   4
      80   Choice (D) (4X20)+(4X2)+(4X1/2) = 80+8+2 = 90
       8   (This is an example of the Distributive Law,
       2   which links the operations of addition and
      90   multiplication.)

9. Answer: (B) (4 X 16) + (4 X 1/2)
   16 1/2 ÷ 4 = $\frac{16\ 1/2}{4}$ = 16 1/2 X 4/1 = (4 X 16) + (4 X 1/2)

10. Answer: (C) .2$\overline{)3.4}$ = 2$\overline{)34}$
    $\frac{3}{4}$ = $\frac{6}{8}$; $\frac{3.4}{.2}$ = $\frac{34}{2}$ = 17

TEST 4

1. Answer: (C)   15
                   X12
                   180
   (A) 10 X 15 = 150   (B) 2 X 15 = 30   (D) 2 X 15 = 30
        2 X 15 = 30   10 X 15 = 150   10 X 15 = 15(0)
                  180   180   180
   The Distributive Law links the operations of addition and
   arithmetic.

2. Answer: (B) 11, 4, 6, 61

9

```
     Partial Sums
        36      (A)  11      (C)  11      (D)  36
       +25          +20          +30          +20
        61           31           41           56
                    +30          +20          + 5
                     61           61           61
```

3. Answer: (A) ten hundred thousand   100,000 X 10 = 1,000,000

4. Answer: (B) dividend, quotient, divisor, minuend
   Division is repeated subtraction

```
                        21    quotient
     divisor 12) 256          dividend
                 24
                 16    minuend - partial dividend
                 12
                  4    partial dividend
```

```
      36 multiplicand
     X45 multiplier                           5 addend
     180 partial product                     +6 addend
     144 partial product                     11 sum
    1620 product
```

```
                              7,485 minuend
                              2,648 subtrahend
                              4,837 remainder (difference)
```

5. Answer: (C) $375

```
        $600        $480        $600        $480
     X    .20     X    .20     - 120       -  96
       120.00       96.00      $480        $384 ( approximately)
```

6. Answer: (C) 9 1/11
   Cost of one dozen $33.00 $2.50
   Selling price of one dozen   30.00   X 12
   Loss $ 3.00 $30.00 sold at close-out sale

   $$\frac{L}{C} = \frac{\$ 3}{\$33} = \frac{1}{11} = 9\ 1/11\%$$

7. Answer: (B) 2:54 p.m.
   A simple way to do this is to add 4 minutes to 10:56 a.m., making
   11:00 a.m.   Adding 3 hours = 2:00 p.m.
   Adding 54 minutes (instead of 58 minutes, to compensate for the
   4 minutes added to 10:56 a.m.) = 2:54 p.m.

8. Answer: (C) $11.74   15¢   31¢ $7.33 $20.00
                         11¢   X 3   + .93   - 8.26
                          5¢   93¢ $8.26 $11.74
                         31¢

9. Answer: (C) $166
   $30.19 x 5 = $150.95 (loan value on $5,00 policy at end of 5 yrs.)
   $150.95 ÷ 10 = $15.10 (approx.) (loan value on additional $500 at
                                    end of 5 years)
   ∴ $150.95 + $15.10 = $166 (approx.)

10. Answer: (C) 32
    We must know that 1 cup = 8 oz. and that 1 qt. = 4 cups or 32 oz.
    Since 1 gal. = 4 qts., 1 gal. = 128 oz. (4 x 32 oz.)
    ∴ 1/2 gal. = 64 oz. and 1 1/2 gal. = 192 oz. (128 + 64)
    Finally, 192 ÷ 6 = 32 (cups)

TEST 5

1. Answer: (B) 35%
   Cost = $36
   Overhead = 10% of Cost, OR $3.60
   Profit = $9.00 (Given)
       Selling Price = $48.60 (36 + 3.60 + 9)
   Markup = $12.60 (48.60 (S.P.) - 36 (Cost))
   Finally, $\frac{12.60 \text{ (markup)}}{36.00 \text{ (cost)}}$ = 35%

2. Answer: (C) 8:3

1st carton

V = 8

2nd carton

V = 3

$$\frac{V1}{V2} = \frac{8}{3}$$

3. Answer: (C) 26   26 X 10 = $2.60 + .50 = $3.10

4. Answer: (C) 1,000 times the value represented by the second digit 3
        (approximately) 300 x 1,000 = 300,000

5. Answer: (C) 360   C = π D
                     C = $\frac{22}{7}$ X 28 = 88"
   1 revolution of wheel covers 88"
   $\frac{1}{2}$ X 5280 X $\frac{12}{1}$ = traveling distance in inches
                                   360 revolutions
   6 X 5280 - 31680 inches   88$\overline{)31680}$
                                 264
                                  528
                                  528

6. Answer: (D) diagonals bisect each other

         triangle = 180°

         parallelogram = 360°

7. Answer: (C) 9 is part of the quotient
   Division is repeated subtraction.
   Below is a division "pyramid," which shows what actually happens
   when we divide.

11

```
           8
          10
         200
   32) 6985    dividend
       6400
        585    partial dividend
        320
        265    partial dividend
        256
          9    partial dividend
```

32 X 100 = 3200
32 X 200 = 6400
32 X 10 = 320

8. Answer: (B) less

Diameter of moon = 2000 miles ; Diameter of earth = 8000 miles

Moon

Earth

The larger the circle, the larger the arc.

$1°$ of arc $= \dfrac{1}{360}$ of circle

Circumference of earth = 25,000 miles
Circumference of moon = 6,200 miles (1/4 of earth)

```
          69+
   360) 25,000
        21 6
         3 40
         3 24
           16
```

$1° = 69+$ miles on the equator (Earth)
$1° = 17+$ miles (Moon)

9. Answer: (C) MCMLVIII

```
   M    = 1000
   CM   =  900
   L    =   50
   VIII =    8
            1958
```

10. Answer: (A) greater

$$\frac{2 + 2}{3 + 2} = \frac{4}{5} = \frac{12}{15} \qquad \frac{2}{3} = \frac{10}{15}$$

EXAMINATION SECTION

DIRECTIONS: Each question or incomplete statement is followed by several suggested answers or completions. Select the one that BEST answers the question or completes the statement. *PRINT THE LETTER OF THE CORRECT ANSWER IN THE SPACE AT THE RIGHT.*

1. $2/3 \times 12$ equals
   A. 4   B. 6   C. 8
   D. 18   E. None of the above   1.___

2.   83.97
       1.78
     14.36
      9.03   2.___

   The sum of the above column is
   A. 99.13   B. 99.24   C. 109.14
   D. 109.23   E. 109.24

3. The value of x in the equation $5x = 75$ is
   A. 13   B. 15   C. 70
   D. 80   E. none of the above   3.___

4. $65.13 \div .13$ equals
   A. .501   B. 5.01   C. 50.1
   D. 501   E. none of the above   4.___

5. The sum of 6 feet 8 inches and 3 feet 4 inches is
   A. 2 ft. 2 in.   B. 9 ft.   C. 10 ft.
   D. 10 ft. 12 in.   E. none of the above   5.___

6. $3/4 - 1/2 + 1/8$ equals
   A. 3/10   B. 3/8   C. 5/8
   D. 1 3/8   E. none of the above   6.___

7. $4\ 5/16 - 2\ 3/8$ equals
   A. 1 15/16   B. 2 1/16   C. 2 1/4
   D. 2 15/16   E. none of the above   7.___

8. $(-12) + (-3)$ equals
   A. -9   B. +15   C. +9
   D. -15   E. none of the above   8.___

9. The ratio of the lengths of two lines is 5 to 3. The length of the shorter line is 30 inches. The length of the longer line is _____ inches.
   A. 18   B. 48   C. 50
   D. 150   E. none of the above   9.___

10. .025 written as a common fraction is   10.___
    A. 25/10   B. 25/100   C. 25/1000
    D. 25/10,000   E. none of the above

11. In the proportion $\frac{5}{2} = \frac{9}{x}$, the value of x is   11.___
    A. 1.8   B. 3.6   C. 22.5
    D. 36   E. none of the above

12. 33 1/3 percent of 3 equals   12.___
    A. 1   B. 10   C. 100/3
    D. 100   E. none of the above

13. $\sqrt{225}$ equals   13.___
    A. 15   B. 20.5   C. 25
    D. 112.5   E. none of the above

14. On the portion of the scale shown at   14.___
the right, the reading to which the
arrow points is _____ units.
    A. 6 3/16
    B. 6 3/5
    C. 6 3/4
    D. 7 5/8
    E. none of the above

15. If $\frac{4x}{5} - 6 = 10$, then x equals   15.___
    A. 15 1/5   B. 5   C. 4
    D. 3 1/5   E. none of the above

16. The difference between 8 hours 0 minutes 6 seconds and   16.___
6 hours 4 minutes 15 seconds is _____ hr. _____ min.
_____ seconds.
    A. 0; 54; 51   B. 1; 54; 51   C. 2; 4; 9
    D. 2; 54; 45   E. none of the above

17. The scores made by nine pupils on a science test are: 2,   17.___
4, 6, 6, 8, 10, 12, 14, 19.
The MEAN score is
    A. 6   B. 8   C. 9
    D. 81   E. none of the above

18. A certain cost formula is   18.___
represented graphically in the
figure at the right.
From the graph, when n = 7,
the value of C is about
    A. 140
    B. 120
    C. 110
    D. 102
    E. none of the above

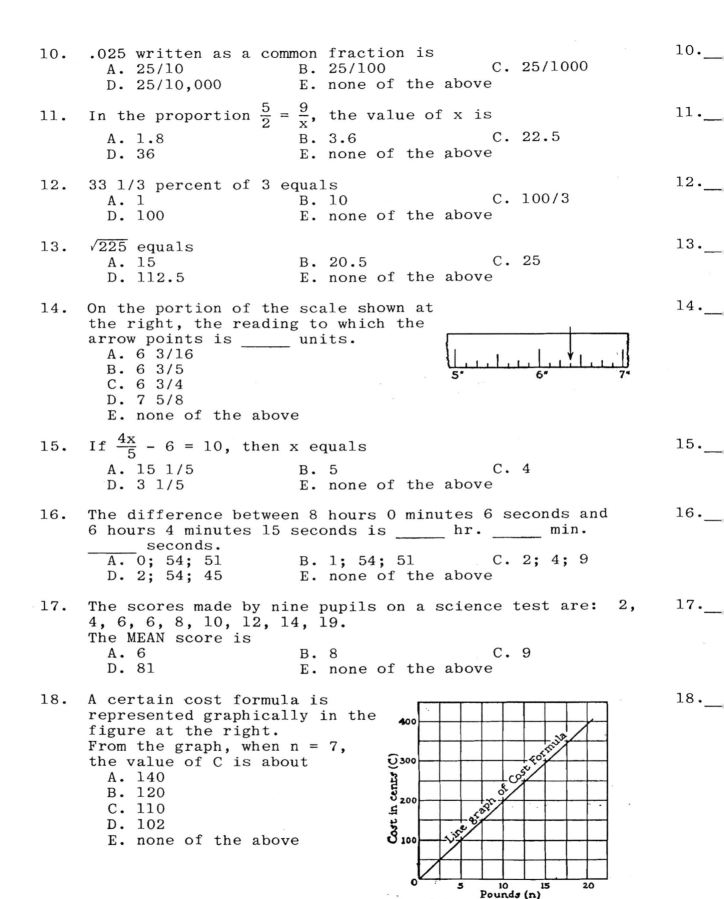

19. A simplified form of the expression $A = \frac{1}{2}bh + \frac{1}{2}ah$ is   19.___
    A. $A = \frac{1}{2}h(b+a)$ B. $A = bh + ah$ C. $A = abh$

    D. $\frac{A}{\frac{1}{2}bh} = \frac{1}{2}ah$ E. none of the above

20. The ratio of 6 inches to 3 feet is   20.___
    A. 6/1   B. 2/1   C. 1/2
    D. 1/18   E. none of the above

21. The value of s in the equation $3s = 12 - s$ is   21.___
    A. 6   B. 4   C. 3 2/3
    D. 3   E. none of the above

22. 16 2/3 percent of what number is 30?   22.___
    A. 5   B. 18   C. 160
    D. 180   E. none of the above

23. The line graph shown at the right represents the temperature readings in Albany, New York, at two-hour intervals from 4 A.M. to 10 P.M. on a certain day in February. The APPROXIMATE change in temperature between 7 A.M. and 9 A.M. is _____ degrees.   23.___
    A. 3.5
    B. 3.0
    C. 2.5
    D. 2.0
    E. none of the above

Questions 24-25.

DIRECTIONS: Questions 24 and 25 are to be answered on the basis of the following figure and information.

In the figure below, a square whose side is b is cut from a square whose side is a.

24. The sum of the perimeters of Section I and Section III can be represented by   24.___
    A. b^2 B. 4a - 2b   C. 2a + 3b
    D. a(a-b)   E. none of the above

25. The sum of the areas of Section II and Section IV can be represented by   25.___
    A. b^2 B. 4a - 2b   C. 2a + 3b
    D. a(a-b)   E. none of the above

26. The temperature reading (F) on the Fahrenheit scale equals 32 more than 9/5 of the Centigrade reading (C). This rule when translated into symbols is expressed by   26.___
    A. F = 9/5C + 32   B. F = 9/5(C + 32)   C. F = 9/5 + 32C
    D. F + 32 = 9/5C   E. none of the above

27. In the equation 6x - 114 = .3x, the value of x is   27.___
    A. 38   B. 20   C. 12 2/3
    D. 2   E. none of the above

28. What percent of 42 is 84?   28.___
    A. ½%   B. 2%   C. 50%
    D. 200%   E. none of the above

29. The CORRECT name of the solid figure at the right is   29.___
    A. semicircle
    B. circle
    C. sphere
    D. cone
    E. cylinder

30. Which of these fractions has the LARGEST value?   30.___
    A. 1/2   B. 5/9   C. 7/12
    D. 2/3   E. 3/4

31. The formula for the area of a circle is A =   31.___
    A. πr^2 B. $2/3\pi r^2$ C. $2\pi r$
    D. bh   E. none of the above

32. The CORRECT name of the figure at the right is   32.___
    A. pentagon
    B. hexagon
    C. rectangle
    D. trapezoid
    E. square

33. The figure at the right is a   33.___
    A. rectangle
    B. square
    C. pentagon
    D. trapezoid
    E. parallelogram

34. If x = -18, y = 3, and z = -2, then x - y + z equals   34.____
    A. 3   B. -3   C. -23   D. -52   E. -56

35. The number 335,560 rounded off to the nearest thousand is   35.____
    A. 335,000   B. 335,500   C. 336,000
    D. 340,000   E. none of the above

36. In the triangle ABC at the right, the sum   36.____
of the angles is _____ degrees.
    A. 360
    B. 180
    C. 90
    D. 45
    E. none of the above

37. According to the map shown at   37.____
the right, the APPROXIMATE
distance between the southern
point of New York City and
Albany is _____ miles.
    A. 50
    B. 75
    C. 130
    D. 180
    E. 200

38. If 6 is added to a certain number n, the result is 1.   38.____
An equation which expresses this relationship is
    A. n + 6 = 1   B. n - 1 = 6   C. 6 - n = 1
    D. n + 1 = 6   E. none of the above

39. In the expression $2n^3$, the 3 is called a(n)   39.____
    A. coefficient   B. factor   C. exponent
    D. multiplicand   E. none of the above

40. The number of inches in n feet is represented by   40.____
    A. 12n   B. 3n   C. n/3
    D. n/12   E. none of the above

41. The simple interest on $600 for 3 months at 4 percent per   41.____
year is represented by 600 × .04 ×
    A. 1/4   B. 1/3   C. 3
    D. 4   E. none of the above

42. The circle graph at the right indicates how a family's annual budget of $3000 was planned.

    Food   40 percent
    Shelter   25 percent
    Clothes   15 percent
    Operating Expenses   10 percent
    Insurance & Savings   10 percent

The part of the circle representing Shelter is _____ degrees.

    A. 25
    B. 45
    C. 90
    D. 250
    E. none of the above

42.___

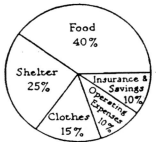

43. In the parallelogram ABCD at the right, each small square represents 4 square inches.
The area of the right triangle AED represents _____ square inches.

    A. 3
    B. 12
    C. 24
    D. 48
    E. none of the above

43.___

44. A surveyor measured angle x with a transit. (See figure at the right.)
Angle x is called

    A. the angle of depression of B from A
    B. an obtuse angle
    C. the supplement of angle y
    D. the angle of elevation of B from A
    E. none of the above

44.___

45. In the figure at the right, AOB is a straight line.
An equation showing the relationship between u and v is

    A. $u = \frac{1}{2}v$
    B. $u = 180 - v$
    C. $u + v = 90$
    D. $v = 3u$
    E. none of the above

45.___

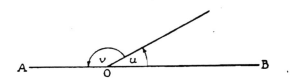

46. If x = 4 when y = 6 and x varies directly as y, then when   46.___
    y = 15, x equals
       A. 20   B. 10   C. 1 3/5
       D. 1 1/3   E. none of the above

47. A discount of 15 percent from a marked price produces a   47.___
    net price which is _____ of the marked price.
       A. .15%   B. .85%   C. 15%   D. 85%   E. 115%

48. When the formula A = P + Prt is solved for t, t equals   48.___
       A. A - P - Pr   B. $\frac{A - Pr}{P}$ C. $\frac{A - P}{1 + r}$

       D. $\frac{A - P}{Pr}$ E. none of the above

49. The Greek letter π 49.___
       A. was assigned the value 3.1416 by the International
          Court of Law
       B. was given an arbitrary value of 22/7 by a famous
          mathematician
       C. was discovered to be exactly 3.142
       D. when multiplied by the radius of a circle equals the
          area
       E. is used as a symbol for the ratio of the circumference
          of a circle to its diameter

50. If the base and altitude of a triangle are doubled, the   50.___
    area
       A. remains constant   B. is multiplied by 4
       C. is doubled   D. is divided by 4
       E. is none of the above

51. Each side of the equilateral triangle in   51.___
    the figure at the right is s inches long.
    The length of an altitude of the triangle
    is represented as
       A. s in.
       B. s$\sqrt{2}$ in.
       C. s$\sqrt{3}$ in.
       D. $\frac{s\sqrt{3}}{2}$ in.

       E. none of the above

52. The length of a meter is about _____ inches.   52.___
       A. 1   B. 6   C. 12   D. 40   E. 100

53. A point which lies on the straight-line graph of the   53.___
    equation 2x - 3y = 12 is
       A. (3,-2)   B. (2,-3)   C. (-4,0)
       D. (0,6)   E. none of the above

54. If the two parallel lines AB and
CD in the figure at the right are
cut by a third line, EF, then the
FALSE statement is
A. $\angle r + \angle s = \angle s + \angle y$
B. $\angle y + \angle w = \angle t + \angle s$
C. $\angle u + \angle w = \angle s + \angle x$
D. $\angle r + \angle x = \angle t + \angle w$
E. $\angle s + \angle u = \angle r + \angle t$

54.__

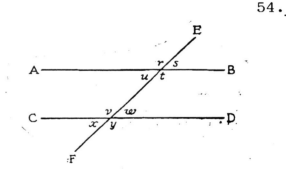

55. The product of n^4 and n^2 equals
A. $2n^8$　　　　　B. $2n^6$　　　　　C. n^8
D. n^2　　　　　E. none of the above

55.__

56. The volume of the rectangular
solid shown at the right is
A. 12 cu. in.
B. 44 sq. in.
C. 48 cu. in.
D. 88 sq. in.
E. none of the above

56.__

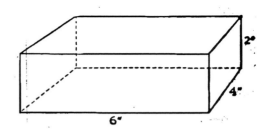

57. Baseball bats listed at twenty-one dollars per dozen are
sold to schools at a discount of 20 percent.
How much do they cost the schools per dozen?
A. $4.20　　　　　B. $16.80　　　　　C. $20.80
D. $25.20　　　　　E. None of the above

57.__

58. Last year a Chicago merchant's total business amounted to
$30,000. For the goods sold, he paid $12,000, for rent
he paid $2500, for clerk services $4742, and for other
expenses $1058.
His average monthly net profit was
A. $676.67　　　　　B. $891.67　　　　　C. $2500.00
D. $9700.00　　　　　E. none of the above

58.__

59. If the marked price of an article is $100 and the first
discount is 10 percent and the second discount 2 percent,
the sale price is
A. $78.20　　　　　B. $88.00　　　　　C. $88.20
D. $88.80　　　　　E. none of the above

59.__

60. Mr. Smith agreed to pay an automobile agency a commission
of 18 percent of the selling price of his car.
If the selling price was $1250, Mr. Smith would receive
A. $225.00　　　　　B. $1025.00　　　　　C. $1227.50
D. $1475.00　　　　　E. none of the above

60.__

61. Mr. Browne receives $30.45 per year on an investment of
$870.
At this rate, if his total investment was $1500, his
annual interest would be
    A. $52.50   B. $62.50   C. $625.00
    D. $655.45   E. none of the above

61.___

62. The Ephrata National Bank discounted a 60-day note for
$3500 at $3\frac{1}{2}$ percent per year.
The proceeds of the note were
    A. $3377.50   B. $3479.58   C. $3520.42
    D. $3622.50   E. none of the above

62.___

63. The normal weight of an adult can be found by using the
formula w = 5.5(20+d), where w represents the weight in
pounds and d the number of inches one's height exceeds
5 feet.
By this formula, the normal weight of an adult who is
5'6" tall is _____ pounds.
    A. 134   B. 140.25   C. 140.8
    D. 143.0   E. none of the above

63.___

64. In the figure at the right,
triangles ACB and ADE are
similar triangles.
The length of side DE is
_____ feet.
    A. 30
    B. 32
    C. 48
    D. 50
    E. none of the above

64.___

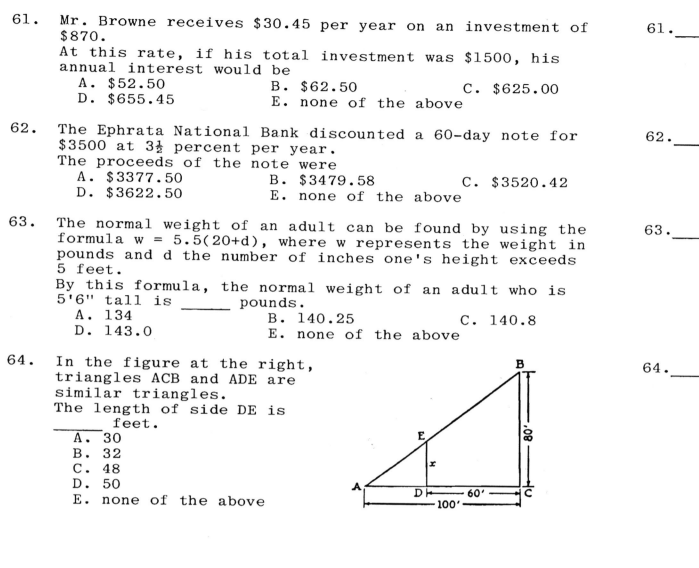

65. A square piece of tin shown in the
figure at the right is used to make
an open box. One-inch squares are
cut from each corner of the piece of
tin and the sides then turned up, to
form a box containing 49 cubic
inches.
The length of a side of the original
square piece of tin required to make
this box is _____ inches.
    A. 5
    B. 7
    C. 8
    D. 9
    E. none of the above

65.___

KEY (CORRECT ANSWERS)

1. C	16. E	31. A	46. B	61. A
2. C	17. C	32. A	47. D	62. B
3. B	18. A	33. E	48. D	63. D
4. D	19. A	34. C	49. E	64. B
5. C	20. E	35. C	50. B	65. D
6. B	21. D	36. B	51. D	
7. A	22. D	37. C	52. D	
8. D	23. C	38. A	53. A	
9. C	24. E	39. C	54. E	
10. C	25. D	40. A	55. E	
11. B	26. A	41. A	56. C	
12. A	27. B	42. C	57. B	
13. A	28. D	43. B	58. E	
14. E	29. E	44. D	59. C	
15. E	30. E	45. B	60. B	

SOLUTIONS TO PROBLEMS

1. $2/3 \times 12 = \frac{2}{3} \cdot \frac{12}{1} = \frac{24}{3} = 8$

2. Adding, we get 109.14

3. If 5x = 75, x = 75/5 = 15

4. 65.13 ÷ .13 = 501

5. 6 ft. 8 in. + 3 ft. 4 in. = 9 ft. 12 in. = 10 ft.

6. 3/4 - 1/2 + 1/8 = 6/8 - 4/8 + 1/8 = 3/8

7. $4\frac{5}{16} - 2\frac{3}{8} = 3\frac{21}{16} - 2\frac{6}{16} = 1\frac{15}{16}$

8. (-12) + (-3) = -15

9. Let x = length of longer line. Then, 5:3 = x:30.
    Solving, x = 50

10. .025 = 25/1000 (Can also be reduced to 1/40)

11. Cross-multiplying, 5x = 18. Thus, x = 18/5 = 3.6

12. $33\frac{1}{3}\%$ of 3 = $(\frac{1}{3})(3)$ = 1

13. $\sqrt{225}$ = 15, since 15^2 = 225

14. The arrow points to $6\frac{3}{8}$

15. $\frac{4x}{5}$ - 6 = 10. Adding 6, $\frac{4x}{5}$ = 16. Then, x = 16 ÷ $\frac{4}{5}$ = 20

16. 8 hrs. 0 min. 6 sec. - 6 hrs. 4 min. 15 sec. can be written as
    7 hrs. 59 min. 66 sec. - 6 hrs. 4 min. 15 sec. to get
    1 hr. 55 min. 51 sec.

17. Mean = (2 + 4 + 6 + 6 + 8 + 10 + 12 + 14 + 19) ÷ 9 = 9

18. When n = 0, c = 0. When n = 5, c = 100. Thus, c = 20n.
    Finally, for n = 7, c = (20)(7) = 140

19. $A = \frac{1}{2}bh + \frac{1}{2}ah = \frac{1}{2}h(b+a)$

20. 6 inches : 3 feet = 6 inches : 36 inches = 1/6

21. Add 5 to both sides to get $4s = 12$, so $s = 3$

22. $16\frac{2}{3}\%$ of x is 30. Then, $\frac{1}{6}x = 30$, so $x = 180$

23. At 7:00 AM the temperature was 12.5°, while at 9:00 AM the temperature was 15°. The change was 2.5 degrees.

24. Perimeter of Section I is 4b and the perimeter of Section III is $2b + 2a - 2b = 2a$. The sum of the perimeters is $4b + 2a$.

25. Area of Section II is $b(a-b) = ab - b^2$ and the area of Section IV is $(a-b)^2 = a^2 - 2ab + b^2$. The sum of the areas is $a^2 - ab = a(a-b)$.

26. Direct translation of words to symbols yields $F = \frac{9}{5}C + 32$

27. Subtract 6x to get $-114 = -5.7x$. Solving, $x = 20$

28. $(84/42)(100)\% = 200\%$

29. The figure is a cylinder.

30. Converting each choice to a decimal, we get $.5$, $.\overline{5}$, $.58\overline{3}$, $.\overline{6}$, $.75$. The largest is $.75$ corresponding to 3/4.

31. For a circle, $A = \pi r^2$.

32. A five-sided enclosed figure with straight sides is called a pentagon.

33. A quadrilateral with opposite sides parallel is called a parallelogram. Rectangles and squares are parallelograms with 90° angles.

34. $x - y + z = -18 - 3 - 2 = -23$

35. Since the digit in the hundreds place is 5 or greater, the answer is 336,000.

36. The sum of the angles of any triangle is 180°.

37. The scale difference is about 2 inches, and since 50 miles corresponds to 3/4 inch, the actual distance is about $(50)(2 \div \frac{3}{4}) = 133\frac{1}{3}$ mi. Closest answer given is 130 mi.

38. 6 added to n means 6 + n. Thus, 6 + n = 1 or n + 6 = 1

39. 3 is an exponent for $2n^3$.

40. 12 inches in 1 foot means 12n inches in n feet.

41. 3 months = 1/4 year.

42. 25% of 360 degrees = 90 degrees

43. Area of $\triangle AED = (\frac{1}{2})(2)(3) = 3$ square units = 12 sq. inches

44. Angle x is the angle of elevation to B from A.

45. Since u + v = 180, we can also write u = 180 - v

46. 4/x = 6/15 Cross-multiplying, 6x = 60. Solving, x = 10

47. 100% - 15% = 85%

48. A = P + Prt becomes A - P = Prt. Dividing by Pr we get:
    t = (A-P)/Pr

49. π = ratio of circumference to diameter of a circle

50. Let B = base, H = altitude. Original area of triangle = $\frac{1}{2}$BH.
    If new base and altitude are 2B and 2H, new area =
    $\frac{1}{2}$(2B)(2H) = 2BH, which is 4 times the value of $\frac{1}{2}$BH.

51. Let x = altitude. Then, $x^2 + (\frac{S}{2})^2 = s^2$. This becomes
    $3/4s^2 = x^2$. Solving, $x = s\sqrt{3}/2$

52. 1 meter $\approx$ 39.37 inches $\approx$ 40 inches

53. Substituting (3,-2), 2(3) - 3(-2) = 12. The other points do
    not lie on 2x - 3y = 12.

54. The false statement is $\angle s + \angle u = \angle r + \angle t$ (It is only true that
    $\angle s = \angle u$ and $\angle r = \angle t$)

55. $n^4 \cdot n^2 = n^6$, since exponents are added in multiplication

56. Volume = (6)(4)(2) = 48 cu.in.

57. ($21)(.80) = $16.80

58. $30,000 - $12,000 - $2500 - $4742 - $1058 = $9700.
    The monthly amount is $9700 $\div$ 12 = $808.33

59. ($100)(.90) = $90. Then, ($90)(.98) = $88.20

60. $1250 - (1250)(.18) = \$1025$

61. $\$30.45/\$870 = 3.5\%$ Then, 3.5% of \$1500 = \$52.50

62. $(.035)(60/360) = .0058\overline{3}$ = discount for 60 days.
The value of the note = $(1 - .0058\overline{3})(\$3500) = \$3479.58$

63. $W = 5.5(20 + 6) = (5.5)(26) = 143$

64. $x/80 = 40/100$. Solving, $x = 32$. Note that AD:AC = DE:BC

65. When folded, each new side is $\sqrt{49} = 7$ inches. Thus, the original length (unfolded) was $7 + 1 + 1 = 9$ inches.

EXAMINATION SECTION
TEST 1

DIRECTIONS: Each question or incomplete statement is followed by several suggested answers or completions. Select the one that BEST answers the question or completes the statement. *PRINT THE LETTER OF THE CORRECT ANSWER IN THE SPACE AT THE RIGHT.*

1. Which of the following fractions is the SMALLEST?

   A. $\frac{2}{3}$ B. $\frac{4}{5}$ C. $\frac{5}{7}$ D. $\frac{5}{11}$ 1.____

2. 40% is equivalent to which of the following?

   A. $\frac{4}{5}$ B. $\frac{4}{6}$ C. $\frac{2}{5}$ D. $\frac{4}{100}$ 2.____

3. How many 100's are in 10,000?   3.____
   A. 10   B. 100   C. 10,000   D. 100,000

4. $\frac{6}{7} + \frac{11}{12}$ is approximately

   A. 1   B. 2   C. 17   D. 19

5. The time required to heat water to a certain temperature is directly proportional to the volume of water being heated.   5.____
   If it takes 12 minutes to heat $1\frac{1}{2}$ gallons of water, how many minutes will it take to heat 2 gallons of water?
   A. 12   B. 16   C. 18   D. 24

6. The cost of an item increased by 25%.   6.____
   If the original cost was C dollars, identify the expression which gives the new cost of that item.
   A. C + 0.25   B. $\frac{1}{4}$C   D. 25C   D. 1.25C

7. Given the formula PV = nRT, all of the following are true EXCEPT   7.____

   A. $T = \frac{PV}{nR}$ B. $P = \frac{nRT}{V}$ C. $V = \frac{P}{nRT}$ D. $n = \frac{PV}{RT}$

8. If a Fahrenheit (F) temperature reading is 104, find its Celsius (C) equivalent, given that $C = \frac{5}{9}(F-32)$ 8.____
   A. 36   B. 40   C. 72   D. 76

9. If 40% of a graduating class plans to go directly to work after graduation, which of the following must be TRUE?   9.____
   A. Less than half of the class plans to go directly to work.
   B. Forty members of the class plan to enter the job market.
   C. Most of the class plans to go directly to work.
   D. Six in ten members of the class are expected not to graduate.

10. Given a multiple-choice test item which has 5 choices, what is the probability of guessing the correct answer if you know nothing about the item content?

    A. 5%   B. 10%   C. 20%   D. 25%

10.____

11. Which graph BEST represents the data shown in the table at the right?

S	T
0	80
5	75
10	65
15	50
20	30
25	5

11.____

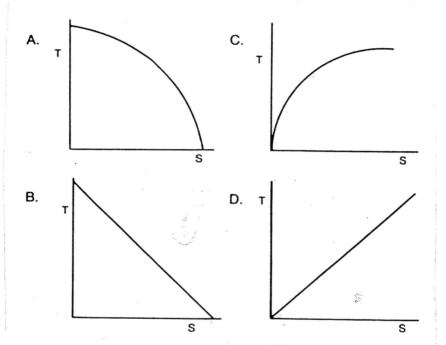

12. If $3(X + 5Y) = 24$, find Y when $X = 3$.

    A. 1   B. 3   C. $\frac{33}{5}$ D. 7

12.____

13. The payroll of a grocery store for its 23 clerks is $395,421.
Which expression below shows the average salary of a clerk?

    A. 395,421 × 23   B. 23 ÷ 395,421
    C. (395,421 × 14) ÷ 23   D. 395,421 ÷ 23

13.____

14. If 12.8 pounds of coffee cost $50.80, what is the APPROXIMATE price per pound?

    A. $2.00   B. $3.00   C. $4.00   D. $5.00

14.____

15. A road map has a scale where 1 inch corresponds to 150 miles.
A distance of $3\frac{3}{4}$ inches on the map corresponds to what actual distance?

    _____ miles

    A. 153.75   B. 375   C. 525   D. 562.5

15.____

16. How many square feet of plywood are needed to construct the back and 4 adjacent sides of the box shown at the right?
_____ square feet.
A. 63
B. 90
C. 96
D. 126

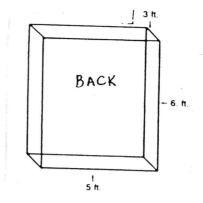

16.____

17. One thirty pound bag of lawn fertilizer costs $20.00 and will cover 600 square feet of lawn. Terry's lawn is a 96 foot by 75 foot rectangle. How much will it cost Terry to buy enough bags of fertilizer for her lawn? Which of the following do you NOT need in order to solve this problem?
The
A. product of 96 and 75
B. fact that one bag weighs 30 pounds
C. fact that one bag covers 600 square feet
D. fact that one bag costs $20.00

17.____

18. On the graph shown at the right, between which hours was the drop in temperature GREATEST?
A. 11:00 - Noon
B. Noon - 1:00
C. 1:00 - 2:00
D. 2:00 - 3:00

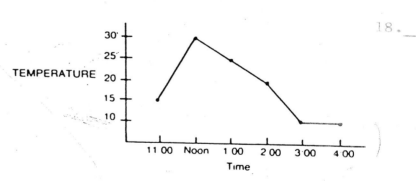

18.____

19. If on a typical railroad track, the distance from the center of one railroad tie to the next is 30 inches, approximately how many ties would be needed for one mile of track?
A. 180   B. 2,110   C. 6,340   D. 63,360

19.____

20. Which of the following is MOST likely to be the volume of a wine bottle?
A. 750 milliliters   B. 7 kilograms
C. 7 milligrams   D. 7 liters

20.____

21. What is the reading on the gauge shown at the right?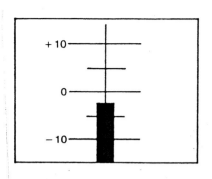
    A. −7
    B. −3
    C. 1
    D. 3

21.___

22. Which statement below disproves the assertion, *All students in Mrs. Marino's 10th grade geometry class are planning to go to college?*
    A. Albert is in Mrs. Marino's class, but he is not planning to take mathematics next year.
    B. Jorge is not in Mrs. Marino's class, but he is still planning to go to college.
    C. Pierre is in Mrs. Marino's class but says he will not be attending school anymore after this year.
    D. Crystal is in Mrs. Marino's class and plans to attend Yale University when she graduates.

22.___

23. A store advertisement reads, *Buy now while our prices are low There will never be a better time to buy.* The customer reading this advertisement should assume that
    A. the prices at the store will probably never be lower
    B. right now, this store has the best prices in town
    C. prices are higher at other stores
    D. prices are always lowest at this store

23.___

24. *Given any positive integer A, there is always a positive number B such that A × B is less than 1.* Which statement below supports this generalization?
    A. $8 \times \frac{1}{16} = \frac{1}{2}$ B. $8 \times \frac{1}{2} = 4$

    C. $\frac{5}{2} \times \frac{1}{10} = \frac{1}{4}$ D. $\frac{1}{2} \times \frac{1}{2} = \frac{1}{4}$

24.___

25. Of the following expressions, which is equivalent to $4C + D = 12E$?
    A. $C = 4(12E - D)$ B. $4 + D = 12E - C$

    C. $4C + 12E = -D$ D. $C = \frac{12E - D}{4}$

25.___

KEY (CORRECT ANSWERS)

1.	D		11.	A
2.	C		12.	A
3.	B		13.	D
4.	B		14.	C
5.	B		15.	D
6.	D		16.	C
7.	C		17.	B
8.	B		18.	D
9.	A		19.	B
10.	C		20.	A

21. B
22. C
23. A
24. A
25. D

SOLUTIONS TO PROBLEMS

1. Converting to decimals, we get $.\overline{6}$, $.8$, $.714$ (approx), $.\overline{45}$. The smallest is $.\overline{45}$ corresponding to 5/11.

2. $40\% = 40/100 = \dfrac{2}{5}$

3. $10,000 \div 100 = 100$

4. $\dfrac{6}{7} + \dfrac{11}{12} = (72 + 77) \div 84 = \dfrac{149}{84} \approx 1.77 \approx 2$

5. Let x = required minutes. Then, $12/1\frac{1}{2} = x/2$
   This reduces to $1\frac{1}{2}x = 24$. Solving, $x = 16$

6. New cost is $C + .25C = 1.25C$

7. For $PV = nRT$, $V = nRT/P$

8. $C = \dfrac{5}{9}(104-32) = \dfrac{5}{9}(72) = 40$

9. Since 40% is less than 50% (or half), we conclude that less than half of the class plans to go to work directly after graduation.

10. The probability of guessing right is $\dfrac{1}{5}$ or 20%.

11. Curve A is most accurate since as S increases, we see that T decreases. Note, however, that the relationship is NOT linear. Although S increases in equal amounts, the decrease in T is NOT in equal amounts.

12. $3(3+5Y) = 24$. This simplifies to $9 + 15Y = 24$
    Solving, $Y = 1$

13. The average salary is $\$395,421 \div 23$

14. The price per pound is $\$50.80 \div 12.8 = \$3.96875$ or approximately \$4.

15. Actual distance is $(3\frac{3}{4})(150) = 562.5$ miles

16. The area of the back = (6)(5) = 30 sq.ft. The combined area of the two vertical sides is (2)(6)(3) = 36 sq.ft. The combined area of the horizontal sides is (2)(5)(3) = 30 sq.ft. Total area = 30 + 36 + 30 = 96 square feet.

17. Choice B is not relevant to solving the problem since the cost will be [(96)(75) ÷ 600][$20] = $240. So, the weight per bag is not needed.

18. For the graph, the largest temperature drop was from 2:00 P.M. to 3:00 P.M. The temperature dropped 20 - 10 = 10 degrees.

19. 1 mile = 5280 feet = 63,360 inches. Then, 63,360 ÷ 30 = 2112 or about 2110 ties are needed.

20. Since 1 liter = 1.06 quarts, 750 milliliters = $(\frac{750}{1000})(1.06)$ = .795 quarts. This is a reasonable volume for a wine bottle.

21. The reading is –3.

22. Statement C contradicts the given information, since Pierre is in Mrs. Marino's class. Then he should plan to go to college.

23. Since there will never be a better time to buy at this particular store, the customer can assume the current prices will probably never be lower.

24. Statement A illustrates this concept. Note that in general, if n is a positive integer, then $(n)(\frac{1}{n+1}) < 1$

   Example: $(100)(\frac{1}{101}) < 1$

TEST 2

1. Which of the following lists numbers in INCREASING order?   1.____
   - A. 0.4, 0.04, 0.004
   - B. 2.71, 3.15, 2.996
   - C. 0.7, 0.77, 0.777
   - D. 0.06, 0.5, 0.073

2. $\dfrac{4}{10} + \dfrac{7}{100} + \dfrac{5}{1000} =$ 2.____

   - A. 4.75
   - B. 0.475
   - C. 0.0475
   - D. 0.00475

3. 700 times what number equals 7?   3.____
   - A. 10
   - B. 0.1
   - C. 0.01
   - D. 0.001

4. 943 - 251 is approximately   4.____
   - A. 600
   - B. 650
   - C. 700
   - D. 1200

5. The time needed to set up a complicated piece of   5.____
   machinery is inversely proportional to the number of
   years' experience of the worker.
   If a worker with 10 years' experience needs 6 hours to
   do the job, how long will it take a worker with 15 years'
   experience?
   - A. 4
   - B. 5
   - C. 9
   - D. 25

6. Let W represent the number of waiters and D, the number   6.____
   of diners in a particular restaurant.
   Identify the expression which represents the statement:
   There are 10 times as many diners as waiters.
   - A. 10W = D
   - B. 10D = W
   - C. 10D + 10W
   - D. 10 = D + W

7. Which of the following is equivalent to the formula   7.____
   F = XC + Y?
   - A. F - C = X + Y
   - B. Y = F + XC
   - C. $C = \dfrac{F\ Y}{X}$
   - D. $C = \dfrac{F\ X}{Y}$

8. Given the formula $A = \dfrac{BC}{D}$, if A = 12, B = 6, and D = 3,   8.____
   what is the value of C?
   - A. $\dfrac{2}{3}$
   - B. 6
   - C. 18
   - D. 24

9. 5 is to 7 as X is to 35.
   X =
   A. 7   B. 12   C. 25   D. 49

9.___

10. Kramer Middle School has 5 seventh grade mathematics
    teachers: two of the math teachers are women and three
    are men.
    If you are assigned a teacher at random, what is the
    probability of getting a female teacher?
    A. 0.2   B. 0.4   C. 0.6   D. 0.8

10.___

11. Which statement BEST describes
    the graph shown at the right?
    Temperature
       A. and time decrease at the
          same rate
       B. and time increase at the
          same rate
       C. increases over time
       D. decreases over time

11.___

Temperature

Time

12. If 3X + 4 = 2Y, find Y when X = 2.
    A. 0   B. 3   C. $4\frac{1}{2}$ D. 5

12.___

13. A car goes 243 miles on 8.7 gallons of gas.
    Which numeric expression should be used to determine the
    car's miles per gallon?
    A. 243 × 87   B. 8.7 ÷ 243
    C. 243 ÷ 8.7   D. 243 − 8.7

13.___

14. What is the average cost per book if you buy six books
    at $4.00 each and four books at $5.00 each?
    A. $4.40   B. $4.50   C. $4.60   D. $5.40

14.___

15. A publisher's sale offers a 15% discount to anyone buying
    more than 100 workbooks.
    What will be the discount on 200 workbooks selling at
    $2.25 each?
    A. $15.00   B. $30.00   C. $33.75   D. $67.50

15.___

16. A road crew erects 125 meters of fencing in one workday.
    How many workdays are required to erect a kilometer of
    fencing?
    A. 0.8   B. 8   C. 80   D. 800

16.___

17. Last month Kim made several telephone calls to New York   17.____
    City totaling 45 minutes in all.
    What does Kim need in order to calculate the average
    duration of her New York City calls?
    The
        A. total number of calls she made to New York City
        B. cost per minute of a call to New York City
        C. total cost of her telephone bill last month
        D. days of the week on which the calls were made

18.   18.____

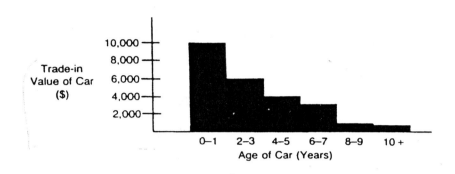

    The chart above relates a car's age to its trade-in value.
    Based on the chart, which of the following is TRUE?
        A. A 4- to 5-year old car has a trade-in value of about
           $2,000.
        B. The trade-in value of an 8- to 9-year old car is about
           1/3 that of a 2- to 3-year old car.
        C. A 6- to 7-year old car has no trade-in value.
        D. A 4- to 5-year old car's trade-in value is about
           $2,000 less than that of a 2- to 3-year old car.

19. Which of the following expressions could be used to   19.____
    determine how many seconds are in a 24-hour day?
        A. 60 × 60 × 24   B. 60 × 12 × 24
        C. 60 × 2 × 24   D. 60 × 24

20. For measuring milk, we could use each of the following   20.____
    EXCEPT
        A. liters   B. kilograms
        C. millimeters   D. cubic centimeters

21. What is the reading on the gauge   21.____
    shown at the right?
        A. 51
        B. 60
        C. 62.5
        D. 70

22. Bill is taller than Yvonne. Yvonne is shorter than Sue. Sue is 5'4" tall.
    Which of the following conclusions must be TRUE?
    A. Bill is taller than Sue.
    B. Yvonne is taller than 5'4".
    C. Sue is taller than Bill.
    D. Yvonne is the shortest.

22.

23. The Bass family traveled 268 miles during the first day of their vacation and another 300 miles on the next day. Maria Bass said they were 568 miles from home. Which of the following facts did Maria assume?
    A. They traveled faster on the first day and slower on the second.
    B. If she plotted the vacation route on a map, it would be a straight line.
    C. Their car used more gasoline on the second day.
    D. They traveled faster on the second day than they did on the first day.

23.

24. *The word LEFT in a mathematics problem indicates that it is a subtraction problem.*
    Which of the following mathematics problems proves this statement FALSE?
    A. I want to put 150 bottles into cartons which hold 8 bottles each. After I completely fill as many cartons as I can, how many bottles will be left?
    B. Sarah had 5 books but gave one to John. How many books did Sarah have left?
    C. Carlos had $4.25 but spent $3.75. How much did he have left?
    D. We had 38 models in stock but after yesterday's sale, only 12 are left. How many did we sell?

24.

25. Let Q represent the number of miles Dave can jog in 15 minutes.
    Identify the expression which represents the number of miles Dave can jog between 3:00 PM and 4:45 PM?
    A. $1\frac{3}{4}Q$ B. $7Q$

    C. $15 \times 1\frac{3}{4} \times Q$ D. $\frac{Q}{7}$

25.

KEY (CORRECT ANSWERS)

1. C	6. A	11. D	16. B	21. C
2. B	7. C	12. D	17. A	22. D
3. C	8. B	13. C	18. D	23. B
4. C	9. C	14. A	19. A	24. A
5. A	10. B	15. D	20. C	25. B

SOLUTIONS TO PROBLEMS

1. Choice C is in ascending order since .7 < .77 < .777

2. Rewrite in decimal form: .4 + .07 + .005 = .475

3. Let x = missing number. Then, 700x = 7. Solving, $x = \frac{7}{700} = .01$

4. 943 - 251 = 692 ≈ 700

5. Let x = hours needed. Then, 10/15 = x/6. Solving, x = 4

6. The number of diners (D) is 10 times as many waiters (10W). So, D = 10W or 10W = D

7. Given F = XC + Y, subtract Y from each side to get F - Y = XC. Finally, dividing by X, we get (F-Y)/X = C

8. 12 = 6C/3. Then, 12 = 2C, so C = 6

9. $\frac{5}{7} = \frac{x}{35}$ Then, 7x = 175, so x = 25

10. Probability of a female teacher = $\frac{2}{5}$ = .4

11. Statement D is best, since as time increases, the temperature decreases

12. (3)(2) + 4 = 2Y. Then, 10 = 2Y, so Y = 5

13. Miles per gallon = 243 ÷ 8.7

14. Total purchase is (6)($4) + (4)($5) = $44. The average cost per book is $44 ÷ 10 = $4.40

15. (220)($2.25) = $450. The discount is (.15)($450) = $67.50

16. The number of workdays is 1000 ÷ 125 = 8

17. Choice A is correct because the average duration of the phone calls = total time ÷ total number of calls

18. Statement D is correct since a 4-5 year-old car's value is $4,000, whereas a 2-3 year-old car's value is $6000.

19. 60 seconds = 1 minute and 60 minutes = 1 hour. Thus, 24 hours = (24)(60)(60) or (60)(60)(24) seconds

20. We can't use millimeters in measuring milk since millimeters is a linear measurement

21. The reading shows the average of 50 and 75 = 62.5

22. Since Yvonne is shorter than both Bill and Sue, Yvonne is the shortest.

23. Statement B is assumed correct since 568 = 268 + 300 could only be true if the mileage traveled represents a straight line

24. To find the number of bottles left, we look only for the remainder when 150 is divided by 8 (which happens to be 6)

———

MATHEMATICAL RELATIONSHIPS AND CONCEPTS

1. SOLVING LINEAR EQUATIONS

When solving simple linear equations, the goal is to rewrite the equation in the form *variable = constant* or *constant = variable*. To achieve the goal, you generally need to add the same quantity to both sides of the equation or to multiply both sides of the equation by the same quantity. Thus, to solve $3x - 6 = 14$, we would add 6, the opposite of −6, to both sides, obtaining $3x = 20$. We would then multiply both sides by 1/3, the *opposite* or *inverse* of 3, to obtain the final answer.

$$3x = 20$$
$$\frac{1}{3} \cdot 3x = \frac{1}{3} \cdot 20$$
$$x = \frac{20}{3} \text{ or } 6\frac{2}{3}$$

Notice that the equation has been reduced to the form *variable = constant*, that is $x = 6\frac{2}{3}$. Here is another example. Solve for x:

Add −7 (the opposite of 7) to both sides	$\frac{2}{3}x + 7 = 18$ $\quad - 7 \quad -7$
This reduces to	$\frac{2}{3}x \quad = 11$
Multiply both sides by $\frac{3}{2}$ because $\frac{3}{2}$ is the inverse of $\frac{2}{3}$	$\frac{3}{2} \cdot \frac{2}{3}x = \frac{3}{2} \cdot \frac{11}{1}$ $x = \frac{33}{2} \text{ or } 16\frac{1}{2}$

Some equations have variables on both sides of the equality symbol.

Problem: Solve for x: $3x + 7 = 5x - 11$
Solution:

Add −3x to both sides	$3x + 7 = 5x - 11$ $-3x \qquad -3x$
This reduces to: Add 11 to both sides:	$7 = 2x - 11$ $+11 \qquad +11$
This reduces to: Multiply both sides by ½: The answer is:	$18 = 2x$ $\frac{1}{2} \cdot 18 = \frac{1}{2} \cdot 2x$ $9 = x$

Problem: Solve for t: $4 + 3(t-2) = t + 1$

Solution: When equations contain parentheses, always remove the parentheses first and then proceed as usual. Here, $3(t-2)$ is equivalent to $3t - 6$. Thus,

$$4 + 3t - 6 = t + 1$$

Reordered:	$3t + 4 - 6 = t + 1$
Reduced:	$3t - 2 = t + 1$
Add $-t$ to both sides:	$-t \qquad\qquad =-t$
The result is:	$2t - 2 \qquad = \qquad 1$
Add 2 to both sides:	$+2 \qquad\qquad +2$
The result is:	$2t \qquad = \qquad 3$
Multiply both sides by $\frac{1}{2}$:	$\frac{1}{2} \cdot 2t = \frac{1}{2} \cdot 3$
The answer is:	$t = \dfrac{3}{2}$

Problem: Solve for x: $0.17x + 1.2 = 6.3$

Solution: Sometimes you must multiply both sides by an appropriate power of ten in order to remove the decimals. Because the equation above has as many as two digits to the right of the decimal point, we multiply both sides by 10^2 or 100.

$$100(0.17x + 1.2) = 100(6.3)$$
$$17x + 120 = 630$$
$$17x = 510$$
$$x = 30$$

EXERCISES

1. Solve for x:
   A. $2x - 3 = 15$
   B. $5x + 8 = 20$
   C. $15 = 3x - 6$
   D. $\frac{2}{3}x - 7 = 4$
   E. $\frac{3}{5}x + 4 = 12$

2. Solve for x:
   A. $3x + 5 = 6x - 1$
   B. $4x - 5 = 12 - 9$
   C. $4 - 2x = 6x + 5$
   D. $12 - x = \frac{3}{2}x + 2$
   E. $300 - 140x = 3860x - 20$

3. Solve for the variable:
   A. $2x - 5 = 4(3x+1) - 2$
   B. $10t + 1 = 2(3t+5) - 1$
   C. $2(x+2) = 1 + 3(1-x)$
   D. $5 - (11-2x) = 7x + 7$

4. Solve for the variable:
   A. $0.42x - 1.2 = 7.2$
   B. $1.1a + 3 = 0.712$
   C. $-6.54 = 1.48t - 3.062$
   D. $\frac{1}{a} + 1 = 3$

2. EVALUATING ALGEBRAIC EXPRESSIONS

Evaluating algebraic expressions is mostly a matter of replacing variables with numbers. You may need to use your equation-solving knowledge to complete the process.

Problem: Find the value of y when x = 3 if x = 3y - 6.

Solution:
   Replace x by 3

$$x = 3y - 6$$
$$3 = 3y - 6$$
$$\underline{+6 \qquad\qquad +6}$$
$$9 = 3y$$
$$\frac{1}{3} \cdot 9 = \frac{1}{3} \cdot 3y$$

   The answer is: $3 = y$

EXERCISES

5. Evaluate the following when a = 2, b = 3, c = 2:
   A. $-3a + 5b$
   B. $a(b+c)$
   C. $3a + 2b + 4c$

6. Find the value of y when x = 3 if
   A. $y = 3x - 9$
   B. $x + y = 11$
   C. $2x + 3y = 7$
   D. $5 - (x+y) = 11$
   E. $3y = 2x$

7. Solve for y if x = 20:
   A. $y = \frac{2}{3}x - 4$

   B. $y = \frac{9}{5}x + 32$

   C. $\frac{1}{3}y + \frac{1}{4}x = \frac{1}{5}$

8. Interest (I) equals principal (P) multiplied by the interest rate per unit of time (r) multiplied by the number of the time periods (t) of the loan: I = Prt. What is the rate per year if an invested principal of \$2000 earns \$320 interest over a 2-year period?

9. What is the value of a if b = 0.2 and $3.2 + a + 0.3b = 0.25$?

3. SOLVING LITERAL EQUATIONS

A literal equation is one involving more than one variable; for example, $3x + 2y = 6$ or $d = rt$. Often literal equations need to be solved for one or another of the variables in the equation, Thus, $d = rt$ is in a form where d is the solution. To *solve for* r, we may divide both sides of the equation by t to obtain $\frac{d}{t} = \frac{rt}{t}$ or $\frac{d}{t} = r$. We might also divide both sides by r to obtain $\frac{d}{r} = t$. Thus, we have three *equivalent* equations: $d = rt$; $\frac{d}{t} = r$; $\frac{d}{r} = t$.

Solving literal equations involves our usual equation-solving techniques: We add (or subtract) the same quantity to both sides of the equation, and we multiply (or divide) both sides by the same quantity.

Problem: Rewrite $2x + 9y - 18 = 0$ in terms of y:

Solution:

$$\begin{array}{rcl} 2x + 9y - 18 &=& 0 \\ +18 & & +18 \\ \hline 2x + 9y &=& 18 \\ -2x & & -2x \\ \hline 9y &=& 18 - 2x \end{array}$$

Now divide both sides by 9:

$$\frac{9}{9}y = \frac{18-2x}{9}$$

$$y = \frac{18-2x}{9}$$

Problem: Solve the following for C: $F = \frac{9}{5}C + 32$

Solution:

$$F = \frac{9}{5}C + 32$$

$$\underline{-32 \qquad\qquad -32}$$

$$F - 32 = \frac{9}{5}C$$

$$\frac{5}{9}(F-32) = \frac{5}{9} \cdot \frac{9}{5}C$$

$$\frac{5}{9}(F-32) = C$$

Problem: Solve for x: $y = 14 - 8x$

Solution:

$$\begin{array}{rcl} y &=& 14 - 8x \\ -14 & & -14 \\ \hline y - 14 &=& -8x \end{array}$$

$$\frac{y-14}{-8} = \frac{-8x}{-8}$$

Multiply numerator and denominator by -1 to eliminate the negative denominator

$$\frac{y}{8} \quad \frac{14}{8} = x$$

$$\frac{14}{8} \quad \frac{y}{8} = x$$

EXERCISES

10. Solve the equations in terms of y
    A. $3x + y = 12$
    B. $xy = 8$
    C. $A = bry$
    D. $4x + 3y = 12$
    E. $4x - 13y = 17$
    F. $3x = 6y$

11. Rewrite $I = Prt$ in terms of P

12. Solve $s = a + (n-1)d$ for d

13. Rewrite $L = a(1+ct)$ in terms of c

14. Suppose $x y z = 10$. Solve for x and then for y

15. Give two equivalent forms of the equation $7x - 2y = 14$ by solving for x and for y

4. DIRECT AND INVERSE VARIATION

If the numbers involved are simple, direct and inverse variation problems can be done mentally.

Consider this problem: Suppose y varies directly as x. If y is 8 when x is 2, what is y when x is 3?

To say, *y varies directly as x* means y is a multiple of x. Now, if y is 8 when x is 2, what multiple of x must y be? Clearly, 8 is 4 times 2 so y must be 4 times x: $y = 4x$. At this point, you can answer the question, *What is y when x is 3?* Since $y = 4x$, it follows that when x is 3, y is 12.

Consider this problem: Suppose y varies directly as x. When $y = 5$, then $x = 10$. What is the value of y when $x = 6$? The variable y varies directly as x. This means that y is a multiple of x. What do you multiply the x-value of 10 by to get the y-value 5? The multiplier is $\frac{1}{2}$ because $\frac{1}{2}$ 10 = 5. Thus, if $x = 6$, then $y = \frac{1}{2} \cdot 6 = 3$.

EXERCISES

16. Solve these direct variation problems. In each case, y varies directly as x.
    A. If y is 3 when x is 1, then y = _____ when $x = 6$.
    B. If y is 10 when x is 2, then y = _____ when $x = 4$.
    C. If y is 2 when x is 4, then y = _____ when $x = 9$.
    D. If y is 5 when x is 15, then y = _____ when $x = 9$.
    E. If y is 3 when x is 2, then y = _____ when $x = 10$.
    F. If y is 12 when x is 4, then y = 15 when $x =$ _____.
    G. If y is 3 when x is 9, then y = 4 when $x =$ _____.

H. If y is $\frac{3}{2}$ when x is 1, then y = 6 when x = _____.

I. If y is 5 when x is 2, then y = _____ when x = 6.

Although many variation problems can be solved or approximated mentally, there are mechanical, rote methods for solving such problems.

Consider problem 16I above: If y is 5 when x is 2, then y = _____ when x = 6. Some people might reason this way: *So y = 5 when x = 2. That means that y equals two and a half times x. So if x = 6, then two and a half x's make 6 + 6 + 3 = 15, so when x = 6, then y = 15.*

Here is a mechanical way to do the same problem. Since y varies directly as x, y is a multiple of x: y = kx. By substituting the known values 5 and 2 for y and x respectively, you can solve for k. We know that y = kx, 5 = k·2. Therefore, 5/2 = k. If y = 5/2x and if x = 6, then y = 5/2·6 = 15. Thus, we have this procedure:

$$\text{Use formula } y = kx \text{ where } k = \frac{\text{known y-value}}{\text{known x-value}}$$

EXERCISES

17. Solve these direct variation problems by using the formula y = kx. In each case, y varies directly as x. For each problem, identify the value of k you used and the value that goes in the blank.
    A. If y is 6 when x is 2, then y = _____ when x = 10.
    B. If y is 6 when x is 3, then y = _____ when x = 18.
    C. If y is 12 when x is 1/3, then y = _____ when x = 5.
    D. If y is 28 when x is -4, then y = _____ when x = 7.
    E. If y is 12 when x is 4, then y = 12.36 when x = _____.
    F. If y is 459 when x is 17, then y = 27 when x = _____.
    G. If y is 100 when x is -10, then y = -10 when x = _____.
    H. If y is 1.4 when x is 7, then y = 10 when x = _____.

18. The salary of an hourly worker varies directly with the number of hours she works per week. According to the records, she worked 24 hours last week and made $108. How many hours would she need to work this week to make $45?

19. The weight of a collection of machine screws varies directly as the number of screws in the collection. If 110 screws weigh 1.1 kg, how many screws are in a collection weighing 0.56 kg.?

By now you have noticed that y varies directly as x, when x increases so does y and when x decreases so does y. For instance, if x doubles then y also doubles. For inverse variations, however, if x doubles, then y decreases by half! Overall, for inverse variations one variable moves in the opposite direction from the other.

Direct Variation: If y = 8 when x = 4, then when x = 8, y = 16.
Inverse Variation: If y = 8 when x = 4, then when x = 8, y = 4.

Direct Variation: If y = 15 when x = 3, then when x = 9, y = 45.
Inverse Variation: If y = 15 when x = 3, then when x = 9, y = 5.

Suppose y is inversely related to x. Then if x doubles, y is $\frac{1}{2}$ its former value. If the value of x is multiplied by 3, then the y-value is multiplied by 1/3, and so forth.

EXERCISES

20. Solve these inverse variation problems mentally. In each case, assume that y varies inversely as x.
   A. If y = 6 when x = 8, then y = _____ when x = 16.
   B. If y = 6 when x = 8, then y = _____ when x = 24.
   C. If y = 6 when x = 8, then y = _____ when x = 2.
   D. If y = 10 when x = 10, then y = _____ when x = 5.
   E. If y = 10 when x = 10, then y = _____ when x = 2.
   F. If y = 24 when x = 6, then y = 12 when x = _____.
   G. If y = 24 when x = 12, then y = 2 when x = _____.
   H. If y = 15 when x = 12, then y = 10 when x = _____.
   I. If y = 1 when x = 1, then y = 1/3 when x = _____.

As is the case with direct variation, there is also a formula (if you need it) for solving inverse variation problems:

$$y = \frac{k}{x} \text{ where } k = \text{(known x-value)} \cdot \text{(known y-value)}$$

Let us solve problem 20C by means of the formula. In this problem, k = 8·6 = 48. Thus, $y = \frac{48}{x}$. So, to find y when x = 2, we calculate y = 48/x = 48/2 = 24.

Let us use the formula to solve 20G. Here, k = 12·24 = 288. So the formula is $y = \frac{288}{x}$. If y = 2, then to find x we proceed as follows:

$$y = \frac{288}{x}$$

$$2 = \frac{288}{x}$$

$$2x = 288$$
$$x = 144$$

21. Solve these inverse variation problems by using the formula $y = \frac{k}{x}$. In each case, y varies inversely as x. For each problem, identify the value of k you used and then the value that goes in the blank.

    A. If y is 12 when x = 2, then y = _____ when x = 1.
    B. If y is 6 when x = 2, then y = _____ when x = 3.
    C. If y is 2 when x = -3, then y = _____ when x = $\frac{1}{2}$.
    D. If y is 6 when x = 4, then y = _____ when x = 3.
    E. If y is 3 when x = 2, then y = 1 when x = _____ .
    F. If y is 10 when x = 9, then y = 45 when x = _____ .

22. The pressure of a gas varies inversely as its volume. If the pressure is 21 pounds per square inch when the volume is 350 cubic inches, find the pressure when the volume is 70 cubic inches.

    In place of phrases *varies directly as* or *varies inversely as*, you may encounter terms like *is directly proportional to* or *is inversely proportional to*. Problems 23-26 use this alternate wording.

23. The time required to heat water to a given temperature is directly proportional to the volume of water being heated. If 1½ gallons of water take 12 minutes to heat, how many minutes will 2 gallons take to heat?

24. The scaled score on a particular test is directly proportional to the raw score. Lee had a scaled score of 500 and a raw score of 40. If Carlos had a scaled score of 375, what was his raw score?

25. The time required to travel one lap on a racetrack is inversely proportional to a car's average speed. A car averaging 90 mph takes 2 minutes to complete one lap. How long will it take to complete one lap at 120 mph?

26. A sociologist has developed a test for measuring *teaching anxiety* among junior high school teachers. She estimates that test scores are inversely related to years of teaching experience. If a teacher with 3 years experience scores 60, how many years experience has a teacher who scores 15?

5. RATIO AND PROPORTION

Ratio may be considered to be another word for *fraction*. The ratio of x to y is written x/y or x:y. Just as the fractions 2/4 and 1/2 are equal, we consider the ratio 2:4 to be the same as 1:2.

Thus, if an office employs 18 men and 15 women, we might report the ratio of men to women as 18:15, but more likely we would use 6:5 (dividing both terms by 3). On the other hand, the ratio of women to men would be 5:6. Watch out for the order of the numbers when writing ratios. The order of terms should match the order of groups or things to which they refer.

EXERCISES

27. Give the ratios required (using lowest terms).
   A. An office employs 10 female employees and 3 males. What is the ratio of males to females?
   B. A rectangle has length 20 and width 15. What is the ratio of length to width?
   C. John spends $200 a month for food and $300 a month for rent. What is the ratio of the amount he spends for food to the amount he spends for rent?
   D. A TV station airs 40 drama shows in a given week and 24 news/sports shows. What is the ratio of news/sports to drama for the TV station?

A proportion is a statement that two ratios are equal. Proportions are commonly used to solve ratio problems. Consider this problem: Bill needs to paint 3 identical bedrooms. He needs 5 gallons of paint for 2 of the rooms. How much paint will he need for all 3 rooms? We express the relationship this way

$$\frac{5}{2} - \frac{x}{3}$$ (Read *5 is to 2 as x is to 3*)

or this way

$$\frac{2}{5} \quad \frac{3}{x}$$ (Read *2 is to 5 as 3 is to x*)

Note that both proportions will yield the same solution for x.

To solve a proportion, simply multiply as follows and solve the resulting equation:

Product: 15   Product: 2x

$$\frac{5}{2} \quad = \quad \frac{x}{3}$$

Thus, $15 = 2x$
             $7\frac{1}{2} = x$

So, $7\frac{1}{2}$ gallons are needed for 3 rooms.

Here is a second problem: 3 is to 7 as 8 is to what?

$$\frac{3}{7} = \frac{8}{x}$$

$$3x = 7 \times 8$$
$$3x = 56$$
$$x = \frac{56}{3}$$

28. A park ranger counts 16 trout out of 30 fish sampled in a given lake. If the lake contains 2000 fish in all, how many would you predict should be trout?

29. The ratio of a person's weight on Mars to the person's weight on Earth is 2:5. How much would a 120-pound Earth person weigh on Mars?

30. A map of your hometown has a scale that reads, *1 inch equals 6 miles*. If two locations on the map are 4½ inches apart, what is the distance between them in miles?

31. Gerry's car burns 1½ quarts of oil on a 700-mile trip. How much oil will be needed for a 3000-mile trip?

32. If a 6-foot person casts a 4-foot shadow, how tall is a tree that casts a 25-foot shadow?

33. The ratio of male to female faculty members in the Delendo School system is 2:5. If there are 36 male faculty, how many female faculty are there?

34. A collection of miniature dinosaur replicas are all constructed on the same scale. One dinosaur, whose length is estimated at 12 feet, measures 4 inches. Another measures 6 inches. Estimate its length in feet.

35. It is estimated that student scores on two different physical skills tests are proportional. John got 20 on the first test and 32 on the second. If Maria got 6 on the first test, estimate her score on the second.

6. PERCENT PROBLEMS

What is 10% of 60? Many percent problems, such as this one, can be done mentally:

> 10% of 60 becomes 1/10 of 60 or 6
> 10% of 90 is 9
> 10% of 463 is 46.3, etc.

More complicated problems involve changing percents to decimals and manipulating the resulting numbers

> 23% of 187 becomes 0.23 × 187 or 43.01
> 102% of 16 becomes 1.02 × 16 or 16.32

Proportions can be used to solve many percent problems. Consider this question: *50 is 25% of what number?* Since 25% = ¼, you could determine the answer in this way: 50 is ¼ of 200. But you could also set up a proportion: 50 is to x as 25 is to 100.

$$\frac{50}{x} = \frac{25}{100}$$

or 50 · 100 = 25x

200 = x

Problem: 10 is 30% of what number?

Solution:

$$\frac{10}{x} = \frac{30}{100}$$

$$1000 = 30x$$

$$\frac{1000}{30} = x$$

$$33.3 = x \text{ (rounding the answer)}$$

So, 10 is 30% of 33.3 (rounded).

Problem: 25 is what percent of 60?

Solution:

$$\frac{25}{60} = \frac{x}{100}$$

$$\frac{2500}{60} = x$$

$$41.67 = x \text{ (rounding the answer)}$$

So, 25 is approximately 41.67% of 60.

EXERCISES

36. What is:
     A. 10% of 50
     B. 1% of 50
     C. 20% of 50
     D. 21% of 50
     E. 25% of 40
     F. 50% of 160
     G. 100% of 86
     H. 150% of 50

37. What is:
     A. 17% of 80
     B. 12% of 116
     C. 8% of 21
     D. 7.5% of $15.60

38. Solve the following:
     A. 16 is 25% of what number?
     B. 13 is 86% of what number?
     C. 10 is what percent of 18?
     D. 17 is what percent of 51?

39. Solve the following:
     Example: A shirt that regularly sells for $15 is on sale for
     $12. What is the percent of the discount?
     The discount is $3 out of $15. 3 is what percent of 15?

$$3 = x \cdot 15$$

$$\frac{3}{15} = x$$

$$0.2 = x$$

So, x = 20%. The discount is 20%.

Example: The sign says that all merchandise is marked down 12%. What should one pay for a dress normally priced $28? 12% of $28 becomes 0.12 · $28 or $3.36. Thus, the sale price of the dress is $28 − $3.36 or $24.64.

A. The price of a $32 shirt has just increased by 16%. What does it cost now?
B. A used car is marked $6200, but the salesman claims that he can deduct another 15%. What would the new price be?
C. A movie ticket that usually sells for $4 now costs $5. What is the percent of the mark-up?
D. A tire selling for $60 has just been reduced to $56. What is the percent of the discount?

40. Three grapefruits weighing 14 oz. each were combined with seven oranges weighing 8 oz. each. What percent of the total weight was provided by
A. the grapefruits?
B. the oranges?

7. EXPRESSING RELATIONSHIPS SYMBOLICALLY

Consider this problem: In Academy School there are twenty times as many students as there are teachers. Express this fact symbolically, letting S represent the number of students and T, the number of teachers. Which of the following answers is correct?

A. $T = S + 20$
B. $S = T + 20$
C. $T = 20S$
D. $S = 20T$

The Academy School problem illustrates what is meant by *expressing relationships symbolically*. When you have taken a relationship expressed in words and have expressed it by means of an equation or formula, it is a good idea to create an example to test your answer to see if it is correct.

Consider the Academy School problem. There are twenty times as many students as teachers at the school. If Academy School had, for example, one teacher, how many students would there be? There would be 20. So, if $T = 1$, $S = 20$. If you take the number of teachers (T) and multiply it by 20, you will identify the number of students (S): $20T = S$. Therefore, choice D above is the correct answer.

Notice how choices A, B, C fail when you substitute $T = 1$, $S = 20$ in the equations. By testing your answer, you can avoid incorrect responses. A person who thought $T = 20S$ was the correct equation should discover the error by responding in this way: *I know that for 20 students I should have one teacher. If I let S = 20 in the equation T = 20S, I would get T = 20 · 20 = 400. Four hundred teachers for 20 students? Something is wrong!*

Problem: An item regularly sells for R dollars but is on sale for S dollars. Which expression gives the percent discount?

  A. $\dfrac{(R-S)(100)}{R}$

  B. $\dfrac{100S}{R}$

  C. $\dfrac{R-S}{100}$

  D. $(R-S)100$

Solution: How do we find percent discounts? Suppose something that normally sells for $10 is on sale for $8. This discount is $2 out of $10 or 2/10, 0.20, or 20%. The strategy used was this: The sale price (S) was subtracted from the regular price (R), then the answer was divided by the regular price (R) to get 2/10 or 0.20. We then moved the decimal point two places to the right to get the answer, 20%. This is the same as multiplying by 100. Thus, the formula is identified this way: R-S/R · 100. The answer is A.

Only practice and some familiarity with frequently encountered situations can help improve formula and equation-writing skills. Remember, if you have any difficulty at all with these problems, begin by creating an example to test your answer. We did this with both problems above.

EXERCISES

41. If 100 pounds of scrap metal cost p dollars, how much is 2 tons worth at the same rate? (Note: 2000 pounds = 1 ton)

  A. $2p$ B. $\dfrac{100-p}{2}$ C. $40p$ D. $\dfrac{2-p}{100}$

42. An item regularly sells for p dollars but is marked *25% off*. Which of the following is not a correct expression for the sale price?

  A. $\dfrac{3}{4}p$ B. $(1-0.25)p$ C. $p - \frac{1}{4}p$ D. $p - 25$

43. Given a car's odometer reading S at the start of a trip, the reading F at the trip's finish, and the elapsed time t, write an expression for the trip's average speed V.

44. The regular price p of an item has been increased by 20%. Write an expression for the new price.

45. If x is positive and increasing in value, then $y = \dfrac{1}{x}$ is

  A. increasing and always positive
  B. increasing and always negative
  C. decreasing and always positive
  D. decreasing and always negative
  E. none of the above

46. If x is positive and increasing in value, then $y = x - \frac{1}{x}$ is
   A. increasing and always positive
   B. increasing and always negative
   C. decreasing and always positive
   D. decreasing and always negative
   E. none of the above

47. Write an expression that gives the total number of jars we need if each jar holds 0.5 liters and we need T liters in all. (Create an example to test your answer.)

48. Louise is trying to write an equation involving P, Q, and R. She has created an example showing that when P and Q are both 1, R must be 4. Which one or more of the following equations indicates this relationship?
   A. R = 5P - Q

   C. $1 = \frac{P+Q+R}{6}$

   B. R = 5(P-Q)

   D. 4Q = PR

49. Which of the following have the property that when x is positive and decreasing, y is positive and increasing?
   A. y = 4 - 1/x
   B. xy = 1
   C. y = (4+x)100
   D. 1/x + 1/y = 3

50. Textbooks you plan to order cost $P. However, you receive a 20% discount on each book after the first 100 ordered. Which of the following will express your dollar cost if you order T textbooks, where T is larger than 100?
   A. 100P + 0.8(T-100)
   B. (100-0.20)PT
   C. 20P + 0.8PT
   D. 100P + 0.8PT

51. Suppose that personal income is taxed at a 15% rate for the first $20,000 and 28% for all income over that amount. Write an expression for the total tax paid on an income of D dollars, where D is larger than $20,000.

8. GRAPHS AND TABLES

For most people, reading graphs and tables is a matter of attention to detail and common sense. Carelessness is the most frequent cause of error. The exercises below will give you some idea of the most frequently encountered ways of displaying data and relationships pictorially.

EXERCISES

52.

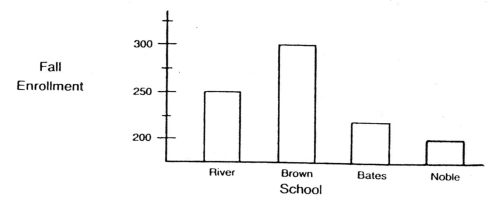

Fall Enrollment

A. What is the total enrollment at the four schools?
B. What, approximately, is the ratio of the enrollment at Noble School to that at River School?
C. How many times greater is enrollment at Brown School than at Noble School?

53. This graph shows spending for the town of Amsden last year. What percentage went for police and fire protection?

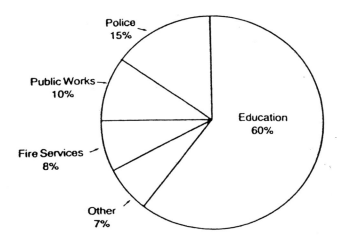

54. The graph below represents milk production for three counties last year. (Each symbol represents 10,000 gallons.) What was the approximate milk production in Balch County last year?

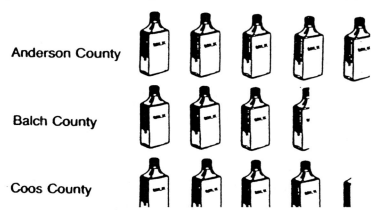

Anderson County

Balch County

Coos County

55. Mrs. Menon's mathematics group has been working independently on some lesson units. Mrs. Menon's record book is shown below. She enters *S* on the day a student starts Unit 1. On the day a student completes a unit, she enters that unit's number in her book.

DAY

	1	2	3	4	5	6	7	8	9	10	11	12	13
Andrew	S	1		2			3		4		5		6
Susan		S	1		2			3			4	5	
Louis				S		1	2		3		4		5
Tomás			S	1		2		3	4		5		6
Fran						S	1	2		4	5		6

UNITS COMPLETED

A. Susan took 11 days to complete units 1–5. How many days did Louis take to complete the same units?
B. At the end of the 11th day, which student had been working at the most rapid pace?

56. The distance (d) a person walks varies directly with time (t). Which graph best represents this situation?

A.

B.

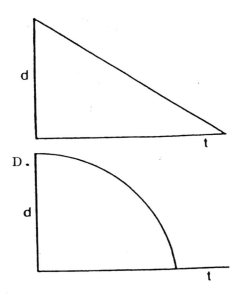

C.

D.

57. Which graph best represents the number of hours (T) from sunrise to sunset in Hartford, Connecticut, from January of one year to January of the next?

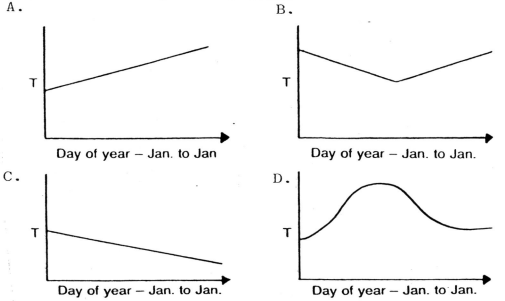

A.

Day of year — Jan. to Jan

B.

Day of year — Jan. to Jan.

C.

Day of year — Jan. to Jan.

D.

Day of year — Jan. to Jan.

58.

TEMPERATURE

City	Noon	6 PM
A	72°	54°
B	80°	70°
C	62°	50°
D	90°	66°

A. In which city did the temperature drop the most rapidly between noon and 6 P.M.?

B. Assuming an equivalent decrease in temperature per hour, what was the rate of temperature decrease in city A between noon and 6 P.M.?

59. Lee has been studying designs for picnic tables as shown below. Which design gives Lee the greatest surface area per dollar?

Design	Surface Area of Table	Cost of Materials
#1	20 square feet	$48.00
#2	18 square feet	$44.00
#3	24 square feet	$60.00

60. Ms. Haddad's 30 students took a standardized examination. The data below indicate the quartile in which each of her students' scores lie.

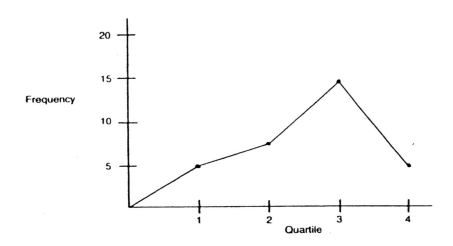

   A. Approximately how many students have scores in the 4th quartile?
   B. What quartile contains more of Ms. Haddad's students' scores than any other?

61. Use the table below to respond to the statements that follow.

SMOKERS BY FAMILY INCOME AND SEX

Family Income	Male	Female
Under $5,000	40%	32%
$5,000 - $14,999	36%	32%
$15,000 - $24,999	36%	30%
$25,000 or more	32%	26%

	Yes	No	Cannot Tell From Table Data
A. 60% of males with family incomes of under $5,000 are non-smokers	___	___	___
B. 58% of the people with family incomes of $25,000 or more are smokers	___	___	___
C. Among those with family incomes of $25,000 or more, more males than females smoke.	___	___	___
D. 36% of those with family incomes of under $5,000 smoke.	___	___	___
E. Among 600 females with family incomes in the $15,000-$24,999 range, there are about 180 smokers.	___	___	___

9. BASIC PROBABILITY CONCEPTS

When a student says, *The probability that I will pass the examination tomorrow is 2/3*, what does that student mean? She means that, were she to find herself in that situation many times, on about 2/3 of those occasions she would pass the exam. On about 1/3 of the occasions she would not pass.

Imagine a person playing a game which involves rolling a die. When he says, *The probability that I will roll a three is 1/6*, what does he mean? In this case, he means that of the six possible outcomes when rolling a die (1, 2, 3, 4, 5, 6), one possible outcome out of six is three. It is also true that, were he to roll that die a large number of times, about 1/6 of the times he would roll a three. (Thus, in 600 rolls, he would expect to get approximately 100 three's.)

Problem: The names of 5 students - Deborah, Andrew, Thomas, Jose, and Maria - are placed in a hat. One name is withdrawn at random. What is the probability that
  A. Deborah's name is chosen?
  B. The name chosen is either Deborah's or Andrew's?
  C. A boy's name is chosen?

Solution: A. Deborah's name is 1 of 5. Thus, the answer to A is 1/5.
  B. 2/5
  C. 3/5

Problem: Consider the data below on 100 different students. If we choose one student at random from the 100 students shown on the chart, what is the probability of choosing
  A. a boy?
  B. a girl?
  C. a student with glasses?
  D. a girl with glasses?

	Glasses	No Glasses
Boys	15	45
Girls	10	30

Solution: A. Of the 100 students, 15 + 45 = 60 are boys. Thus, the probability of choosing a boy is 60/100 = 6/10 = 3/5.
  B. There are 10 + 30 = 40 girls. Thus, 40/100 = 2/5 is the probability of choosing a girl. You could also reason this way: The probability of choosing a boy is 3/5. The probability of not choosing a boy is, therefore, 1 - 3/5 = 2/5.
  C. 15 + 10 = 25 out of 100 students. Thus, the answer is 25/100 = 1/4.
  D. 10/100 or 1/10.

EXERCISES

62. A hat contains six tickets numbered 1, 1, 2, 2, 3, 3, respectively. One ticket is withdrawn at random. What is the probability that the ticket drawn
    A. is a 1?
    B. has an even number on it?
    C. is either a 2 or 3?
    D. has a 5 on it?
    E. has a number less than 3 on it?

63. Kim keeps records of his hens' daily egg production for 3 weeks and identifies the results listed in the table below. Based on these data, answer the questions that follow.

Eggs Laid Per Day	Number of Days
1	//
2	////
3	++++ //
4	/
5	///
6	//
7	//

    A. What is the probability of getting 5 or more eggs on a given day?
    B. What is the probability of not getting exactly 4 eggs on a given day?

64. Here are some data on student test performance at a particular school. Based on the data, answer the questions that follow.

	Above Mean	Below Mean
Boys	246	54
Girls	280	20

    A. What is the probability that a randomly chosen student scored above the mean?
    B. What is the probability that a randomly chosen female student scored below the mean?

65. The science students at our school have kept records indicating that the probability of rain at noon on a given day is 1/3 during the month of October.
    A. We have 21 school days this October. How many of rainy-days-at-noon do we anticipate?
    B. What is the probability of no rain at noon during October?
    C. Suppose that the probability of the sun shining at noon is 1/6 during October. What is the probability of neither rain nor sun at noon during October?

66. Here is a summary of student performance on a statewide test. Based on the data, answer the questions that follow.

Class	Number Passed	Number Failed
Ms. Adams	20	5
Ms. Blake	18	6
Ms. Gomez	22	2

A. What is the probability that a randomly chosen student has passed the exam?

B. What is the probability that a student who has failed belongs to Ms. Adams' class?

67. Based on statewide test data, here are probabilities of scoring in certain categories:

Score	Probability
0-50	0.16
51-60	0.24
61-70	0.30
71-80	0.20

A. If 5,000 students took the test, how many would you predict had scores below 51?

B. Eighty students at School A took the test. Fifteen students scored 50 or below. Is this better or worse than the state as a whole?

C. Overall, what was the probability of scoring above 80 on the statewide test?

10. NEEDED AND EXTRANEOUS INFORMATION IN PROBLEM SOLVING

Problems with missing or with extra information are very common in real-life situations, but relatively rare in textbooks. These problems may not be necessarily difficult, but they often trap unwary readers whose schooling has led them to expect that all school problems and test problems contain precisely the information needed for a solution. But that is not always so. It is important to read problems carefully and use your common sense; imagine you are not faced with a *mathematics* problem on a test, but have encountered the problem in your daily life. Ask yourself, what information would you need to solve it?

EXERCISES

68. Pedro wants to tile a rectangular floor measuring 7.2 m by 5.4 m. Tiles cost 35¢ each at a store. What additional information will Pedro need before he can tell how much he needs to spend on tiles at a store?

69. Consider this situation: A manager bought 100 identical video cameras for $2,568. He sold them for $5,042. This situation includes three numerical pieces of information, not all of which may be needed to answer the questions below. What are the answers? What information is extraneous in each case?

	Answer	Extraneous Data
A. What was the total profit?	_____	_____
B. What was the selling price of each camera?	_____	_____
C. What did the manager pay for the cameras?	_____	_____
D. What was the manager's profit per camera?	_____	_____

70. Identify the additional information, if any, needed for each of the following problems.
    A. When mixing concrete for a patio, a contractor uses sand and gravel in a ratio of 3 to 4. How many cubic yards of gravel did the contractor use?
    B. The distance from Ampex to Bodwick is 38 miles. The distance from Bodwick to Cranmore is 20 miles. How far is it from Ampex to Cranmore?
    C. Ten percent of Ms. Mora's fourth graders failed the state's mastery test in reading. Four percent of Mr. Gomez's class failed. What was the total number of failing students in the two classes?
    D. All the rooms in Lauren's house are the same size. To paint two of those rooms she needs three gallons of paint. How many gallons does she need to paint all her rooms?
    E. A team wins 105 games. This is 70% of the games they played. How many games did they lose?

71. Identify any extraneous data.
    A. Of 180 class days last year, Lisa missed 9. If the probability of her missing school that year was 1/20, what was the probability of her being in school on a given day?
    B. The 30 students in Ms. Gato's class paid an average of $12.50 each during the year for special class materials, fees, etc. How much more, on the average, would each student need to pay for the class average to be $14 per student?
    C. A car averaged 20 miles per hour traveling from point A to point B. On the return trip, it averaged 40 miles per hour and took 2½ hours. How far did the car travel for the entire trip?
    D. Tickets to the student production of OUR TOWN sell for $3 each. Yesterday, 30 students and 7 teachers bought tickets. Today $123 worth of tickets were sold, including another 30 student tickets. How many nonstudents bought tickets these two days?

KEY (CORRECT ANSWERS)

1. A. $x = 9$

    B. $x = \dfrac{12}{5}$

    C. $x = 7$

    D. $\dfrac{2}{3}x = 11$, so $x = \dfrac{3}{2} \cdot \dfrac{11}{1} = \dfrac{33}{2}$

    E. $\dfrac{3}{5}x = 8$, so $x = \dfrac{5}{3} \cdot \dfrac{8}{1} = \dfrac{40}{3}$

2. A. $x = 2$
    B. $x = 2$
    C. $x = -\dfrac{1}{8}$

    D. $x = 4$

    E. $x = \dfrac{320}{4000} = \dfrac{2}{25}$

3. A. $x = -\dfrac{7}{10}$

    B. $t = 2$
    C. $x = 0$
    D. $x = -\dfrac{13}{5}$

4. A. $x = 20$

    B. $a = -\dfrac{52}{25}$ or -2.08

    C. $t = -\dfrac{3478}{1480} = -\dfrac{47}{20}$

    D. $\dfrac{1}{a} = 2$, so $a = \frac{1}{2}$

5. A. 9
    B. 10
    C. 20

6. A. 0
   B. 8
   C. $\frac{1}{3}$
   D. -9
   E. 2

7. A. $\frac{28}{3}$

   B. 68

   C. $- \frac{72}{5}$

8. $320 = \$2000 \ x r x \ 2$, so $r = \frac{320}{4000} = \frac{32}{400} = \frac{8}{100} = 8\%$

9. $a = - \frac{301}{100} = -3.01$

10. A. $y = 12 - 3x$

    B. $y = \frac{8}{x}$

    C. $y = \frac{A}{br}$

    D. $y = \frac{12-4x}{3} = 4 - \frac{4}{3}x$

    E. $y = \frac{17-4x}{-13} = \frac{4x-17}{13}$

    F. $y = \frac{3x}{6} = \frac{1}{2}x$

11. $P = \frac{I}{rt}$

12. $\frac{s-a}{n \ 1} = d$

13. $L = a + act; \ L - a = act; \ \frac{L-a}{at} = C$

14. $x = \frac{10}{yz}; \ y = \frac{10}{xz}$

15. $x = \frac{14+2y}{7} ; \ y = \frac{14-7x}{-2}$ or $y = \frac{7x-14}{2}$

16. A. 18   D. 3   G. 12
    B. 20   E. 15   H. 4
    C. $4\frac{1}{2}$ F. 5   I. 15

17. A. $k = \frac{6}{2} = 3$, so $y = 3x$ and $y = 30$

   B. $k = \frac{6}{3} = 2$, so $y = 2x$ and $y = 36$

   C. $k = 12 \div \frac{1}{3} = 12 \times \frac{3}{1} = 36$, so $y = 36x$ and $y = 180$

   D. $k = \frac{28}{4} = -7$, so $y = -7x$ and $y = -49$

   E. $k = \frac{12}{4} = 3$, so $y = 3x$ and $12.36 = 3x$. Therefore, $x - 4.12$

   F. $k = \frac{459}{17} = 27$, so $y = 27x$ and $27 = 27x$. Therefore, $x = 1$

   G. $k = \frac{100}{10} = -10$, so $y = -10x$ and $-10 = -10x$. Therefore, $x = 1$

   H. $k = \frac{14}{7} = 0.2$, so $y = .2x$ and $10 = .2x$. Thus, $100 = 2x$ and
       $x = 50$

18. $k = \frac{\text{known } y\text{-value}}{\text{known } x\text{-value}} = \frac{24}{108} = \frac{2}{9}$, so $y = \frac{2}{9}x$. If $x = 45$, then $y = \frac{2}{9} \cdot \frac{45}{1} = \frac{90}{9} = 10$. She needs to work 10 hours this week. If you reversed the x's and y's, you should have obtained $k = \frac{108}{24} = \frac{9}{2}$, so, $y = \frac{9}{2}x$. When $y = 45$, we have $45 = \frac{9}{2}x$ and, multiplying both sides by $\frac{2}{9}$, we get $\frac{2}{9} \cdot \frac{45}{1} = x$, so $x = 10$.

19. If $y = 110$ when $x = 1.1$, then what is y when $x = .56$?
     $k = \frac{110}{1.1} = \frac{1100}{11} = 100$ and $y = 100x$. So, when $x = .56$, then $y = 100 \times .56 = 56$.

20. A. 3
     B. 2
     C. 24
     D. 20
     E. 50
     F. 12
     G. 144
     H. The value of y has been multiplied by 2/3. The value of x will therefore be multiplied by 3/2 (or $1\frac{1}{2}$). Since $x = 12$ and $1\frac{1}{2}$ twelves are 18, the answer is $x = 18$.
     I. 3

21. A. k = 12 × 2 = 24, so $y = \frac{24}{x}$. Thus when x = 1, y = 24.

    B. k = 6 × 2 = 12, so $y = \frac{12}{x}$. Thus when x = 3, y = 4.

    C. k = 2(−3) = −6, so $y = -\frac{6}{x}$. Thus when x = ½, y = −6 ÷ ½ = $-\frac{6}{1} \times \frac{2}{1} = -12$.

    D. k = 6 · 4 = 24, so $y = \frac{24}{x}$. Thus when x = 3, y = 8.

    E. k = 3 · 2 = 6, so $y = \frac{6}{x}$. Thus if y = 1, we have $1 = \frac{6}{x}$ and x = 6 .

    F. k = 10 · 9 = 90, so $y = \frac{90}{x}$. Thus if y = 45, we have 45 = $\frac{90}{x}$ and x = 2 .

22. If y is 21 when x = 350, then what is y when x = 70?
    k = 21 · 350, so $y = \frac{21 \cdot 350}{x}$. If x = 70, then $y = \frac{21 \cdot 350}{70}$
    21 · 5 = 105 pounds per square inch.

23. If y = 1½ when x = 12, then when y = 2, what is x?
    Here, 1½ · 8 = 12, so 2 · 8 = 16. Therefore, x = 16 when y = 2.

24. Let y represent the scaled score and x represent the raw score.
    Then, $k = \frac{500}{40} = \frac{25}{2}$, so $y = \frac{25}{2}x$. Thus, if y = 375, we have
    $375 = \frac{25}{2}x$. Therefore, $x = \frac{2}{25} \cdot 375 = 30$.

25. Let y represent the speed and x the number of minutes. Notice that 90 plus one-third of 90 is 120. So, since y has increased by $1\frac{1}{3}$ (or $\frac{4}{3}$), x will decrease by $\frac{3}{4}$. $\frac{3}{4} \cdot 2 = \frac{6}{4} = \frac{3}{2}$, so the answer is $\frac{3}{2}$ minutes, or 1½ minutes.

26. Going from 60 to 15 represents a decrease by a factor of ¼. Thus, the years of experience will increase by a factor of 4, and the answer is 12.

27. A. three to ten or $\frac{3}{10}$ or 3:10

    B. $\frac{20}{15} = \frac{4}{3}$ or 4:3 or four to three

    C. $\frac{200}{300} = \frac{2}{3}$ or 2:3 or two to three

    D. $\frac{24}{40} = \frac{3}{5}$ or 3:5 or three to five

28. 16 trout out of 30 fish. How many trout out of 2000 fish? $\frac{16}{30} = \frac{x}{2000}$, so $16 \times 2000 = 30x$ and $x = \frac{32000}{30}$ trout. Since $\frac{32000}{30} = 1066.7$, the ranger would estimate that roughly 1067 trout are in the lake.

29. $\frac{\text{Mars}}{\text{Earth}} = \frac{2}{5} = \frac{x}{120}$ so $240 = 5x$, and $x = 48$ pounds.

30. $\frac{1}{6} = \frac{4\frac{1}{2}}{x}$, so $x = 6 \times 4\frac{1}{2} = 27$ miles.

31. $\frac{1\frac{1}{2}}{700} = \frac{x}{3000}$, so $1\frac{1}{2} \times 3000 = 700x$ or $4500 = 700 x$ and $x = \frac{45}{7} = 6\frac{3}{7}$ quarts.

32. $\frac{6}{4} = \frac{x}{25}$ and $6 \cdot 25 = 4x$. Therefore, $x = \frac{150}{4} = 37\frac{1}{2}$ feet.

33. $\frac{2}{5} = \frac{36}{x}$, so $2x = 180$ and $x = 90$ females.

34. $\frac{12 \text{ feet}}{4 \text{ inches}} = \frac{x \text{ feet}}{6 \text{ inches}}$, so $12 \cdot 6 = 4x$, and $x = 18$ feet.

35. $\frac{20}{32} = \frac{6}{x}$, so $20x = 192$, and $x = \frac{192}{20} = 9.6$.

36. A. 5   D. 10.5   G. 86
    B. 0.5   E. 10   H. 75
    C. 10   F. 80

37. A. 13.6   C. 1.68
    B. 13.92   D. $1.17

38. A. Mental solution: 16 is $\frac{1}{4}$ of what? Answer: 4×16 or 64

   Algebraic solution: $\frac{16}{x} = \frac{25}{100}$; $1600 = 25x$, therefore $x = \frac{1600}{25} = 64$

   B. $\frac{13}{x} = \frac{86}{100}$; $1300 = 86x$, so $x = \frac{1300}{86}$ or approximately 15.1

   C. $\frac{10}{18} = \frac{x}{100}$, so $x = \frac{1000}{18} = 55.55....$ Thus, x is approximately 55.6%

   D. $\frac{17}{51} = \frac{x}{100}$, so $x = \frac{1700}{51} = 33.33....$ Thus, x is approximately 33.3% (or exactly 33 1/3%).

39. A. 16% of \$32 = 0.16 × 32 = \$5.12. The shirt now costs
       \$32 + \$5.12 or \$37.12
    B. 15% of \$6200 = 0.15 × 6200 = \$930. The new price would
       be \$6200 - \$930 = \$5270
    C. The mark-up is \$1. The percent mark-up is \$1 out of a
       price of \$4 or $\frac{1}{4}$ = 0.25 = 25%
    D. The discount is \$4 out of a price of \$60 or 4/60 = 0.0666...
       or approximately 6.7%

40. A. The total weight is 3 × 14 + 7 × 8 = 98 oz. Of the total,
       the grapefruits provide 42/98 = 0.4285...or approximately 43%
    B. If the grapefruits provide 43% of the total weight, then the
       oranges must provide the rest: 57% because 43% + 57% = 100%

41. C

42. D

43. We use the formula d = rt, except that we are interested in
    the rate of travel r. Thus, r = d/t. In terms of this
    problem, r is denoted by V and we have V = F-S/ t

44. p + 0.2p or 1.2p

45. C

46. e. Let x be $\frac{1}{2}$, 1, 2. The corresponding y values are $-1\frac{1}{2}$,
    0, $1\frac{1}{2}$. The expression x - 1/x is always increasing but it is
    negative when x is less than 1 and positive when x is larger
    than 1.

47. T/0.5 or 2T

48. If you let P = 1 and Q = 1, then R = 4 for equations a, c, d

49. b, d (Try substituting some positive, decreasing values for
    x; for example, x = 10, 2, 1. What happens to y?)

50. Total Cost   100 × P   \$P each for 100 books
                     +(T-100).8P   80% of P (.8P) for each
                     ─────────────   book over 100(T-100)
                     100P + (T-100).8P

    100P + (T-100).8P = 100P + T × .8P - 100 × .8P
                      = 100P + .8TP - 80P
                      = 20P + .8TP
    Therefore, c is the correct response.

51. .15 × 20,000 + .28 × (D-20,000)
    = 3000 + .28D - .28 × 20,000
    = 3000 + .28D - 5600
    = .28D - 2600

52. A. approximately 975 students
    B. 200 to 250 or 4:5
    C. $1\frac{1}{2}$

53. 23%

54. 35,000 gallons

55. A. 10 days
    B. Fran

56. Choice A is correct: If t doubles, d doubles, etc.

57. Choice D

58. A. City D
    B. 18 degrees/6 hours = 3 degrees per hour
       (The rate of decrease for city D was 4 degrees per hour.)

59. #1 gives 20/48 square feet per dollar (20/48 = 5/12)
    #2 gives 18/44 square feet per dollar (18/44 = 9/22)
    #3 gives 24/60 square feet per dollar (24/60 = 2/5)
    Comparing the order of these fractions, 2/5 is less than 9/22,
    which is less than 5/12. Thus, 5/12 square feet per dollar
    is the best Lee can do. Choice #1 is best.

60. A. 5
    B. The third quartile

61. A. Yes
    B. No. The correct figure will lie somewhere between 26% and 32%,
       depending on the ratio of men to women. Suppose, for example,
       that there are 200 males and 100 females in the $25,000 plus
       category. Of the males, 32% or 64 smoke. Of the females,
       26% or 26 smoke. Altogether 90 out of 300 smoke, that is,
       90/300 = 30/100 = 30%. Thus, 26% of the females are smokers,
       32% of the males are smokers, and 30% of the entire group
       smokes. (Note that 30% is closer to the male percentage of
       32% than it is to the female percentage of 26%. This is
       because there are more males than females in the entire
       population.)
    C. You cannot tell. A higher percentage of males are smokers,
       but the absolute number of males who smoke could be smaller.
       Perhaps there are 300 people in this category; for example,
       100 males and 200 females. 32% of 100 means 32 males smoke.
       26% of 200 means 52 females smoke.
    D. You cannot tell. The correct figure will lie somewhere
       between 32% and 40%, but will not be 36% unless the number
       of males equals the number of females in the under $5,000
       category. (See the answer to B above)
    E. Yes.

62. A. 2/6 or 1/3
    B. 2/6 or 1/3
    C. 4/6 or 2/3
    D. 0/6 or 0
    E. 4/6 or 2/3

63. A. On 7 of the 21 days, egg production was 5 or more dozen. Thus, the probability is 7/21 or 1/3.
    B. The probability of getting exactly 4 dozen eggs is 1/21. The probability of not getting 4 dozen is 20/21.

64. A. There are 600 students in all (246 + 54 + 280 + 20 = 600). Of these, 246 + 280 = 526 scored above the mean. The probability would be 526/600 (or 263/300).
    B. 20/300 or 1/15

65. A. 7
    B. 2/3
    C. The probability of either rain or sun is 1/3 + 1/6 = 1/2. The other half of the time you get neither rain nor sun. The probability of neither rain nor sun is 1/2.

66. A. 60 out of 73 students passed: 60/73
    B. 5/13

67. A. 0.16 × 5000 = 800
    B. 15/80 = .1875, which is larger than the statewide figure of .16. Since a score below 51 is presumably not good, your students did worse than the state as a whole.
    C. The probability of scoring in the 0-80 range is .16 + .24 + .30 + .20 = .90. The missing .10, therefore, must have scores above 80.

68. He needs to know the size of a tile so that he can decide how many tiles he needs.

69. A. $2474; 100 cameras
    B. $50.42; $2568
    C. $2568; 100 and $5042
    D. $24.74; no extraneous data

70. A. How many cubic yards of sand did the contractor use or how many cubic yards of both sand and gravel did the contractor use?
    B. We need to know where Ampex and Cranmore are in relation to Bodwick. Do the three towns lie on a line with Bodwick in the middle (Figure 1) or with Cranmore in the middle (Figure 2)?

Figure 1

Figure 2

Do the three towns form the vertices of a right triangle, etc.?

C. What is the number of students in each class?
D. How many rooms are in that house?
E. No information is needed. 105 = .70x so 1050 = 7x and x = 150. The team played 150 games and won 105. They lost 45 games.

71. A. The information in the first sentence is extraneous. Alternately, if you use the information in the first sentence, then 1/20 is extraneous.
B. The 30 is not needed.
C. The first sentence is irrelevant.
D. We don't need to know that yesterday 30 students bought tickets; only the non-student data are relevant.

ESSAY WRITING

THE WRITING PROCESS

Under ideal conditions, writing involves a series of steps:

1. Pre-writing activities which facilitate understanding the purpose and the audience for a particular piece of writing and which might include generating ideas through brainstorming, notes, reflection, research, or discussion;

2. Focusing the material generated in step one by framing a thesis (controlling idea) and a direction (organization);

3. Getting the first draft on paper, using standard grammar, correct mechanics, and accurate spelling;

4. Assessing the success of the first draft by yourself or in consultation with a reliable reader;

5. Revising the draft by clarifying the thesis, topic sentences, supporting detail, and word choice; and

6. Proofreading for mistakes in grammar and spelling.

Ideal conditions do not always exist in the real world. Often you have to write under pressure and produce a clear statement. This is the case in a test situation. You must streamline the writing process to compose an acceptable essay in approximately one hour. This section will help you to practice necessary strategies by describing how you might do the following:

1. Turn the directions into a purpose statement.
2. Brainstorm for material to put in the essay.
3. Group and focus your ideas.
4. Compose your essay with clear signals for the reader.
5. Proofread for word choice, grammar, and mechanics.

TURN DIRECTIONS INTO PURPOSE STATEMENTS

For each of the following sets of essays, the directions specify a topic, an audience, and some possible ways to develop the essay. You have some choice about how to develop the essay, but you must stick to the topic given and a style appropriate to the audience. The directions consist of four sentences which give

1. an indication of audience,
2. a description of the topic,
3. suggestions for development, and
4. a restatement of the topic.

You can distinguish the sentences that suggest development because they contain words which give options rather than commands; for example, the sentences that give you commands about the topic will look like this:
In writing, tell the panel why you are considering teaching as a career.

On the other hand, sentences that suggest development will look like this:
The reasons may include...
You might want to consider...
The experiences could be...

Your first step, then, is to sort out the essential commands in the directions and convert them into a clear purpose statement such as *I will explain my reasons for choosing teaching as a career.* The purpose statement must cover all the essential parts of the assignment.

EXERCISE B

For each of the following sets of directions, underline the sentences that give you commands about the topic and write a purpose statement, using your own words if possible.

Prompt 1
A committee of teachers and administrators is reviewing your qualifications for a scholarship. In writing, tell the committee about a special activity you engage in, either in school or outside of school. It could be a job, an organization you belong to, a hobby or sport you participate in, or something you do with your family. Tell the committee what your special activity is and explain why this activity is important to you.

Prompt 2
A superintendent of schools has reviewed your application for a teaching position. Before holding a formal interview with you, the superintendent wants you to provide a writing sample that tells what motivated you to choose teaching as a profession. You might want to discuss a special learning experience you had or your interest in a chosen field or subject. Tell the superintendent what your motivation is and explain why your learning experience or your interest in a special field or subject is important to you.

Prompt 3
Your college advisor has just notified you that the college has instituted an open curriculum. As a result, you may choose any three courses or activities you wish to take next semester. You will be given equal course credit for academic subjects and activities such as sports, cultural activities (music, theater, art), school newspaper or literary magazine activities, fraternities, sororities, community projects, or any other activity whose importance you can justify. In writing, indicate what three courses or activities you would select and how each one would make you a better person.

Prompt 4

You have just been given the opportunity to write a letter of application to the Director of Admissions at the college of your choice. Imagine that cost is not a concern to you; you may choose a college that offers a traditional liberal arts curriculum or one that allows you to study only those courses that relate to your field of interest. In your essay, tell the Director of Admissions the type of college you are choosing and identify the reasons for your choice.

Prompt 5

A committee of teachers is reviewing your application for admission into the teacher education program of your choice. The committee has asked you to write an essay that describes a book that made the most lasting impression on you or from which you believe you learned some valuable lesson. The book may be on any subject, fiction or nonfiction, that is meaningful to you. The book need not be something you read for a course. Explain to the committee what your impression or lesson is and why it is important to you.

BRAINSTORM FOR MATERIAL TO PUT IN THE ESSAY

The directions on the subtest often contain suggestions for areas to explore. The sample directions which ask for an essay on your reasons for choosing a teaching career suggest that you consider *examples set by other people, benefits you expect from a teaching career, or the challenges you think teaching offers*. Remember that these suggestions are only suggestions. Before you respond to them, you should think about how you would accomplish the writing task if the suggestions had not been made. To be convincing, the material in your essay must come from your own experiences and knowledge. Brainstorming can help you accomplish this.

There are different ways to brainstorm. Some people prefer to write freely for 5-10 minutes. Others like to make lists or sketches. Others mull over ideas and ask themselves questions before jotting down a few key words. If you have a method that works for you, stick with it. If you don't, try one of the three approaches just mentioned.

EXERCISE C

1. Think about your reasons for wanting to teach and jot down a list of those reasons.

2. Compare your list with the suggestions given for considering teaching as a career: (examples, benefits, and challenges).

3. Which reasons fit the category of the rewards of teaching?

4. Which reasons could be labeled challenges of teaching?

5. Which reasons are related to examples set by other people?

6. What labels or categories do your other reasons fall under?

7. Are some of your reasons related to experiences that you have had as a learner or teacher (e.g., sports, scouting, 4-H, religious classes)?

8. Are some of your reasons related to your interest in a particular subject such as mathematics or art?

9. Are some of your reasons related to particular qualities you possess such as patience, enthusiasm, or tolerance?

LISTEN TO YOUR INNER VOICE

The purpose of brainstorming is to come up with enough detail or elaboration to satisfy the evaluation requirements. You should aim to produce enough material for an introduction and at least three additional paragraphs. Once you list a few initial ideas, the best way to generate more detail is to imagine a voice saying, *Tell me more about that*. Let's suppose that your initial list of reasons for wanting to teach looked like this:

- I like kids.
- Summers off.
- Make a contribution to society.
- Encouragement from teachers.

Responding to that imaginary voice saying, *Tell me more*, might help you elaborate on the first reason as follows:

I like kids...
    because they all have some undeveloped potential.
    because their responses aren't always predictable.
    because they get so excited when they learn something new.

Another way to elaborate on the first reason is through examples:

- The two boys I used to babysit.
- The girl I helped to get over her fear of water.
- The special education student who was my *little brother*.

Imagine the voice asking for more information until you believe you have enough for a satisfactory essay. Not every statement will give you as much room for development as others, but you can expand upon all of the statements. Each time you elaborate, your writing becomes more specific. Including specific detail makes your ideas concrete and your writing more convincing. Specific detail is one of the criteria for evaluating your essay.

EXERCISE D

1. Go back to the list of purpose statements that you developed in Exercise C, and brainstorm for material you might include in an essay.

2. Go back to your list of reasons for wanting to teach and elaborate as much as you can on each one.

GROUP AND FOCUS YOUR IDEAS

A good essay is unified by a controlling idea or thesis which dictates a pattern of organization. The thesis should be stated in one or two sentences. The words you choose to write the thesis statement should repeat or echo the directions for the essay. This strategy will ensure that you state the topic clearly. One way to write a thesis is to do one of the following:

1. Look at your purpose statement.
   Example 1: I must explain my reasons for choosing teaching as a career.
   Example 2: I must explain how a learning experience motivated me to go into teaching.

2. Look at the list of ideas you generated by brainstorming and try to sum up the ideas in a sentence or two:
   Sample Thesis 1: I have chosen teaching as a career because I enjoy young children, particularly those who have a learning disability. Teaching is a career that will enable me to make a contribution to society.
   Sample Thesis 2: The experience that I had as a *big brother* to a special education student helped me to realize that everyone has the potential to learn. This experience strengthened my interest in teaching as a career.

The thesis prepares the reader for what is to follow. It is a promise that you will discuss certain ideas and not others.

You will not always use all the material you generated during the brainstorming step. In the sample that we have been discussing, you might have decided not to use material related to summers off or the encouragement of teachers. However, if you decide that there is some material you want to include in the body of your essay material which is not indicated by the thesis, you need to revise the thesis. Suppose you decide to include the information about summers off and the encouragement of teachers, how could you revise the thesis? Here is one possibility:

Revised Thesis: There are many reasons why I have chosen teaching as a career. The pleasure of working with children, the opportunity to make a contribution to society, the encouragement of teachers, and time during the summer to continue my own education and interests are a few of them.

You should understand that it is not necessary or advisable to give every reason why you would like to teach. Be selective. Choose reasons on which you can elaborate and ones you feel strongly about. This will make a more convincing essay.

OUTLINING

There are different ways of grouping brainstorming ideas. The traditional format is the outline. Here is one example, based on the thesis we have been discussing.

Thesis: There are many reasons why I have chosen teaching as a career; some of them are the pleasure of working with children, the opportunity to make a contribution to society, the encouragement of teachers, and time during the summer to continue my own education and interests.

I. I enjoy working with children.
   A. All children have potential.
   B. Their responses are unpredictable.
   C. They are excited when they learn something.

II. I will make a contribution to society.
   A. Many jobs have questionable social value even if they have high salaries.
   B. Teachers can help children develop a good self-image and give them necessary skills.

III. Teachers have encouraged me.
   A. They say I can express myself clearly.
   B. They see that I am enthusiastic about learning.

IV. Summers will be time to continue my education and interests.
   A. Teachers must be lifelong learners.
   B. Intensity of teaching requires time for pursuing other interests.

CLUSTERING

Another way of grouping ideas is using clustering or an idea wheel. The controlling idea is at the center, in the hub of the wheel.

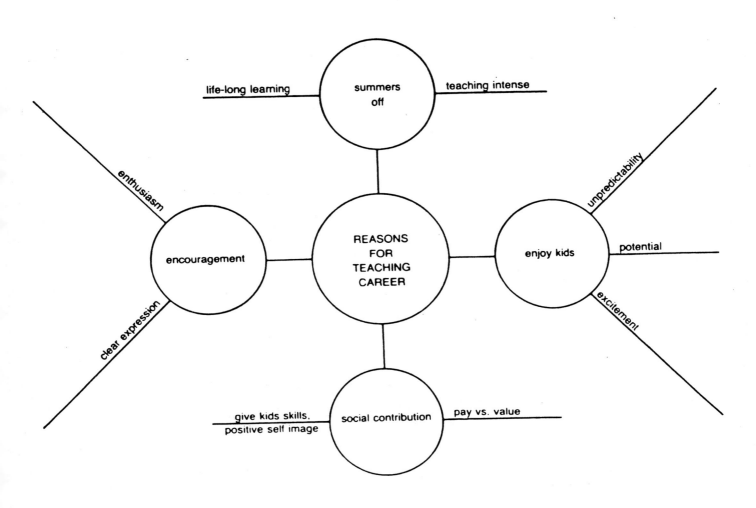

FLOW CHARTS

Still another way to map ideas is with the help of a flow chart. The main idea is placed in a box at the top, and other categories branch off below.

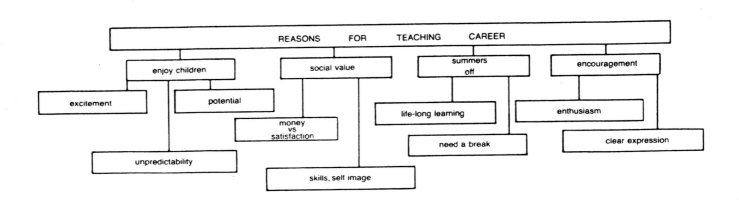

INFORMAL LISTS

An informal list is an easy way to group ideas.

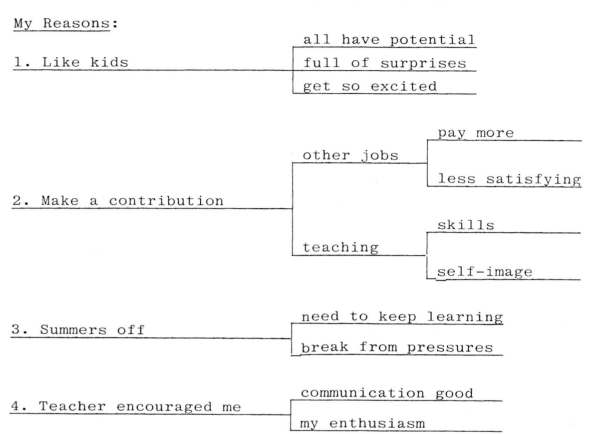

My Reasons:

1. Like kids
   - all have potential
   - full of surprises
   - get so excited

2. Make a contribution
   - other jobs
     - pay more
     - less satisfying
   - teaching
     - skills
     - self-image

3. Summers off
   - need to keep learning
   - break from pressures

4. Teacher encouraged me
   - communication good
   - my enthusiasm

Regardless of which method you use to group your ideas, the goal is to pull together related bits of information and sketch the paragraph structure for your essay before you actually start writing your essay in the test booklet.

EXERCISE E

1. Go back to the material that you produced through brain-storming in Exercise D.2 and group the ideas by using one of the formats illustrated.

2. Using one of the strategies mentioned previously, group the ideas given below in each set. For each set, read through the ideas in the set and identify or create a thesis state-ment; group related sentences; and find or create a sentence or phrase that will hold each group of sentences together.

SET A.

1. TV cartoons show characters recovering quickly from serious injury.
2. Mr. Rogers never loses his temper.
3. Ads associate happiness and good times with possession of a product.
4. The ads show cereal boxes opening by themselves and dancing on the table.
5. TV gives children a distorted sense of reality.
6. Mr. Rogers always takes off his shoes when he comes inside.
7. A character falls off a mountain top, shakes his head, and gets up.
8. Positive role models, like Mr. Rogers, are unlike any real-life adult.
9. Mr. Rogers never raises his voice.
10. The ads are deceptive and manipulative.
11. Characters who smash into walls are never badly hurt.

SET B.

1. I felt welcome when I went to see my math teacher during his office hours.
2. The activity fair during orientation week had something to offer everyone.
3. The counselors were helpful.
4. Many teachers ask if students need help rather than wait for the students to get in trouble.
5. The counselors helped with course selection.
6. Resident advisors counsel students about adjustment problems.
7. The counselors provided placement testing.
8. Teachers talk to students after class rather than just rushing off.
9. Students on campus are friendly.
10. My experience at Winona College has been good, and I would recommend it to others.
11. Teachers go over sample tests before you take the first test.
12. The dorm council plans activities and projects to bring students together.
13. The counselors offer minicourses on taking notes and tests.

SET C.

1. I don't belong to any organizations.
2. I'm not involved in any special activities.
3. I go to classes, work at the store, and see my friends on weekends.
4. My job isn't special.
5. I work at a supermarket.
6. I need the job for spending money and college expenses.
7. I have learned some things from working.
8. It's not like school.
9. You have to be there to get paid.

10. The boss isn't always fair.
11. Sometimes she is impatient.
12. As a lowly clerk, you don't get any respect.
13. The boss seemed annoyed when I brought back the shopping carts.
14. There were long lines at the registers.
15. She told me to help bag groceries.
16. There's a pecking order in most companies.
17. My boss is under pressure from the manager.
18. I'm trying to stay on top of the situation rather than just reacting.
19. I ask the boss how things have been going.
20. I try to anticipate what she'll ask me to do and offer to do it first.
21. Sometimes I feel frustrated about being low on the totem pole.
22. The manager doesn't even know who I am.
23. There's not much incentive to do good work.
24. You can always be replaced by another minimum wage worker.

SET D.

1. DEATH OF A SALESMAN is a book that influenced me because of the connections between the play and my own life.
2. Each time I had a different reaction.
3. I read the play once in high school, again in college, and then saw it on TV.
4. In high school, Biff was a good-looking football hero.
5. The play is about a salesman named Willy, his wife, and two sons, Biff and Happy.
6. Happy was just an ordinary kid, living in his brother's shadow.
7. When Biff learned that his father was not perfect, he began to drift around.
8. I realized I was only hurting myself.
9. I had an older brother who was a star.
10. I was always trying to get my parents' attention.
11. I even tried to get their attention by doing poorly in school.
12. At first, I identified with Happy.
13. Biff had a big ego because of all the attention he received.
14. Biff became a bum because of all the attention he received as a teenager.
15. When I read the play in college, I sympathized with Willy.
16. He never received any respect from his boss.
17. I have been working at a supermarket.
18. Clerks are a dime a dozen, just like salespeople.
19. I want a career where a paycheck is not the only satisfaction you receive.
20. The TV version made me admire the mother.
21. She held the family together.
22. She was completely loyal to Willy.
23. We all want someone to stick by us like she did.

SET E.

1. Earning credit for my choice of courses and activities will give me a chance to integrate course work and real experience.
2. Reading Methods is a required course.
3. I'll learn how to assess a student's reading level.
4. I'll learn about various methods for teaching reading skills.
5. I plan to work as a literacy volunteer.
6. I want to know why people don't learn to read.
7. I'll learn about methods for teaching adults.
8. I'll learn how illiteracy affects a person's life.
9. I'll realize what's at stake if the education system fails.
10. I want to take either an advanced composition course or an independent study in composition.
11. I would like to keep a journal of my experience as a literacy volunteer.
12. I would like to write about the connections I see between the methods course and my tutoring experience.
13. I would like to write some feature stories about illiteracy for the college newspaper.

COMPOSE YOUR ESSAY WITH CLEAR SIGNALS FOR THE READER

Your essay is judged on how well the essay communicates a whole message. If you keep the reader in mind, your essay is likely to communicate more effectively. The most important signals to use are topic sentences to state the main idea of each paragraph and transitions to link sentences within the paragraphs. One basic pattern you might use in composing your paragraphs is the five paragraph essay. Here is one example of such an essay written in response to Prompt 1, Exercise B. Study the way in which the topic sentences give the reader a preview of what will be discussed.

Paragraph I.   Lead and thesis statement.

Lead

Some students may have the time for sports, clubs, or volunteer organizations. Unfortunately, my schedule of classes and part-time work does not give me much time to devote to other activities. However, my job has been quite a learning experience. Although I am just a supermarket clerk, I have gained insight into the demands of a job, the behavior of supervisors, and my ability to influence a situation.

Thesis

Paragraph II.   Topic sentence developed with sufficient detail.

Topic
sentence

I realized that the demands of a job are not always like the demands of school. Maybe that is something that other people know from the start, but it did not work that way for me. In fact, I can remember how the equation between work and pay dawned on me; If I missed an afternoon of work, I missed an equivalent amount of money in my paycheck. The connection between work and rewards is not quite so clear in school. A student can study hard for a test and do poorly. On the other hand, a student can sometimes bluff through a test and get a good grade.

Paragraph III.   Another topic sentence with supporting detail.

Topic
sentence
          <u>I did not work for very long before I also realized that bosses can be difficult.</u> At first, my supervisor seemed like a nice enough person. However, I had a look at her other side one day when I returned to the store, pushing a long line of shopping carts which she had told me to gather from the parking lot. Lines had formed at all the registers, and she snapped at me to bag for one of the cashiers. It was as if it was my fault that she had sent two of the cashiers out for supper just as it was getting busy in the store.

Paragraph IV.   Another topic sentence followed by detail.

Topic
sentence
          <u>After my initial anger at the boss's behavior, I decided to try to influence the situation rather than just reacting to it.</u> I realized this approach might work as I was bagging groceries. I saw the store manager peering down at my boss from her office window. My boss had a boss who had a boss who had a boss. She was part of the pecking order just like me. Now I try to make small talk with her, ask how things have been going, and so forth. Also, I try to anticipate what she might ask me to do and then offer to do it first. This gives me the feeling that I can be an actor rather than just a puppet.

Paragraph V.   Conclusion with restatement of thesis.

          Sometimes I still get frustrated at work. As a lowly clerk, I do not get much respect in a large, impersonal company. <u>However, my job has shown me that even the
Thesis
restated
most ordinary parts of my life can give me an opportunity to learn something about myself and other people.</u>

     Topic sentences do not always occur at the beginning of paragraphs. In fact, at times it seems stilted to put the topic sentence at the start of a paragraph. You may need a sentence or two that makes a bridge with the preceding paragraph. For example, the fourth paragraph in the sample essay above might have been written more chronologically, following the sequence of events more closely.

Example: After my initial anger, I noticed the store manager
                  peering down at my boss from the upstairs office window.
                  I realized that my boss had a boss who had a boss; She
                  was just a part of the pecking order like me. <u>I decided</u>
Thesis   <u>to try to influence the situation instead of just reacting</u>
statement   <u>to it.</u>

Placing the topic sentence at the start of a paragraph gives the
clearest signal to a reader, but it is not always essential to place
the topic sentence at the beginning. It is important, however, to
have a sentence that holds the rest of the paragraph together. It can
come at the beginning, the middle, or the end of the paragraph. Here
is a paragraph without a topic sentence:

Ms. Rodriquez always had a word of encouragement on each test
she handed back. Furthermore, she taught me the difference
between an intelligent mistake and a dumb one. An intelligent
mistake occurs when a learner applies a rule or procedure to a
special situation where it does not apply. For example, if a
young child says, "I taked the book," she is applying the rule to
use a "d" sound for a past action. Ms. Rodriquez also had a way
of making math problems exciting mysteries. We watched her solve
equations on the board like Sherlock Holmes in pursuit of a suspect.
The work was never easy, but she always made us feel that it was
possible to succeed if we put in enough time.

One way to phrase a topic sentence for the paragraph above would
be: <u>Ms. Rodriquez was one of the best teachers I ever had.</u>

Even if you think that the point of the paragraph is perfectly
clear without a topic sentence, put one in. You are not writing this
essay for a sophisticated magazine; you are taking a test to show that
you can get an idea across clearly to a reader.

EXERCISE F

1. Each paragraph below lacks a topic sentence. Create a topic
sentence for each paragraph and decide where best to place it.

    a. I would be happy if I could make some difference in the
        lives of the students I will teach. It might just mean
        making them more curious about the world or more accept-
        ing of themselves. I realize that it is difficult to
        reach each student, but that does not mean that I will
        not try.

    b. Mr. Wright began every class by putting the homework on
        the board. Then he would announce what we were going to
        do that day. Usually, we went over the homework problems
        first. Students were asked to put their solutions on the
        board. After discussing them and making necessary correc-
        tions, Mr. Wright would turn to the new material. Using

three or four pieces of colored chalk, he illustrated and commented on the examples in the book. Finally, if we finished all of the scheduled lesson, there was time at the end of class to start on the homework.

c. Every teacher spends a minimum of 35 hours in school. In addition, teachers must often supervise activities such as the drama club or school newspaper. Conferences with parents, staff meetings, and required professional development activities also add to the total hours required A teacher usually has three different course-related preparations, each of which may take an hour or more, depending on the teacher's experience. English teachers who have 25 to 30 students per class may assign a short piece of writing each week, and may spend 4 to 5 minutes reading each paper. This may add 13 hours of additional work per week.

2. Go back to the material that you brainstormed and organized in Exercise D.   Pick at least one batch of material and turn it into an essay following the pattern of the five-paragraph essay described previously.

TRANSITIONS

Transitions are signals to your reader about how your ideas are connected. Certain words and phrases prepare the reader for what is to follow. Examples of important transitions to use in your essay are:

1. Words that indicate sequence of events or ideas: first, second (etc.), finally, last, ultimately, eventually, later, meanwhile, afterwards;

2. Words that indicate examples: for instance, for example, specifically, in particular;

3. Words that indicate addition of similar ideas: and, also, furthermore, moreover, similarly, equally important, another;

4. Words that indicate addition of contrasting ideas: however, but, on the other hand, on the contrary, still, yet, in contrast, nevertheless

Transitions between sentences can also be achieved by repeating key words, using synonyms, or using pronouns:

1. Example of a repeated key word: *Literacy* is not just a matter of learning the ABC's. *Literacy* means having sufficient control of the language to function in one's society.

2. Example of use of a synonym: *Literacy* is not just a matter of learning the ABC's. One's ability to read and write must be equal to the demands of one's society.

3. Example of use of a pronoun: *Literacy* is not just a matter of learning the ABC's. *It* means having sufficient control of the language to function in your society.

EXERCISE G

1. Look at the paragraphs you wrote in Exercise F and underline all the transitions.

2. Go back to the essay you wrote in Exercise F. Underline any transitions you used. Find places where you might insert additional transitions.

PROOFREAD FOR WORD CHOICE, GRAMMAR, AND MECHANICS

Under ideal conditions, you would complete a first draft and then evaluate it for content and structure. However, a subtest, lasting approximately one hour, does not allow time for true revision. You may want to think of your brainstorming as a type of first draft and your focusing as a type of revision. As you focus and compose your essay, you will do a certain amount of revision, deciding to change the order of paragraphs, inserting or deleting details, trying out sentences in your head before you put them down on paper. Once you have completed the essay, you need to proofread to make sure you have used words correctly and avoid errors that will detract from your essay and subsequently from the score you receive for your essay.

WORD CHOICE

In choosing words to express your ideas, keep in mind that the directions on the examination writing subtest are likely to specify an audience that requires you to use a professional tone. You should avoid slang and cliches. On the other hand, don't go overboard and complicate your essay with fancy terms and inflated language. Aim for a clear and direct expression of your ideas.

Here are a few examples of the kinds of words and expressions to avoid:

1. One activity that I've really *gotten into* lately is sailing. (Substitute *become involved in*, *become interested in*, *become enthusiastic about*).

2. The person sitting behind me talked *a lot* during the class. (Try to be as specific as possible about what *a lot* means in the sentence where you are tempted to use it. Here, you might use *continuously* or *incessantly*, but at other times, you might want to substitute *a great deal* or *often*.)

3. My first class was *awful*. (General words such as *awful*, *perfect*, *beautiful*, etc. are acceptable if you are going to follow up with more specific description. However, it is almost always better to use specific language. In what respect was the experience or the person awful, perfect, or beautiful? In the example above, was the class dull, disorganized, too demanding?)

4. I was faced with a *number of alternatives*. (Strictly defined, an alternative is a choice between two things. If you mean more than two, use *options* or *choices*.)

5. Computers are a *new innovation* in the classroom. (Innovation means *new*; therefore, the phrase is redundant. The same would be true of expressions such as *personal friend* and *advance planning*.)

Our language is constantly changing. At any period in history, some words and expressions are considered suitable for formal writing while others are considered colloquial and appropriate only for informal settings. As you prepare for the writing subtest, you might want to use a dictionary or a glossary of usage in a handbook. These references will provide guidance in currently acceptable choices. You might also want to keep in mind that no references will be available during the test. Therefore, if you have any doubt about the appropriateness of a word or phrase, you might want to avoid using it, and choose words about which you feel more confident.

Excess words are as much a problem as inexact words. When people don't know what to write, they often try to pad the paragraphs with sentences that say the same thing in slightly different words or fill up the sentences with empty phrases. Superfluous words and sentences may bore, frustrate, or even confuse your reader. You will be spared these problems if you practice brainstorming for relevant and interesting details before you compose your essay. Here are some examples of padded writing:

<u>Wordy</u>: Education faces a crisis today. At the present time, a number of problems are troubling concerned citizens. Not a day goes by that you do not hear about one problem or another.
<u>To the Point</u>: Many problems in education call for our attention.

<u>Wordy</u>: Due to the fact that a problem arose concerning the time our committee should meet, we decided in the final analysis that it would be best to postpone our decision until the new chairperson took over.
<u>To the Point</u>: Unable to agree on a meeting time, our committee postponed the decision until the new chairperson took over.

EXERCISE H

1. Find places in your own writing where you could eliminate words without losing meaning.

2. Trim unnecessary words from the following sentences and rewrite.

   a. The aspects of teaching that I imagine I will most enjoy are the diversity of students and the freedom to organize my own classes.

   b. The problem that I foresee causing the most difficulty in the future is that a few years from now we are going to have even more non-native English speaking students than we do now and people don't understand the need for bilingual education.

   c. In conclusion, the final point that I want to make is to say that the productivity of our economic system will decline unless we do something to tackle the problem of illiteracy among the many people who can't read at all or who can barely read.

EXERCISE I

There are a number of commonly confused words. Use a dictionary or handbook to check the correct choice for each of the sentences that follow.

1. I _____ your invitation to the party. (accept, except, expect)
2. I _____ to do well on my math exam. (accept, except, expect)
3. Everyone is going _____ Susan. (accept, except, expect)
4. I went to my guidance teacher for some good _____. (advise, advice)
5. I always _____ my students to take French literature. (advise, advice)
6. The _____ of the hurricane was horrendous. (affect, effect)
7. Does this test _____ my grade? (affect, effect)
8. _____ never too late to try. (Its, It's)
9. The committee reported _____ decision. (its, it's)
10. Please place the books over _____. (there, they're, their)
11. _____ my brother's friends. (There, They're, Their)
12. The boys have lost _____ shoes. (there, they're, their)
13. Most of the students could not choose _____ the four answers. (between, among)
14. Mary is trying to decide _____ two majors: History and French. (between, among)
15. John arrived at the game, _____. (to, too, two)
16. Please place _____ books on this corner. (to, two, too)
17. David gave the ball _____ Mark. (to, two, too)

18. Peter ran the mile _____. (bad, badly)
19. I feel _____ when it rains. (bad, badly)
20. Teachers often have to _____ packaged materials to the special needs of their students. (adopt, adapt)
21. Our school would like to _____ a dress code for all students. (adopt, adapt)
22. This corner will be the _____ for the reading materials. (site, cite)
23. Students must learn how to _____ source materials in a research paper. (site, cite)
24. Individualized activities are needed to _____ group activities. (compliment, complement)
25. Teachers should _____ children often on the work that they successfully complete. (compliment, complement)

GRAMMAR AND MECHANICS

An occasional error in grammar or mechanics in an essay written without access to a dictionary will not result in failing the writing portion of the exam. However, frequent errors will detract from the effectiveness of your message and can cause failure. There are so many possible errors, that they cannot be covered in this brief guide. A discussion of the most serious errors will be followed by a set of sentences you can use to test your proofreading skills.

1. <u>Sentence boundaries</u>. Running two or more independent clauses together without linking words or proper punctuation violates basic rules. A grammatically incomplete sentence is equally distracting.

   a. Run-on, fused sentence, or comma splice: Teaching is not an easy field, the rewards aren't always there. (A comma is not sufficient to separate two independent clauses. Substitute a period, a semi-colon, or a linking word, such as *because* for the comma.)

   b. Fragment: The best example being the difference between the way we see a character on TV and the way we visualize a character in a story. (The *ing* form of the verb creates a fragment. Substitute *is* for *being* to correct the sentence.)

2. <u>Agreement of sentence elements</u>. Verbs must agree with their subjects; pronouns with the nouns to which they refer. Similar elements must have parallel structure. Parts of the sentence must fit together grammatically.

   a. Lack of subject-verb agreement: The problems that young readers have seems to come partly from the environment. (*Problems* calls for the verb form *seem* not *seems*. In sentences where several words come between subject and verb, it is easy to lose track of the elements.)

b. Lack of pronoun agreement: Everyone wants to achieve their potential. (*Everyone* is singular and calls for *his/her*, not *their*.)

c. Lack of parallel structure: I learned to operate the computer, write some simple programs, and the fundamentals of word processing. (*Operate* and *write* set up a pattern which calls for a similar word. Therefore, the last part of the sentence should be rephrased to include a verb; for example, ...*and use the fundamentals of word processing*.)

d. Lack of grammatical fit: While taking an elective course in design my freshman year sparked my interest in art. (The introductory phrase, *While taking an elective course*, calls for a subject to come before the verb. This sentence could be revised in at least two ways:
While taking an elective course in design my freshman year, I became interested in art.
Taking an elective course in design my freshman year sparked my interest in art.

SELECTED CAPITALIZATION RULES

A few of the rules governing capitalization are reviewed below. Consult a dictionary or handbook for more complete coverage of this topic.

1. Capitalize proper nouns and adjectives.
   <u>Example</u>: Capitalize: *Judy Blume* and *Southington High School*. Do not capitalize *the author* or *my high school*.

2. Capitalize titles when they precede proper names, but not when they follow proper names or are used alone.
   <u>Example</u>: Professor Kent Curtis
   Kent Curtis, professor of history
   the history professor

3. Do not capitalize the names of academic years or terms.
   <u>Example</u>: spring semester
   my sophomore year

4. Capitalize the names of specific courses, but not fields of study unless they are languages.
   <u>Example</u>: Capitalize *English*, *Spanish*, and *Math 101*.
   Do not capitalize *math*, *physics*, or *education*.

5. Capitalize the important words in titles of books and underline the titles.
   <u>Example</u>: <u>Catcher in the Rye</u>
   <u>Grapes of Wrath</u>

PUNCTUATION

Punctuation is another area that you should review with the help of a good handbook or dictionary. One simple rule to remember is: Do not use the dash as a substitute for the proper punctuation. Example of a punctuation error: Although I took up swimming - the doctors said it would be good exercise - but I found that I did not have the ability to make the team.

(The problem with relying on dashes is that, as in the example, dependence can lead to sloppy sentence construction. The sentence above should be revised: I took up swimming because the doctors said it would be good exercise, but I found that I did not have the ability to make the team.)

EXERCISE J

1. Proofread the following essay to identify errors in grammar, mechanics, and word use. Underline or cross out all errors.

2. Rewrite the essay, using correct grammar, mechanics, and wording.

The extent of illiteracy in the Country is documented in Illiterate America - a book by Jonathan Kozol. When I read this book and realized the extent of illiteracy gave me a shock. Kozol claims that 25 million people can not read warning labels or a simple news story, another 35 million do not read well enough to survive in the Modern Age - Like being able to follow printed instructions. For someone who can't read and has to support himself or a family could be a real disadvantage.

The problem of illiteracy will be difficult to solve. There being many causes that go deep into our society. Schools have failed to halt the problem and may be contributing to it. My parents say that the problem with schools today are a lack of respect for authority. Years ago, everyone know what would happen if they disobeyed a teacher. Today, teachers must contend with students who are often bored, rarely prepared and frequently they defy the teacher. Some respect and discipline is needed to create a learning environment.

Another problem with the schools is poorly prepare teachers. Students graduating from college without being able to read or write well. During the 1960s was the decline of strict academic standards. Students failed to learn what they should of learned. The decline may be ending, new tests and requirements are in place. For example, the college of arts and sciences at Northeastern State University changed their requirements because entering students were so poorly prepared. Some of them unable to identify Sophocles or locate spain on a map.

Kozol's book interested me in the larger issues of literacy – it is more than learning the ABCs. Literacy is when you can read and write well enough to survive in a complex technology and making informed opinions about government policies. Teachers can help to create a literate America. After reading about the problems of illiteracy facing this country, I want to become one.

PUTTING IT ALL TOGETHER

PRACTICE TOPICS

You will not know in advance the topic on which you will be asked to write an essay for the examination. However, the topic is likely to involve your education, education in general, or your choice of a career.

The best way to prepare for the writing subtest is to practice the skills presented in this book and to write whole essays under conditions similar to those found in examinations. Below are several topics you may use for practice.

Practice Prompt 1

The Academic Standards Committee of your college is considering changes in the current grading system and they have asked you to write a statement about the impact of the letter grade system (ABCDF) on learning. You may want to consider how the letter grade system affects certain types of students, how it is viewed by students, teachers, or prospective employers, whether there is a practical alternative, or whether modifications should be made. Write a statement of your opinion of the letter grade system and the reasons for your opinion.

Practice Prompt 2

A screening committee is reviewing your application for a teaching position and has asked you to submit a statement of your strengths and weaknesses for the position. Imagine a specific teaching position for which you might apply and write a statement about how well you qualify for that particular job. You might want to consider how your educational background, work experiences, internships, or special interests make you a suitable candidate. You might also want to consider whether there is anything about the position, the type of students you might face, the location, or the responsibilities that might be a challenge to you. Describe the teaching position for which you are applying and explain why you would be a good candidate for the position.

Practice Prompt 3

The committee considering your application to enter a teacher training program wants to learn about your awareness of students' non-academic needs. They have pointed out that a teacher must often do more than teach subject matter. Consider the psychological, physical, social, and economic problems that affect a student's ability to learn. Describe your understanding of the ways in which the role of a teacher goes beyond teaching academic subjects.

Practice Prompt 4

Your college is hosting a conference for state high school teachers to address the problem of the inadequate preparation of the average student for college work. The conference is focusing on the average student because college teachers are concerned about the many students entering freshman courses who are unable to meet the demands of college. You might want to describe how serious the problem is, whose problem it is, and to what extent high schools should consider changing what they are doing. Use your experience, observations, and knowledge to write a statement which gives your perspective on the gap between the academic requirements in high school and those in college.

POSTTEST

WRITING SUBTEST DIRECTIONS

This part of the examination consists of one writing exercise. You should allow approximately 60 minutes to complete this assignment. You may NOT use a dictionary during the subtest. Make sure you have time to plan, write, review, and revise what you have written.

Before you begin to write, read the topic carefully and take some time to think about how you will organize what you plan to say. Your writing exercise will be evaluated on the basis of how effectively it communicates a whole message to the intended audience for the stated purpose. Your writing exercise will be judged on the success of its total impression by a panel of language arts experts. When evaluating your ability to communicate a whole message effectively, the scorers will also consider your ability to:

1. state and stay on the topic;
2. address all specified parts of the writing assignment;
3. present your ideas in an organized fashion;
4. include sufficient detail and elaboration to statements;
5. choose effective words;
6. employ correct grammar and usage; and
7. use correct mechanics (spelling, capitalization, paragraph form).

PROMPT

   The screening committee considering your application for a teaching position is concerned about teacher stress and burn-out. They would like to learn about your awareness of this problem and your susceptibility to it. You might want to discuss how you have handled stressful situations in the past and any techniques that you use to cope with stress. Describe in writing how you would confront the problem of stress and burn-out in the teaching profession.

NOTES/OUTLINE

KEY (CORRECT ANSWERS)

In some cases where there is no one right answer, possible answers are given. If your answer is significantly different, discuss it with a teacher or tutor.

EXERCISE B

1. I must describe an activity and tell the committee why it is important to me.

2. I must explain to the superintendent why I want to teach and how an experience or subject helped me make this decision.

3. I have to select three courses or activities and justify why they would be worthwhile.

4. I have to write a letter to the director of admissions at the college of my choice and explain why I want to go there.

5. I have to describe to the committee a significant book and concentrate on what I got out of it.

EXERCISE C

Answers will vary.

EXERCISE D

Answers will vary.

EXERCISE E

1. Answers will vary.

2. A. An idea wheel:

B. A flow chart:

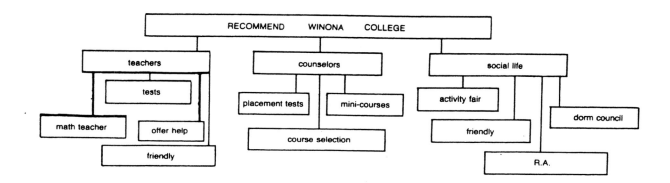

C. Using an outline:

Thesis: My job as a clerk has taught me about the reality of work and how to get along with supervisors.

  I. I don't have time for special activities.
      A. School
      B. Need job
      C. Friends

  II. Work is not like school because if you don't work, you don't get paid.

  III. Boss is not always fair.
      A. No respect for clerks
      B. Gets impatient
      C. Got annoyed about lines

  IV. I'm trying to get on top of the situation rather than just reacting.
      A. Boss is part of pecking order.
      B. Make small talk.
      C. Anticipate orders.

  V. I am still frustrated.
      A. No recognition
      B. No incentive
      C. Easily replaced

D. Using a list:
<u>Death of a Salesman</u> - connections between the play and my life.

  1. Different readings - different reactions

  2. Describe characters
      Willy: salesman
      Linda: wife

                    Biff: good looking, football hero
                           breaks with Willy, drifts around
                    Happy: ordinary, shadowed by Biff

        3. Identified with Happy
            my older brother
            wanted parents' attention
            school troubles
            realized I was hurting myself
            attention hurt Biff

        4. Sympathy for Willy
            no respect from boss
            my job as clerk, dime a dozen
            want more than a paycheck

        5. TV version – admiration for Linda
            held family together
            loyal to Willy
            want someone like her

    E. Another list:
        Choices: integrate courses and experiences

        1. Reading Methods required – would choose it
            what I'll learn; assessment, skills

        2. Activity – literacy volunteer
            why don't people learn
            how to teach adults
            effect on a person's life
            failure of system

        3. Course or individual study in writing
            keep journal
            make connections
            write feature stories for newspaper

EXERCISE F

    1. Answers will vary.

    2. A. One benefit of teaching is personal satisfaction.

        B. Mr. McGrath ran a tightly structured class.

        C. Many teachers work harder than people realize.

EXERCISE G

1. Example: furthermore, for example, also, like, but

   A. but

   B. then, after, finally

   C. in addition, also, another

2. Answers will vary.

EXERCISE H

1. Answers will vary.

2. A. I will enjoy the diversity of students and the freedom to organize my own classes.

   B. The failure of people to understand the need to provide bilingual education to the increasing numbers of non-native English speaking students will be our biggest problem.

   C. Finally, failure to tackle the various forms of illiteracy will cause a decline in our economic productivity.

EXERCISE I

1.	accept	16.	two
2.	expect	17.	to
3.	except	18.	badly
4.	advice	19.	bad
5.	advise	20.	adapt
6.	effect	21.	adopt
7.	affect	22.	site
8.	It's	23.	cite
9.	its	24.	complement
10.	there	25.	compliment
11.	they're		
12.	their		
13.	among		
14.	between		
15.	too		

EXERCISE J

The extent of illiteracy in this ~~C~~country [c] is documented in

<u>Illiterate America</u> ~~/~~ a book by Jonathan Kozol. When I read this

book and realized the extent of illiteracy ~~gave me a~~ shock~~/~~ [, I was ... ed.] Kozol

claims that 25 million people can not read warning labels or a simple

news story~~/~~ [;] another 35 million do not read well enough to survive in

the Modern Age ~~/-like-being~~ [because they are un]able to follow printed instructions.

~~For~~ [S]~~/~~someone who can't read and has to support himself or a family [or her]

~~could-be~~ [is at] a real disadvantage.

The problem of illiteracy will be difficult to solve. ~~There~~

~~being-many~~ [Its] causes ~~that~~ go deep into our society. Schools have failed

to halt the problem and may be contributing to it. My parents say

that the problem with schools today ~~are~~ [is] a lack of respect for

authority. Years ago, ~~everyone~~ [students] knew what would happen if they dis-

obeyed a teacher. Today, teachers must contend with students who

are often bored, rarely prepared[,] and frequently ~~they-defy~~ [defiant of] the

teacher. ~~Some~~ [R]~~/~~respect and discipline ~~is~~ [are] needed to create a learning

environment.

Another problem with the schools is poorly prepare[d] teachers.

Students graduat~~ing~~ [e] from college without being able to read or write

well. During the 1960s ~~was-the-decline-of~~ strict academic standards~~/~~ [declined.]

Students failed to learn[what] they should ~~of~~ [have] learned. The decline may

be ending~~/~~ [because] new tests and requirements are in place. For example,

the ~~c~~[C]ollege of ~~a~~[A]rts and ~~s~~[S]ciences at Northeastern State University

changed ~~their~~ [its] requirements because entering students were so poorly

prepared. Some of them [were] unable to [identify] Sophocles or locate ~~s~~[S]pain on a map.

Kozol's book interested me in the larger issues of literacy, ~~it~~
Literacy means
~~is~~ more than learning the ABCs. ~~Literacy-is-when-you-can~~ It means read~~ing~~ and
write well enough to survive in a complex society and making~~ing~~ informed
opinions about government policies. Teachers can help to create a

literate America. After reading about the problems of illiteracy
a teacher
facing this country, I want to become ~~one~~.

ANSWER SHEET

TEST NO. _____ PART _____ TITLE OF POSITION _____

PLACE OF EXAMINATION _____ DATE _____

(CITY OR TOWN)   (STATE)

RATING

USE THE SPECIAL PENCIL.   MAKE GLOSSY BLACK MARKS.

	A	B	C	D	E		A	B	C	D	E		A	B	C	D	E		A	B	C	D	E		A	B	C	D	E
1	::	::	::	::	::	26	::	::	::	::	::	51	::	::	::	::	::	76	::	::	::	::	::	101	::	::	::	::	::
2	::	::	::	::	::	27	::	::	::	::	::	52	::	::	::	::	::	77	::	::	::	::	::	102	::	::	::	::	::
3	::	::	::	::	::	28	::	::	::	::	::	53	::	::	::	::	::	78	::	::	::	::	::	103	::	::	::	::	::
4	::	::	::	::	::	29	::	::	::	::	::	54	::	::	::	::	::	79	::	::	::	::	::	104	::	::	::	::	::
5	::	::	::	::	::	30	::	::	::	::	::	55	::	::	::	::	::	80	::	::	::	::	::	105	::	::	::	::	::
6	::	::	::	::	::	31	::	::	::	::	::	56	::	::	::	::	::	81	::	::	::	::	::	106	::	::	::	::	::
7	::	::	::	::	::	32	::	::	::	::	::	57	::	::	::	::	::	82	::	::	::	::	::	107	::	::	::	::	::
8	::	::	::	::	::	33	::	::	::	::	::	58	::	::	::	::	::	83	::	::	::	::	::	108	::	::	::	::	::
9	::	::	::	::	::	34	::	::	::	::	::	59	::	::	::	::	::	84	::	::	::	::	::	109	::	::	::	::	::
10	::	::	::	::	::	35	::	::	::	::	::	60	::	::	::	::	::	85	::	::	::	::	::	110	::	::	::	::	::

Make only ONE mark for each answer.   Additional and stray marks may be counted as mistakes.   In making corrections, erase errors COMPLETELY.

	A	B	C	D	E		A	B	C	D	E		A	B	C	D	E		A	B	C	D	E		A	B	C	D	E
11	::	::	::	::	::	36	::	::	::	::	::	61	::	::	::	::	::	86	::	::	::	::	::	111	::	::	::	::	::
12	::	::	::	::	::	37	::	::	::	::	::	62	::	::	::	::	::	87	::	::	::	::	::	112	::	::	::	::	::
13	::	::	::	::	::	38	::	::	::	::	::	63	::	::	::	::	::	88	::	::	::	::	::	113	::	::	::	::	::
14	::	::	::	::	::	39	::	::	::	::	::	64	::	::	::	::	::	89	::	::	::	::	::	114	::	::	::	::	::
15	::	::	::	::	::	40	::	::	::	::	::	65	::	::	::	::	::	90	::	::	::	::	::	115	::	::	::	::	::
16	::	::	::	::	::	41	::	::	::	::	::	66	::	::	::	::	::	91	::	::	::	::	::	116	::	::	::	::	::
17	::	::	::	::	::	42	::	::	::	::	::	67	::	::	::	::	::	92	::	::	::	::	::	117	::	::	::	::	::
18	::	::	::	::	::	43	::	::	::	::	::	68	::	::	::	::	::	93	::	::	::	::	::	118	::	::	::	::	::
19	::	::	::	::	::	44	::	::	::	::	::	69	::	::	::	::	::	94	::	::	::	::	::	119	::	::	::	::	::
20	::	::	::	::	::	45	::	::	::	::	::	70	::	::	::	::	::	95	::	::	::	::	::	120	::	::	::	::	::
21	::	::	::	::	::	46	::	::	::	::	::	71	::	::	::	::	::	96	::	::	::	::	::	121	::	::	::	::	::
22	::	::	::	::	::	47	::	::	::	::	::	72	::	::	::	::	::	97	::	::	::	::	::	122	::	::	::	::	::
23	::	::	::	::	::	48	::	::	::	::	::	73	::	::	::	::	::	98	::	::	::	::	::	123	::	::	::	::	::
24	::	::	::	::	::	49	::	::	::	::	::	74	::	::	::	::	::	99	::	::	::	::	::	124	::	::	::	::	::
25	::	::	::	::	::	50	::	::	::	::	::	75	::	::	::	::	::	100	::	::	::	::	::	125	::	::	::	::	::

ANSWER SHEET

TEST NO. _____ PART _____ TITLE OF POSITION _____

PLACE OF EXAMINATION _____ DATE _____

(CITY OR TOWN)   (STATE)

RATING

USE THE SPECIAL PENCIL.   MAKE GLOSSY BLACK MARKS.

	A	B	C	D	E		A	B	C	D	E		A	B	C	D	E		A	B	C	D	E		A	B	C	D	E
1						26						51						76						101					
2						27						52						77						102					
3						28						53						78						103					
4						29						54						79						104					
5						30						55						80						105					
6						31						56						81						106					
7						32						57						82						107					
8						33						58						83						108					
9						34						59						84						109					
10						35						60						85						110					

Make only ONE mark for each answer.   Additional and stray marks may be counted as mistakes.   In making corrections, erase errors COMPLETELY.

	A	B	C	D	E		A	B	C	D	E		A	B	C	D	E		A	B	C	D	E		A	B	C	D	E
11						36						61						86						111					
12						37						62						87						112					
13						38						63						88						113					
14						39						64						89						114					
15						40						65						90						115					
16						41						66						91						116					
17						42						67						92						117					
18						43						68						93						118					
19						44						69						94						119					
20						45						70						95						120					
21						46						71						96						121					
22						47						72						97						122					
23						48						73						98						123					
24						49						74						99						124					
25						50						75						100						125					